Second Wounds

Second Wounds

Victims' Rights and the Media
in the U.S.

Carrie A. Rentschler

DUKE UNIVERSITY PRESS
Durham and London 2011

© 2011 Duke University Press. All rights
reserved. Printed in the United States of
America on acid-free paper ∞. Designed
by Jennifer Hill. Typeset in Arno Pro by
Tseng Information Systems, Inc. Library of
Congress Cataloging-in-Publication Data
appear on the last printed page of this
book.

For Jonathan

acknowledgments

This book was a long time in the making; Claude Lévi-Strauss would say it has been heavily cooked. While convention dictates that I recognize its beginnings in my dissertation, "Crime Victims and U.S. Public Culture," the book really started when I was a nineteen-year-old undergraduate student at the University of Minnesota. At the time I knew nothing of the victims' rights movement. I was part of a growing generational movement that, for many young women starting university in 1989, was propelled to consciousness by the killings of fourteen female engineering students at the École Polytechnique in Montréal, Quebec. Writing in Montréal on the twentieth anniversary of those murders, I realize that my authorship of this book became possible through my participation in the vibrant political and intellectual environment that formed in the wake of this event. In 1990 I signed up for peer counselor training at at the Sexual Violence Program and joined the school of Feminist Eclectic Martial Arts under the direction of *sensei* Koré Grate. In those transformative spaces I first learned how victimization and awareness of it catalyze social activism and collective organizing, contrary to the critics spouting cranky platitudes about victim mentalities and their supposedly depoliticizing effects on public culture. The work we were doing and the consciousness we were building so clearly proved them wrong.

From these early beginnings, several smart, generous people taught me how to translate the insights I gained through my activism and educational work into forms of feminist inquiry. A group of dedicated women faculty in particular gave me the kind of support of which many students can only dream. They were a key part of my graduate training and continue to provide me with wise expertise and an open ear. My doctoral adviser, Angharad Valdivia, offered guidance both inspirational and pragmatic on writing, research, and publishing and never hesitated to assuage my occasional late-night, long-distance freakouts. Andrea Press kept the political and ethical stakes of this research central in my thinking, offering me innumerable hours of personal and professional advice. Melissa Orlie taught me how to embody playfulness and sincere commitment to the political role of ideas and thought; she has been a model mentor and interlocutor. I thank her for telling me when I was wrong and for cultivating, in her gentle way, my proclivities toward contrarianism.

Carol Stabile, while never a professor of mine, has been a central figure in my life and academic training since 1993, when she started a Marxist reading group in Champaign, Illinois. We have since published together and worked alongside each other as colleagues at the University of Pittsburgh. While we never made the relationship official, she has always been an unwavering, honest, challenging, and deeply committed mentor of mine, and I value our friendship. Paula Treichler is one of my favorite interlocutors—she may actually laugh as much as I do. I especially appreciate her keen sense of what is interesting and her eye for the unexpected. Amanda Anderson taught a feminist theory seminar at the University of Illinois that changed my thinking on so many things, in ways she probably does not even know. I benefited from frequent lively conversations over tasty meals with Janet Lyon and Michael Bérubé. Cheryl Cole pushed me to contextualize the victims' rights movement within the politics of imprisonment in the U.S.

John Nerone always modeled the academic life I wanted to lead. I continue to admire his generosity, his egalitarian ethos, and his profound gift of understatement. Dilip Gaonkar mentored me early on in graduate school, where I learned that the study of communication is, at its best, the study of philosophy. James Hay, my M.A. adviser, shaped my thinking on questions of geography and social space, a mutual interest we continue to share. I am pleased to have him as a friend. I have especially enjoyed tarrying with Cary Nelson over a variety of political and academic topics. I listened attentively when he encouraged me to delve deeper into my research on journalistic trauma training. Most important, I thank him for his impeccable professional advice, his keen sense of the value of academic labor, his recognition of its gendered nature, and his unwavering support. While I took only one graduate seminar with Larry Grossberg on the occasion of a brief return he made to Illinois in the summer of 1995, he has been a major force in my development as a scholar and an academic citizen. I thank him for recognizing the importance of love and family in the life of an academic. Bruce Williams's advice on how to navigate the field in tandem with an academic partner kept my sanity intact. Cameron McCarthy enlivened my graduate studies by maintaining a reading group in which I began to work out the ideas that appear in this book.

Other teachers deserve additional mention here for the ways they permanently left their marks on me: Steve Macek, whose chain smoking and intense lectures on Foucault and the gendered history of medicine, among other topics, convinced me to pursue an education in cultural studies. John Archer gave form to my naïve ramblings on geography and architecture in an honors thesis I wrote on the social space of striptease in Minneapolis. I got the graduate school bug after he invited me to talk to his graduate seminar about my undergraduate research. Richard Leppert channeled my predilections for theory toward feminist thought and poststructuralism as my undergraduate adviser. I will never forget his course "The Body and the Politics of Representation." Gary Thomas deserves my thanks for not throwing me out of his classroom and for accommodating my "live in-class performances." His course "Gay Men and Homophobia in the Modern West" changed my life. Bruce Lincoln made me fall in love with Marx; Prabhakara Jha expanded that love to include Voloshinov, Bakhtin, and Bourdieu. Bruce Holsinger surprised me, an advanced student, out of my slumber with his passion for teaching. Each of these professors provided me with the best undergraduate education imaginable, all while Lynne Cheney tried to shut our program down as an example of the downfall of the humanities. What folly!

A project like this one is not possible without the particular generosity of the people I interviewed and visited in various victim advocacy organizations and antiviolence activist groups. They have my unending gratitude and admiration. Diane Alexander of the National Center for Victims of Crime spent several hours with me over three years, explaining the contours of the crime victim movement and the media practices and training being developed there. She was particularly giving of her time, resources, and connections, opening the door to this research project by putting me in touch with other key sources in national victim advocacy. Others working in the crime victim movement, in antiviolence activism, and in journalism education have shared their expertise and resources with me along the way: Anne Seymour, a communication consultant and longtime victim activist; Roger Simpson of the Dart Center of Journalism and Trauma at the University of Washington; Bruce Shapiro, contributing editor of *The Nation* and executive director of the Dart Center for Journalism and Trauma; John Stein of the National Center for Victim Assistance; Marcia Kight of Families and Survivors United; Cressida Wasserman of the National Center for Victims of Crime (formerly of Safe Horizons, Inc.); Stephanie Frogge of Mothers Against Drunk Driving; Professor Kole Kleeman of the University of Central Oklahoma; Professors Meg Moritz and Beth Gaeddert of the University of Colorado; Nancy Ruhe, executive director of Parents of Murdered Children (POMC); Mary Elledge and Patricia Gioia, chapter leaders of POMC in Portland and Albany, respectively. I give special thanks to Bill and Debbie Brown for their permission to use a photograph of their daughter Shannon and the memorial text that appears on the POMC memorial webpage created to commemorate her life after she was murdered by her former boyfriend. Anna Del Rio and LaWanda Hawkins graciously gave me permission to publish an image of the first billboard erected by Justice for Murdered Children in Los Angeles, in which photographs of their children appear: Anna's daughter Theresa Del Rio, and LaWanda's son Reginald Reese. Thanks to Walter Stachnik for granting permission to publish the photograph of John Heffernan, the guitarist for the band The Bullys, who died on 9/11.

The members of my writing groups in Pittsburgh and Montréal provided exceptional feedback along the way. They include Jody Baker, Jenny Burman, Alice Crawford, Andrew Haley, Kelly Happe, Mark Harrison, Allen Larson, Sheila McBride, Dan McGee, Anne McKnight, Derek Nystrom, Norma Rantisi, Yumna Saddiqi, Dawn Schmitz, Pete Simonson, Gretchen Soderlund, Carol Stabile, and Jonathan Sterne.

Darin Barney has been a wonderful faculty mentor at McGill. He, along with Jonathan, my editor Courtney Berger at Duke University Press, and my two anonymous readers, read the entire manuscript. With his gift of excisional vision, Darin helped me see the path to the end of the book. My colleague Marc Raboy has given me excellent professional and personal advice since I've been at McGill; he and Elaine Arsenault are wonderful friends who remind me that this really is the good life I'm leading, though I could learn to take more vacations. Will Straw, who hired me at McGill, is a fantastic friend and the perfect colleague. It is so enjoyable to work alongside another scholar as interested in crime media and their many weirdnesses. Jenny Burman, theory maven extraordinaire, is an amazing friend and confidante. She and Derek Nystrom read a great majority of the book in process and they always had the very best advice. Becky Lentz brings abundant energy and political vision to my work and personal life. I am lucky to be surrounded by additional colleagues who make the Department of Art History and Communication Studies the perfect intellectual community it is: Cecily Hilsdale, Mary Hunter, Tom Lamarre, Hajime Nakatani, Charmaine Nelson, Andrew Piper, Christine Ross, Richard Taws, and Angela Vanhaelen; my former colleagues Cornelius Borck, Ting Chang, and Bronwen Wilson have both gone on to other positions. The labors of Maureen Coote, Maria Gabriel, Susana Machado, and Jennifer Marleau have not gone unnoticed. I am grateful to them for all the work they do to make my job possible.

I have also found a significant intellectual community and support system at the Institute for Gender, Sexuality and Feminist Studies, formerly the McGill Centre for Research and Teaching on Women. Several colleagues and staff there deserve special mention: Natalie Amar, Marguerite Deslauriers, Elizabeth Elbourne, Michelle Hartman, Erin Hurley, Piper Huggins, Patricia Kirkpatrick, Julia Krane, Shree Mulay, Alanna Thain, Elaine Weiner, and Caili Woodyard.

I have been lucky to be surrounded by smart, socially and politically engaged friends, former fellow students and colleagues in Minneapolis, Champaign-Urbana, Pittsburgh, and Montréal who deserve special mention here: Charles Acland, Lisa Barg, Shannon and Craig Bierbaum, Kathy Blee, David Brackett, Jack Bratich, Dave Breeden, Lisa Brush, Kevin Carollo, Danae Clark, Nicole Couture, Rob Danisch, Melissa Deem, James Delbourgo, Manon Desrosiers, Nick Dew, Greg Dimitriadis, Rachel Dubrosky, Ariel Ducey, Greg Elmer, Jennifer Fishman, Zack Furness, Yuriko Furuhata, Bill Fusfield, Loretta Gaffney, Paula Gardner, Kelly Gates, Jessica Ghilani, Ron Greene, Paul Griffiths and Karola Stotz, Jayson Harsin, Michelle Hartman, Rob Henn, Toby Higbie, Amy Hribar, Adrienne Hurley, Nan Hyland, Steve Jahn, Bridget Kilroy, Lisa King, Nick King, Sammi King, Laura Kopp, Christine Lamarre, Joan Leach and Phil Dowe, Craig Mattarese and Anna Hulseberg, Shoshana Magnet (and Robert), Dan McGee, Nicole McLaughlin, Gordon Mitchell, Radhika Mongia, Negar Mottahedeh, Jessica Mudry, Dave Noon, Jeremy Packer, Laila Parsons, Tom Robbins and Andrea Beck, Kelli Robertson, Gil Rodman, Joseph Rosen, Wayne Schneider and Lisa Friedman, Maxwell Schnurer and Elena Cattaneo, Michelle Silva, Johanne Sloan, Rob and Heather Sloane, Gretchen Soderlund, Michelle Stewart, Zack Stiegler, Joe Terry, Andrea Tone, Mrak and Tony Unger, Dan Vukovich, Fred Wasser, Haidee Wasson, Andrew Weintraub, Greg Wise, Robert Wisnovsky, Mike Witmore, and Mary Vavrus. I especially thank the Graduate Employees' Union at UIUC for the best friendship network ever.

Several people have invited me to give talks, participated on conference panels with me, and have otherwise been part of my circle of dialogue over the years. Our encounters have been especially productive to my thinking: Kate Crawford, Catharine Driscoll, and Joan Leach, who collectively invited me to Australia; Paul Frosh and Amit Pinchevksi for inviting me to Villa Vigoni to talk about witnessing; Fred Turner for being the fabulous, insightful, and generous person he is (and for showing me how to think like a writer); Margaret Schwartz, for great conversations about the lively topic of death; Barbie Zelizer, for just being who she is and for her great work on witnessing; Lisa Henderson for her unique perspectives on the work of affect and the optimism that blooms in the spaces of cultural production; John Peters, for his intellectual engagement and compassionate manner; Haidee Wasson and Charles Acland, for inviting me to join in some very thrilling discussions at their symposium on useful cinema; and Gretchen Soderlund, for inviting me to a symposium on news at the University of

Chicago. Thanks to Vanessa Schwartz for her sage advice on my *next* book project, the subject of which is Kitty Genovese.

My graduate students are an inspirational, creative, and supportive bunch. I am so lucky to be working with them. I thank them for their active engagement and willingness to debate with me many of the ideas that structure this book. They are Andrea Braithwaite, Danielle Chassin de Kergommeaux, Anna Feigenbaum, Natalie Kouri-Towe, Anna Leventhal, Christine Maki, Lena Palacios, Liz Springate, Cee Strauss, Sam Thrift, Jessica Wurster, and Laurel Wypkema. Additional thanks go to the many wonderful students who have taken my graduate seminars over the past six years; I've learned so much from you. Andrea Braithwaite, my research assistant for nearly six years, deserves extra special mention for midwifing this project through to completion with me. I have taken to calling her my own private detective. I also want to thank the outstanding group of undergraduate students I have taught and supervised while at McGill: Amy Hasinoff, Ren Haskett, Ainsley Jenicek, Theresa Knoppers, Taylor Lewis, Natalie Marshik, Sarah Woolf, and the students who took my seminar in affect theory. They are the reasons why I do what I do and enjoy it so much.

Courtney Berger, my editor at Duke University Press, is totally amazing. She is the perfect critic and has believed in the project since our first meeting, when I nervously proposed the book to her. I have taken her advice on everything, and the book is so much better for it. It has been a great experience working with her and the staff at the press, all of whom have been so helpful and accommodating. I also thank my two anonymous reviewers for the significant direction they provided in my revision of the manuscript.

I developed my antiviolence philosophies and pedagogic orientation to its teaching at the Champaign-Urbana Women's Martial Arts School and Women on the Horizon women's self-defense teaching collective. Jacq Madden is an impressive martial artist and an inspirational *sensei* who commands presence in the classroom. More than anyone, she taught me how to teach as an embodied practice. Katherine Coyle, Donna Hoeflinger, and Diane Long are three powerhouse women from whom I have learned many a life's lesson. Together we made feminism a daily, lived practice while teaching other women and girls how to do the same.

I am grateful for funding that supported parts of the research and writing of this book, including McGill University, for an internal Social Science and Humanities Research Council grant, Media@McGill, the Canadian Social Sciences and Humanities Research Council's standard research grants program, and the Fonds du Quebec de Recherche sur la Société et Culture and their Nouveaux Professeurs-Chercheurs program. My success with grants-womanship is due in no small part to Jo Ann Levesque, director of the Office for Research Opportunities, and her excellent staff. Thanks also to Linda Kemp and Rupa Narasimhadevara in the Research Grants Office. Some of the material in chapter 4 appeared in "Victims' Rights and the Struggle over Crime in the Media" in the *Canadian Journal of Communication* 32:2 (2007), 239–59; in another form still, it appeared in an article titled "Trauma Training and the Reparative Work of Journalism" in *Cultural Studies* 24 (2010).

My family has been supportive and ever present. I am grateful to my parents, Kay Larsen and Louis Rentschler, for their unending support and for teaching me independence at a very early age. Judy Andersen, my mother's life partner, and Dianne Rentschler, my father's wife, have both been significant in so many ways, right down to the smallest details of daily life. I love talking politics with both of them! My grandmother, Sara Louise Larsen, reminds me that the teaching and research I do is a big deal. I wish my other grandparents were alive to see this book reach fruition; they are Louis Rentschler Sr., Laverne Rentschler, and Orville Larsen. I thank all of my family scattered across the United States from Alaska to New Jersey but centered primarily in Minnesota, Iowa, and South Dakota. Muriel Sterne, my mother-in-law, and Phil Griffin, my late father-in-law, are true intellectuals and committed citizens. Words really cannot express how much I love and cherish them, and how much I have enjoyed and appreciated their passion for life, justice, and the pursuit of ideas.

This book is dedicated to Jonathan Sterne, my life partner and closest confidante. We have shared a fabulous life together over the past twenty years. Jonathan has nourished me in countless ways, reading multiple drafts of every chapter of this book, spending hundreds of hours in conversation with me, cooking tasty meals, and reveling in my favorite trashy action and sci fi films, TV shows, and heavy music. Even when they make me groan, I love his silly puns. I'm glad he chose me to accompany him through life. Now, when shall we write that book together?

The Victims' Rights Movement and the Second Wound

My story begins with two female crime victims: Kitty Genovese and Elizabeth Smart. Genovese was the victim of a high-profile murder in 1964. Smart was the victim of a kidnapping in 2002 and survived to be returned to her family. The Genovese case marks the first stirrings of victims' rights activism, a tale in which the murder victim was, according to one reporter, "never the story" (see *CQ Researcher* 1994; Rasenberger 2006, 65). Genovese's story is told through journalists' racialized imagination of street crime, its victims and villains, in New York City, the same year in which two of the city's boroughs erupted in riots. The Smart case, a media-saturated story of abduction, polygamy, and sexual assault, signals the dominance of a victims' rights orientation to the representation of crime, forty years after Genovese's murder. Smart's story is told through the perspective of crime's secondary victims, that circle of family and other intimates who claim and occupy victim status as people who are physically, affectively, and often financially altered by the victimization of their loved ones.

In the movement for victims' rights in the U.S., the families of crime victims assert their rights to recognition and participation in the criminal justice system and in the media. In addition to the movement's reform efforts aimed at emboldening these families' rights to speak during trials, to give impact statements at sentencing hearings, to be present at parole hearings, and to have access to victim compensation, among other things, they have also transformed how the news and other media represent and interact with crime victims and their representatives. The victims' rights movement represents a whole way of thinking about the politics of victim recognition and the practices of depicting victims in a media culture saturated with images of crime scenes, "perp walks," and the grief-stricken families of dead victims. In the process, the movement has amplified the familial voice of victims and changed the story of crime in the United States.

While other books detail the development of victims' rights as a national and international social movement, my interest lies in how victims' rights constitutes a historically specific political grammar for representing crime, a way of talking about and depicting crime victims organized around the figures of the secondary victim and the affective qualities of secondary victimization (Roach 1999; Rock 1990; Weed 1995). This book examines the movement's redefinition of victimization and its mobilization and amplification of secondary victims' voices from 1964 to the present in order to evaluate how their visibility and the visibilities of the harms they are said to suffer in the wake of crime have changed the story of crime. The movement matters in this book for the ways it creates, distributes, and uses political resources and representational practices for publicly framing the issues of crime and criminal justice around the perspective of victims' rights. It constitutes what David Altheide refers to as the "institutional arrangements" that "promote [crime's] social definitions" (1992, 69). Organizations within the victims' rights movement became public carriers of and points of access to images of and information about crime victims. They help news media gain access to crime victims' families. They help script commemorative news stories on dead victims' lives in a recent genre of news story I call profiles of life. They help families deliver victim impact statements to judges and juries who are preparing to sentence convicted criminals. And perhaps most important, they train journalists and journalism educators to identify with the families of crime victims as potential victims themselves in order to cover crime from the perspective of its victims in the news. Through the circulation and use of their material and discursive artifacts, the movement changed how and through what means victims and victimization are represented in the United States.

Organizations within the movement do all sorts of media work. They share the power to define victimization in mass culture because of their close proximity to media and policy institutions. Many act as sources for major and local news media. They function as flak machines, responding to news stories that misrepresent victims, their organizations, and new legislation. They criticize particular news workers and television programming for insensitive treatment of victims. They serve as consultants for television and Hollywood dramas on crime and victims' rights. They train victims to become media spokespeople. They produce major public service campaigns. Their names, toll-free numbers, and printed publicity materials appear in news specials, made-for-television movies, and Hollywood films. Many publicly criticize the practices of the news media, some turning such criticism into a primary form of activism. The group Parents of Murdered Children (POMC), a national victim support organization, runs a program called Murder Is Not Entertainment. Through a major letter-writing campaign and publicity blitz, POMC convinced major retailers not to carry Benetton clothing in response to a special photo essay magazine Benetton published on death row inmates. POMC's countercampaign turned into a publicity battle over who the victims of murder are and who has the right to depict them, a story I tell in chapter 6.

The movement's shift from the direct victim of crime to that of the secondary victims or covictims marks the single most important feature in the changing story of crime in the United States and the visibility of victims therein. It comes out of a political struggle staged between the time of the Genovese murder in 1964 and the Smart abduction case in 2002. My book explains this shift, how and why it happened through the victims' rights movement and how it has, since the mid-1960s, changed the public's understanding of what crime and victimization mean and why they matter. The victims' rights movement has expanded the concept of victims to include both crime victims and those close to them. It has shown that forms of institutionalized encounter can produce victimization beyond the event of crime itself; and it has worked to change the representation of victims that comes out of these encounters. The movement reworked the politics of representation in crime politics in the U.S., first, in terms of the strategic outlook and tactical planning it did to retell the story of crime from a victim perspective and, second, as an orientation toward a more robust and complex depiction of crime's victims and the experiential dimensions of victimization. As a multifaceted concept, victims' rights signifies a framework for defining crime through a victim perspective, a kind of participatory practice delineated through social and legal claims for victims' rights to representation in the courtroom and in the news, and a means of claiming victim status for the families of crime's victims.

Two White Female Victims, Two Different Stories of Crime

Two stories, set almost forty years apart, illustrate the ascendancy of secondary victims and the transformation brought about by the victims' rights movement in the story of crime as it has appeared in the news. At 3 A.M. on 13 March 1964, twenty-eight-year-old bar manager Catherine "Kitty" Genovese was stabbed several times, sexually assaulted, and left to die by a twenty-nine-year-old accounting machine operator named Winston Moseley on Austin Street, just outside of Genovese's apartment building in the Kew Gardens section of Queens, N.Y. After Moseley had stabbed Genovese, he left the scene when a neighbor yelled, "Leave that girl alone!," only to return shortly thereafter to assault her again by knife and rape her when he realized no one was going to intervene any further. After a news brief on the murder ran in the *New York Times* on 14 March, an article published on 27 March headlined "Thirty-seven Who Saw Murder Didn't Call Police" (Gansberg 1964, 1) set the narrative arc of the murder story from then on.

Occurring on the cusp of the U.S. declaration of a war on crime in 1968 and in the midst of the race riots of 1964 in New York City; Rochester, N.Y.; Paterson, N.J.; Chicago; and Philadelphia, the murder of Kitty Genovese portrayed a picture of racialized urban violent crime in which the (white) victim is mostly absent from the telling. Genovese functioned as a backdrop to a much larger tale of public apathy, fear of crime, and the mental state of a serial killing black man, a "crime that became a metaphor for the failure of urban residents to help fellow citizens in trouble" (Fried 1995,

B4). In the absence of a discourse of victims' rights, Genovese's "character, her likes and loves," as one reporter put it, could not "speak to the complexity of flesh and blood behind those who have the good or bad fortune to become symbols" (Rasenberger 2006, 67). Lacking any family remembrances of her life or the sense that her family was also victimized by her murder, the accounts of the death of Kitty Genovese represented the old way of reporting on crime, which left the victim out of the story. At the time of her murder there was no discursive apparatus through which her family spoke to and for her innocence against the guilt of the offender. The Genovese family did not speak out until 1995, when Genovese's brother Vincent began to testify at Moseley's annual parole hearings. The family now speaks (and claims rights to speak) at each of his hearings.

It took forty years for personal aspects of Genovese's life to be revealed in press coverage. Today, personal stories about victims and their families are a regular feature of reporting on crime. In March 2004, news audiences learned that at the time of her murder Genovese was living in a committed relationship with her lesbian lover, Mary Ann Zielonko. In an interview published in the *New York Times* Zielonko revealed, "We were lovers together. Everybody tried to hush that up" (Rasenberger 2004, 14). Zielonko, who identified Kitty's remains at the city morgue the night of her murder, was featured in a moving public radio feature, "Remembering Kitty Genovese," on 13 March 2004: "Kitty was the most wonderful person I've ever met. I still remember her face. I can see it in my mind: very Italian looking, very chiseled features, dark hair, like only about five feet tall. And very likeable person, very vibrant, where I'm very quiet, so we were complementary. . . . Being a gay woman in that society was very hard, so we were in the closet a lot. In fact, her family didn't know. I mean, they know now, but there was denial there. It was very hard then" (from soundportraits.org).

Genovese's murder illustrated the problem of the press's indifference to victims of crime. Today their visibility in high-profile cases is a reality of crime coverage that the families of highly publicized victims have found particularly hurtful (see F. Rose 1989). The only newspaper that interviewed a member of Genovese's family, her brother William, at the time of her murder was the neighborhood paper *The Long Island Press*. In all the other press coverage of the story, Genovese barely counted as a victim worthy of recognition after Moseley's violent murder.

The story of Elizabeth Smart's abduction and rescue in 2003, on the other hand, illustrates the success of the victims' rights movement in changing the media's representations of victimization and crime. Smart's story included all of the elements of a victims' rights representation of crime. The victim—fourteen years old, female, presumably or potentially heterosexual, white, a member of a very religious family—sat center stage. Whereas the reporting on Genovese's murder was defined by the victim's absence, Smart's rescue story presumed that there was no alternative to portraying white female victims, particularly with the help of their families. While both Smart and Genovese were young white female victims of sexualized violence who came from middle-class families (Genovese was raped while she lay dying from multiple stab wounds; Smart was sexually assaulted while living as the "second wife" of her captors), only Smart's story constitutes a victims' rights narrative of crime and presumes its very grammar in its coverage. The victims' rights movement would mobilize discourse around crime toward a model in which the victim's life and harrowing experience of victimization could be redeemed through its representation. Victims' rights, in other words, marked a shift from a crime model of victimization that often disappeared the victim to a trauma model that amplified the voices of victims and the affective dimensions crime had on the family. This victims' rights representation of crime is aptly portrayed in the rescue narrative of Elizabeth Smart.

When a homeless man the family had hired to do construction work abducted Smart from her bedroom in her family's home in Salt Lake City, all of the elements for telling a crime story from a victims' rights perspective were in place. *People* magazine for 31 March 2003, called her "the miracle girl." Despite depressing statistics on the survival rate of abducted children who have gone missing for more than twenty-four hours, Smart lived through her nine-month sequestration by a couple the press described as "polygamous Mormon fanatics." Like Genovese's killer, both of Smart's captors had histories of mental illness, and the husband took to calling himself Immanuel. According to media reports, the police stopped and arrested Brian David Mitchell and his wife, Wanda Barzee, after three people separately identified the unkempt and unusually costumed pair and the girl outside of a Kinko's photocopy center in Sandy, Utah. A clerk in a convenience store referred to Mitchell as Jesus when he shopped for beer, as Barzee and Smart waited by the cash register. *People* magazine described each of the three witnesses as fans of the television show *America's Most Wanted*. All three had watched the show's profile of the Smart case and of Mitchell in particular just prior to Smart's rescue on 12 March 2003.

While the story of Smart's rescue drew on frontier narratives of female captivity by savage natives and their calls for the protection of white femininity (see Faludi 2007; Fitzpatrick 1991; Kolodny 1981; Pearce 1947; Slotkin 1973; Sturma 2002; I. M. Young 2003), it also drew on a different set of plot elements and characters than coverage of the Genovese murder: the victims' rights movement, its familial orientation to crime's victims, and its present powers of publicity. Two characters in the movement became especially visible in Smart's story: John Walsh, the host of Fox Television's *America's Most Wanted* and a leading advocate for victims' rights and the plight of missing children in the United States (and the organization he helped found, the National Center for Missing and Exploited Children), and Smart's father, Ed. Walsh was photographed with Ed at a celebratory rally in Salt Lake City two days after the girl's rescue, but in addition his presence in the story linked the search for the missing Elizabeth to the larger construction of the problem of America's missing children around which much of the activism of victims' rights advocates occurs. The photograph-heavy spread in *People* also illustrated the racial politics of dominant public discourses on crime and anticrime activism at the heart of victims' rights discourse in the United States. For this rescue from captivity of a white fifteen-year-old girl provided a broader platform for the cases of twelve other missing children, only one of whom was a young white girl.[1]

Smart's story demonstrates how some victims, white female victims in particular, come to occupy central character roles in the story of crime, and, moreover, how the family is recognized and portrayed as a victim of crime. Smart's family, which is Mormon and by all accounts typically suburban and middle class, sat at the very center of press coverage of the girl's abduction. Her mother and father (especially her father) served as the principal sources of information about Elizabeth's life, and they were highly visible in the intensive coverage of her case over the period of her disappearance. If, as the legal theorist Markus Dirk Dubber argues, the white female child murder victim is "the paradigmatic victim of the victims' rights movement in the United States" (2002, 189), overwhelmingly it has been through the representation of white child victims and white women who have gone missing or been murdered that the ideological and political stakes of crime have been most powerfully articulated (e.g., Stabile 2006; Wood 1999).

These are children like Adam Walsh, the six-year-old son of John Walsh, whose disappearance and murder by a serial killer during the summer of 1981 fed Walsh's desire to commit his life's work to publicizing what he describes as the heinousness and monstrosity of America's "most wanted" criminals. Walsh has since published the books *Tears of Rage* (1997), *No Mercy* (1998), and *Public Enemies* (2002), overseen the production of two made-for-television movies about his son's murder, hosted *America's Most Wanted*, and produced safety training DVDs for kids. Similarly, the father of Polly Klass, a twelve-year-old girl who lived in Petaluma, Calif., and was abducted from her bedroom during a slumber party and murdered later that night by her abductor, became an outspoken advocate for three-strikes legislation in California — state legislation that sets mandatory (and often life-long) prison sentences for three-time convicted felons — and received regular media attention. That is, until he had a change of heart and began to oppose the legislation on the grounds that it would not have prevented his daughter's murder. Jennifer Levin, a middle-class, seventeen-year-old girl from Long Island, was sexually assaulted and murdered in 1986 in Central Park by Robert Chambers, a nineteen-year-old young man whom she met at a bar. Her mother, Ellen Levin, is a victims' rights advocate who founded the pro–death penalty victims' rights organization Justice for All. Nancy Spungen was a psychologically troubled American teenager who fell in love with Sid Vicious of the Sex Pistols; Vicious stabbed her and left her to die in a hotel room the two were sharing in New York. Nancy's mother, Deborah Spungen, became a victims' rights advocate in the wake of her daughter's murder. She is a former chapter leader of POMC and the founder of the Philadelphia organization Families of Murder Victims. She has written two books: *And I Don't Want to Live This Life* (1983) on Nancy's life up until her murder and *Homicide: The Hidden Victims* (1998), a book that forcefully makes the case that the families of murder victims are victims too.

The concepts of covictim and the second wounds around which this book is organized depict victimization as connective and vicarious, as transportable and transposable experiences that mark mothers, fathers, lovers, sisters, and brothers as the victims of crime. These concepts are predicated on three distinct ideas of the victim — that of the victim of *crime*, that of the victim of *criminal justice*, and that of the victim of *trauma*. The last can and often does include victims of both crime and criminal justice, but it casts their victimization in primarily affective and psychological terms. It is the particular quality of their victimization and its effects that defines the victim of trauma, rather than a particular criminal event or institutional encounter with the criminal justice system. The covictims of crime become victims by virtue of their relationship to the primary victim of crime. In this way, they too are said to be victims of crime. Covictims experience the traumatic, grief-ridden dimensions of crime as the caregivers of wounded primary victims, as the bearers of primary victims' testimonials to their experiences of crime, as witnesses to crime's aftereffects, and as dependents of or providers to the primary victim (e.g., who might suffer the loss of financial or other kinds of support or who have provided the direct victim with support). Many of these experiences result not directly from the crime itself, but from harms that emerge from the emotional and financial economies of dependency and care that can change form in the aftermath of crime.

In representing murder victims within the criminal justice system, secondary victims can experience forms of harm that come from their encounters with the system itself, such as being denied what they claim is their right to speak in courts of law. The victims' rights movement deems this encounter with law's denial of victim representation as itself harmful and victimizing. In this way, the parents and families of crime victims are said to become victims of criminal justice, the most significant form of victimization from the perspective of the victims' rights movement. According to survivors, it is seen as the most undeserved and inexcusable form of harm they suffer after crime itself. Advocates also understand it as the most reformable and the most useful for law-and-order advocacy.

Movement, Media, Message

The notion of secondary victim differs from the term *survivor* because it does not signify only those who remain alive after suffering a violent assault or the living family left in the wake of their family member's killing. Secondary victims and their second wounds emerge from a combined discourse of crime and trauma that exceeds what is conventionally understood to constitute survivor discourse. Secondary victims name a particular register, scale, and affective orientation of victimization and its specific harms that the term survivor does not. Where the language of survival is the language of living, the language of secondary victims and their secondary wounds is that of injury, victimization, and grief. Sometimes the language of secondary victims also articulates a language of life, as it does in the profile of life. This language of life, however, does the grief work of commemoration that seeks to remember the dead from the perspective of their survivors. Victims' rights discourse is by necessity a survivor discourse because it is the living that can speak for the dead. But its modes of representation encompass more than the grammar of survival, with its testimonials and speak-outs, its renarration of violence and survival from the perspective of its experiential traumas, and the confessional modes of its deployment (see, e.g., Alcoff and Gray 1993; Moorti 1998).

This book analyzes the political ascent of secondary victims and the redefinition of victimization by the victims' rights movement and its representational strategies. It examines the effects these changes have had on the conditions and practices for representing crime in the United States. The families of crime victims have become the key representatives of victims' rights and the movement portrayals of crime. They are its most visible activists, the authors of its key texts and its media personalities. The movement's claim that families are also victims of crime reconceptualizes victimization beyond the criminal event toward the radiant injuries the media and criminal justice system can inflict. Through the movement's activism, the category of victim opened up to include those who mourn and grieve for people who have been murdered or injured by violent crime.

Secondary victimization and its second wounds constitute the most significant conceptual move made by advocates of the victims' rights movement. Secondary victimization happens specifically around practices and relations of representation—within those relations of speaking and prosecuting in the courtroom and in the processes of news making about crime. The term *covictim*, or *secondary victim* signifies that victimization is structured by the institutional practices of representing crime and justice before the law and before publics. Its secondary nature speaks to its production through the mediations of criminal justice institutions and media institutions.

The secondary nature of victimization not only signifies the families of primary crime victims; it also denotes the additional, or secondary, harms created through encounters with the legal and media systems responsible for representing crime. It names criminal justice and the mass media as institutions capable of harming those who have already been victimized by crime directly and those who have been vicariously victimized through their familial relation to crime. Victimization in this sense does not signify the production of a particular kind of person; it signifies the harm-producing quality of relations of representation and the forms of personal and institutional injuries they can produce. The making of victims is a structure of the politics of representation, of who can speak for whom and in what conditions. The victims' rights movement politicized victimization as an affective experience of institutional encounter. It redefined victimization from the harms caused to victims by crime to harm created by criminal justice and media representation, within people's intimate, dependency-based relations to each other as victims of crime.

The movement's reformist approach to criminal justice and the mass media opened the door to more radical political uses of secondary victimization in prison abolition and anti–death penalty activism that this book also explores. If secondary victimization is victimization caused by the system, then families of murder victims and families of men and women living on death row can both argue that they are secondary victims of murder and of the criminal justice system. Organizations such as Murder Victims' Families for Reconciliation and Murder Victims' Families for Human Rights represent coalitions of families who identify as victims of murder and the death penalty, but from different sides of the crime couplet of "criminal" and "victim." They argue for their rights as familial victims of murder in order to speak against the death penalty, sharing common ground as families of murder and its punishment by the state. Through their example, one can see victimization as a condition of harmful encounters that moves, resonates with, and traffics between people as they become the familial victim subjects of criminal justice. Even those who are cast in apparent opposition between the positions of victim and criminal in murder cases recognize a common language in secondary victimization for organizing against state murder in the death penalty. Victimization is not an experience contained or possessed within bodies and minds, the experiential stuff of primary or direct victims alone; it is also a structural relation formed between families vis-à-vis criminal justice and media representation.

Victims' rights advocates take cultural change and the work of representation seriously. Their publicity strategies are directed at changing how the criminal justice system creates victims and grants them status. They seek to transform how reporters interact with crime victims and their families. They intervene in and change public discourse on crime to reflect their perspectives on victims' rights. They change the public's consciousness about crime by reframing its social construction around the position of victim through training texts they developed for the purpose not only of representing victims' rights' perspectives on crime, but also of directing those perspectives through movement-based textual and representational regimes. They do so by targeting their publicity work at the "transformation in habitual norms and codes of conduct" of those representatives who come to speak for crime through their victims and by "tinkering with practical arrangements rather than epic struggles for consciousness" about crime, victimization, and trauma (T. Bennett 1992, 399, 406). Through this work, the victims' rights movement reveals a network of middle-range organizations and interinstitutional networks that has transformed the representation of crime's victims in the United States.

The middle range is the space where activism happens, a discursive register that operates on a different scale and in different sites from those of major political economic institutions—in the homes of female activists who lead local chapters of victim advocacy organizations, in the libraries of national victim advocacy organizations, and on memorial websites for crime victims, to name a few. An analysis of major media institutions and central institutions within the criminal justice system alone would fail to explain the registers and networks of victim activism with which these systems come in contact, in part because the movement also shaped them. Attending to this middle range of activist labor marks a shift from analyzing what appears in mainstream media representations of victim activism to seeing these representations as an epiphenomenon of the largely invisible work activists do.

Seeing this labor requires that one look at diverse kinds of documents and movement-based media artifacts that bear its marks. My book analyzes this middle range of activist-oriented social relations between the macroinstitutional registers of the criminal justice system and mainstream media institutions and the microlevel, back-channel registers of activists' talk and action. In the middle range one finds all of the messy, often banal, and sometimes unexpected practices of communication rarely seen in mainstream media representations, but which do much of the behind-the-scenes work that shapes the media languages of crime and criminal justice.

Viewing the movement from the middle range, one can see how it produced a way of talking about and portraying victims' rights in victim advocacy organizations and deployed it in federal criminal justice agencies and media organizations. At this level, one can examine the work of translation the movement, criminal justice, and media institutions have done to tune the pitch of victims' rights into a broad-reaching public discourse on crime and justice. It also enables one to hear the dissonant chords that sound alternative tunings within the movement. The movement for victims' rights orchestrated the conditions for what is sayable and doable around secondary victims and their struggles for representation. This is not to say that the movement acted like a puppet master behind the curtains of the war on crime; rather, it functioned as a visible conductor for a large group of actors and organizations who played different, yet constitutive, parts in the overall movement for victims' rights, often in service to the war on crime, but sometimes not. The oeuvre that developed from the movement constitutes what actually gets said and done in the name of victims' rights. This movement renders secondary victims as political subjects who can speak as victims through its adaptations to the story of crime. In the process, the very representation of crime victims and the political cultures surrounding them has changed.

My focus on the movement's discourse of victims' rights is twofold: I examine the circuits of publicity built and maintained by the movement that have developed around victims' rights and the specific representational frameworks through which victims' rights activism brought families-as-victims into representation. As a discourse, victims' rights are not reducible to speech or language or even a group of signs, but are instead "practices that systematically form the objects of what they speak" (Foucault 1972, 49): the victims of crime and criminal justice and the harmful encounters that constitute them. Victims' rights discourse constitutes what is sayable about crime and criminal justice, by whom, and about whom. It is a language and set of practices that make victims more visible in narratives of crime; it also strategically makes invisible other victims, those who, because of their skin color, sexual orientation, or class status, appear less innocent in the moral economies of crime. I ask not only how the "crime victim has become a dominant symbolic reference point in criminal justice"

(Walklate 2005, 92), but also what kinds of political, cultural, and institutional work make visible certain victims and their representatives? *Who* and *what* constitute a crime victim in the public culture of the United States?

To examine the movement's discourse of victims' rights, this book draws on several sets of textual materials that include movement publications, training documents, media planning texts and press kits, online victim memorials and movement-based interventions into media stories on crime and the professional training of crime and disaster journalists, and policy reports. As forms of discourse, these documents textualize victims' rights approaches to talking about and depicting crime's victims. In them the discourse of victims' rights takes tactical and highly mobile form. They represent the precise linguistic and textual means through which victims' rights discourse could be mobilized and reproduced. In my usage, discourse is a material thing found in language and physical documents and in practices such as training regimens. More important, it is also an analytic construct, a way of theorizing power and social struggle at the level of discursive strategies and tactics, whose locations are primarily institutional and whose field of play is contentious and often warlike.

This book approaches victims' rights as a discourse rather than as a system of representations. Victims' rights is part of the world of discourse on crime that has achieved high-profile visibility and federal institutionalization. The movement's texts are important sources within this economy of discourse, revealing the discursive strategies actors in the movement used to codify new ways of talking about families as crime victims. They also define the anchor, or support, of the discourse of victims' rights: the family as secondary crime victim. For Foucault, the family organization constituted the support for the maneuvers the Malthusian state made around its discourse of population, birthrate, and the medicalization of sex (1990, 100). Such supports are "the object at once studied and invented by the discourse that surrounds it" (Edwards 1996, 38). Victims' rights discourse both invented and revised the feminist concept of secondary victimization around which the family as crime victim became its material and discursive support.

Texts such as those produced and used by the movement, as Susan Gal (2003) argues in the context of Hungarian feminism, textualize political discourse and make it mobile across different print cultures. In victims' rights, movement documents do this strategic work. Both the National Center for Victims of Crime (NCVC), a national resource organization, and the smaller but nationally networked National Organization for Victim Assistance (NOVA), which conducts postcrisis intervention, produce major training texts that teach victim advocates how to use the news media. These organizations occupy the central sites of training in the movement and are key producers of training material. They provide resources and information to victim service providers, policymakers, prosecutors, criminal justice agencies, and the news media and are central to the political and movement-building agenda of the victims' rights movement.

In addition to analyzing the training texts of these two organizations, my interviews with their communication staff and directors, respectively, unearthed some of the ways in which they think about the power of the media and the targets of their media activist efforts that remain unstated in their training documents but are crucial to understanding them. My interviews with communication staffers like Diane Alexander at the National Center for Victims' Rights and longtime media activists for victims' rights like Anne Seymour afforded me insight on how movement activists and their organizations do media work and why. Alexander and Seymour each represent over twenty-five years of institutional movement memory, constituting a living archive of victim activism and its changing strategies.

POMC, a national organization headquartered in Cincinnati, provides services for families of murder victims and engages in policy work that is specific to victim-oriented legislative reform, including the passage of state-based victims' bills of rights that symbolically codify covictims' rights to participate in the criminal justice system as well as a national campaign that seeks to amend the U.S. Constitution to substantially enforce victims' bills of rights and victims' rights statutes. They also advocate for the prevention of early release of offenders convicted of murder. They are unique in their media activism, running their flak campaign Murder Is Not Entertainment (MINE), which sends out regular alerts on media practices that portray murder as entertainment. Like some other organizations that advocate for murder victim's families, they have built an online murder victim memorial and a traveling murder wall. These forms of activist commemoration of victims of murder are now common throughout the movement and, notably, in the press. I interviewed chapter leaders of POMC, including Patricia Gioia and Mary Elledge, and the executive director, Nancy Ruhe, to further probe the thinking behind their organization's media strategies, ideas that were not evident in their online materials or in the press coverage of their flak-based letter-writing campaign against Benetton. These women also revealed the affective and political commitment they have made to their advocacy in the name of murder victims. Gioia has survived the killing of her daughter and has published a book on her daughter's case. Ruhe is an overworked powerhouse of an activist who first worked in the feminist antirape movement before taking over as executive director when the founders of the organization, Charlotte and Bob Hullinger, left it in 1986.

Another set of organizations, including Murder Victims' Families for Reconciliation and Murder Victims' Families for Human Rights, articulates a politics of anti–death penalty victims' rights, counter to the claims made in POMC's campaign against Benetton. These organizations advocate from the position of the families of both murder victims and prison inmates for the abolition of the death penalty and mandatory minimum sentencing, respectively, articulating two very disparate political meanings of victims' rights. I analyze texts produced by these other organizations, for, unlike those of any other victims' rights organization, their texts make visible the faces of the families of murder victims alongside the families of men and women living on death row. That is, rather than representing murder victims in their position as the family, they represent themselves in the name of their murdered family member and in their own names. They also articulate an anti–death penalty stance through the language of victims' rights.

Additionally, such policy texts as the *Final Report of the Attorney General's Task Force on Violent Crime* (1981) and the *Final Report of the President's Task on Victims of Crime* (1982) portray the "governing mentalities" that came to identify victims' rights at the federal level (see Campbell 2000). Reports like that of the 1982 task force coded into their very format idealized portraits of victims and their speech. Filling the margins with testimonials taken from victims' statements made at public hearings, the 1982 task force's report held to a fictional victim composite that, in purporting to depict the typical American victim portrayed by the victims' rights movement, instead depicted a highly fictionalized and exaggerated tale of repeated victimizations by numerous individual and institutional aggressors. The report thereby took the form of a worst-case fantasy scenario that points to the government's inabilities to prevent secondary victimizations (see chapter 1). Policymakers use such fantastical portraits of the harms committed against fictional victims to define and direct their governance strategies.

These organizations and their media strategies reveal the activist labor that orients the victims' rights movement to the media in the United States. They reveal the movement infrastructures they built that enabled them to translate their strategies into media representations. And they evidence, along with the policy texts that signaled the nationalization of the movement, the policy apparatus that provided some of the language and governmental space that built the movement into the publicity machine it has become.

The Politics of Movement Documentation

To understand the shifts in the representation of crime through the mobilization and amplification of victims' representation in the documents mentioned above required that I attend to their representations and interpret what they signify; it also required a change in perspective from which to view the work and struggles that occur over representation there. Victims' rights activism exceeds any meaning one might attribute to the content of their portrayals and their conventions of depiction. For this reason, my book is not primarily a study of media representations of victims. Rather, it directs most of its analysis toward the movement labor conducted around crime victim representation that has transformed its portrayal. I emphasize the materiality of this work and the contentiousness of its struggles by considering each as conscious forms of deliberative and representational labor. The specificity of what victims' rights activists and their documents say is crucial, but the structures through which they circulate and are deployed also matter a great deal. Above and beyond the content of what advocates' texts and policy documents say, this book analyzes the form their representation takes. By *work*, I refer to the works of depiction that constitute representation and the labor that goes into their construction and deployment. Through this perspective, I account for the dimensions of their communicative labor that are not reducible to symbolism and meaning, such as the midlevel scale of their communication, its movement and distribution, the speed and uneven rhythm of its movement, its resonances, and the character of its technosocial "couplings."[2]

I emphasize the materialities of the movement's communication and its labors, drawing links between the form representations take in victims' rights texts, the physical documents in which they are housed and travel, the organizational structures that produced the representations in their documentary forms, and the national infrastructures and networks built so that organizations could distribute and share ideas and strategies and thereby access their institutionalized forms of power more effectively. I refigure the work of interpreting what it is that social movements do and are capable of doing, to effect change in how the social problem of crime and other forms of victimization are portrayed (see, e.g., Gumbrecht 1994; Gaonkar and Povinelli 2003). In order to make the activism of the victims' rights movement more visible within the changing history of crime's portrayal, my analysis shuttles between the visibilities of victims' rights in policy discourse and mainstream news media portrayals and the texts of the movement that circulate out of sight but that make such media visibility and policy presence possible.

Studying the politics of movement discourse requires not only an ability to map how they move, in their textualized and artifactual forms, but also analysis of what they say and mean. One must "follow the memos" that evidence the practices of decision making that orient institutional practice within relations of power (see Enloe 2000) — to see how they move and what they say. But it is not enough to point to what movements say and show how they deploy and accumulate power. The question is: how did it happen? And how does knowing "the how" enable one to not only make sense of it, but also to historicize and challenge it when necessary?

To treat movements and social institutions in this way is to insist that the processes of their decision making are neither mysterious nor magical. Memos, reports, letters, and other forms of bureaucratized textual production evidence the maneuvers that movements and other social institutions make as well as the disagreements that shape and sometimes interrupt them. They are artifacts of institutionalized knowledge and orientation, planning, decision making, and directives. Their value comes from what they say, certainly, but also from how they move and direct action (see, e.g., Guillory 2004). Movement texts in this way reveal "the arts of transmission," those textual cultures of circulation that mark the boundaries of what is actionable and sayable within and beyond their organizations (Guillory 2004, 108; see also Gaonkar and Povinelli 2003; Warner 2002). Their print cultures and distribution networks do the work of large-scale organization that "inscribes its processes into textual modes" through specialized practices of documentation (D. Smith 1990, 213; Guillory 2004, 112).

Most of the media work analyzed here occurs out of public sight, in the back channels that advocates, volunteers, counselors, and educators form through the organizations and institutions in which they work. The movement produces a great deal of its media material for the purpose of training victim advocates, policymakers, and members of the media; these documents are not aimed at mainstream media audiences. Movement-based communication networks are especially significant because they enable the movements to politically organize outside of, parallel to, against, and through mass-mediated public debates on crime (see, e.g., Herbst 1994, 128–30). In its back-channel networks, the victims' rights movement developed its own social scripts of crime, its own language, images, metaphors, and story forms for constructing crime as an issue of victims' rights. The materials that circulate in these networks offer rich documentary evidence of how the movement organizes itself to define and mobilize secondary victims into the criminal justice system and mass media.

I originally came to my study of the victims' rights movement thinking I would write a devastating critique of its law-and-order politics and its anti-victim uses of crime victims and their experiences, work other authors have since addressed (see Dubber 2002; Cole 2006). I started from an established set of truisms about victims' rights that have cast it as a movement oriented predominantly around law-and-order political initiatives. I did find these tendencies within the movement, but I also found other political visions of victims' rights activism. I found activists who work outside of victims' rights organizations who use victims' rights discourse to assert their claims against the death penalty and against what they perceive as the militarism of the United States. To call victims' rights a law-and-order movement without recognizing its other political orientations is to ignore the political complexity of its social activism, the concrete struggles over the meaning and political solutions to the violence of crime and state action and inaction, and the different ends to which its claims making is directed. The political divergences in victims' rights are in part what make it such an interesting movement to examine in light of current social activism.

Rather than treat victims' rights as strictly a law-and-order movement, I asked how victims' rights became oriented to law-and-order politics, even before the movement existed, through the crime policy of the 1960s and 1970s.[3] I asked how law-and-order activism helped create the movement and its key terms. Then I began to follow more closely the movement and its production, distribution, and use of victims' rights texts and the other activist and policy texts with which they came into contact. I became very curious about the texts I was coming across, how they talked about classes of secondary victims and the institutional harms they faced. This curiosity then led me to a whole body of documents that have given shape to and deployed victims' rights stories and the cultural figures—the secondary victims—on which their activism so centrally depends. These texts began to help me understand the changes I saw and heard in the media's stories of crime in which the victims took center stage, from the nightly news to cop shows like NBC's *Law and Order* that started to incorporate talk about victim services into their plots.

As a result of the echoes I heard between popular culture depictions of crime victims and victims' rights advocacy texts, I reoriented my analysis more centrally on movement documents and their training protocols. I began to see how movement texts not only depict movement-based thinking and strategy (that is, as representations of the movement), but also function as central forms of agency and distribution in the politics of victims' rights. They actively represent the movement as inanimate proxies. Through them I also heard the different political voices of victims' rights expressed by the various organizations examined in this book. These texts span diverse document types, such as pocket-sized training booklets for journalists that prescribe tips on how to cover victims from a victims' rights perspective; victim advocates' large, three-ring binders of training materials on how to develop communication strategies and use media resources; training DVDs that use experimental forms of filmmaking; free online curricular modules directed at media personnel; yearly victims' rights week press kits; and many other artifacts of activists.

The movement has developed an orientation toward training—media training in particular—as a means to change how criminal justice, victim advocacy, and media institutions construct and depict victims. They have established a pedagogy of victims' rights, a means of educating activists and journalists into an activist grammar of victims' rights that extends from the dominant law-and-order concepts of legal permissiveness and defendants' rights discussed in chapter 1 to include post-traumatic stress disorder, secondary victimization, and terms such as *violence* (instead of *crime*) and *abolitionism* that also now circulate in journalism education as a result of a series of pedagogic encounters between victim advocates, journalists, journalism educators, and trauma specialists (see chapter 4). There is, in other words, an active "pedagogy of the concept" occurring in, around, and through the victims' rights movement (see Deleuze and Guattari 1994, 16). The movement makes teachable a set of problems it has identified with criminal justice and its system of representation that, unless rectified, are defined as making victims. Advocates respond by learning how to think differently—and politically—about how to represent victims when the stakes of victims' rights are defined in terms of victims' capacities for representation. They develop a collective way of talking about and depicting victims' rights that also happens to be a contentious site of political struggle within and around the movement.

In choosing to look at activist texts and other forms of strategic documentation, I was attempting to get at what is unseen in media representations of victims: the work of and references to victim advocacy. To get behind them required a new way of interpreting their content: when I read them, one thing I looked for was their connections to other texts within and outside of victim advocacy—that is, the ways in which they referenced each other as part of a shared universe of discourse. What I found behind these texts was the sociality of the relations in which they are produced, their historicity, and what Sara Ahmed describes as their "conditions of arrival" (2006, 549).

I also analyzed the ways in which these texts' activism produced gender as a particularly meaningful feature of victims and their advocates. Gender matters in multiple ways within the victims' rights movement, in its texts and the staffers and activists who make up its networks. The secondary victims who constitute the main activist voice of victims' rights, for instance, appear most often as political mothers (far more often than fathers), whose maternal grief fuels the crusading energy of victims' rights reforms. Embedded within gendered constructions of the secondary victim is the idea that the reproductive family is the true victim of crime (see, e.g., Jermyn 2003; A. Williams 1993). Within its dominant law-and-order political orientation, victims' rights activism is predicated on racialized and sexualized models of criminals and victims that signify their social differences in moral form: victim innocence is often coded through whiteness and femaleness, while offender guilt is often coded through dark skin and maleness, as evidenced in the racial androcentrism of so much crime news (see Stabile 2006; see also Dubber 2002; Wood 2005).

Feminist activism has been and still is one of the key strands in the political genealogy of victims' rights. In its own genealogies, the movement admits as much (see "Movement's Birth," *CQ Researcher* 1994, 633). The movement has benefited greatly from the work of feminist antirape advocacy and its movement building; it has also used, and sometimes abused, this advocacy to its own ends. The concept of secondary victimization on which victims' rights discourse depends was appropriated and reworked from feminist antirape activists' concept of the second rape. The second rape signified the ways in which women who had been victimized by rape were injured again through social blame, police indifference, and legal indifference to and legitimation of male sexual violence in marriage, for instance. In its appropriation of the term, however, the victims' rights movement expunged the radical feminist social critique of the institutional structures that denied rape victims' victimization and cast women as the ones to blame for their sexual assault by men (see chapter 1). The point, however, is that this appropriation signals how central feminist concepts and frameworks of victimization have been to victims' rights advocacy, in spite of the ways in which some feminist work has been marginalized, while others, more invested in crime control, have been more directly brought into the center of the movement. Victims' rights discourse has also given some anti–domestic violence advocates a renewed language of punishment that fits neatly into calls for increasing the criminalization of violence against women (see, e.g., Bumiller 2008; Rapping 2003).

The great majority of movement activists and movement organization staff also happen to be women. The staff and activists whom I interviewed at the National Center for Victims of Crime, the National Office for Victim Advocacy, Mothers Against Drunk Driving (MADD), and Parents of Murdered Children (POMC) were all, save for one, women. Many of them came to the movement out of antirape organizing and victim-specific groups like MADD. While their sex and gender performance matters, how their sex, gender, and race signify in and through the movement positions they occupy is what is most significant for the book's analysis—for instance, as political forms of primarily middle-class motherhood and activist modes of authorship. Women wrote many of the movement texts I collected and analyzed, as evidenced in those texts where authorship was revealed. Many of the key media strategists in the movement are white women, like Anne Seymour, who at the time I interviewed her had been working as a victim advocate for twenty years. She runs national training seminars on using the media in victim advocacy. Or Deborah Spungen, who wrote an essential book on the covictims of homicide. On the other hand, those victims' rights activists who have become media celebrities are just as likely (if not more so) to be men, such as John Walsh of *America's Most Wanted*. Currently, however, the outspoken victims' rights media personality Nancy Grace of her eponymous show on CNN *Headline News* is unquestionably the most visible victims' rights media celebrity and propunishment spokesperson for the movement.

My feminist analysis in this book is integrated throughout—in my attention to the action of movement infrastructures and the forms of documentation that structure them and in the figures that speak through them, from the political mother to anti–death penalty activists and beyond. It accounts for the affinity I felt for the grieving activist mothers who believed, to my dismay, that seeing their children's killers put to death might lessen the pain they felt. I related in complicated ways with the female staffers and political mothers of the movement. Their understanding of the politics of victimization in the United States is based both upon a feminist analysis of the systemic nature of social violence and the social construction of crime and on years of hard work trying to change law and policy so that they can serve victims better, in often highly compromised circumstances. Some of them believe that punishment is a necessary part of the social redress for crime and its effects on people's lives, which in turn orients them to anticrime work rather than to prevention-based antiviolence initiatives. While I may not always identify with the politics these women share or their life experiences, this book seeks to account for their political passions, their shrewd strategies, their commitments to their own sense of justice, and the profound depths of grief I heard in their stories. I have sought to take their passions and grieving seriously, and I have given them the space they deserve here.

Why Victim Politics?

In light of the large body of cultural criticism and scholarship that is antivictim and opposed to the very lexicon of victimization, I argue that one must account for the political language of victims' rights in order to recognize and understand the important representational work and institutional change it enables: to examine the punitive and reparative work being undertaken by collectives of secondary victims and their representatives (see Sedgwick 2003). I do so in order to take the category of victim more seriously as a form of political and activist subjectivity. I portray how the current terrain of representations of victimization depicts an experiential and political depth too often missing in critiques that seek to dismiss all talk of being victimized in the United States. I recognize that "the stories people tell about themselves, about their troubles, and their social worlds, and about their society's problems are entangled and weave between what is immediately available as a story" of crime's victims "and what their imaginations are reaching toward" (Gordon 2008, 4). Some activists reach for progressive political alternatives to the otherwise punishing vision of victims' rights—alternatives that embrace the subject position of victim, the language of victimization, and, sometimes, the language of victims' rights.

For these reasons, I do not dismiss victim politics or argue against "victim identities." Rather than argue for the need to protect public culture from "a nation of victims" or a spectacular, fear-inspiring "wound culture" (see, e.g., Sykes 1992; Seltzer 1998), the formation of public cultures of secondary victims demonstrates the considerable amount of political work happening around claims to the significance of bringing crime victims into representation. For antivictimists like Charles Sykes, there ought to be no place or time to dwell in the affective and political spaces of grief and loss that come from violent crime and cultural disasters such as Hurricane Katrina.

The antivictimist stance is epitomized in such books as Sykes's *Nation of Victims* (1992), Frank Furedi's *Culture of Fear* (1997), Naomi Wolf's *Fire with Fire* (1993) and Wendy Brown's *States of Injury* (1995), among many others. In all of these texts, *victim* represents a position of undeserved and harmful political power that rests in subjects' claims to injury and powerlessness. These authors argue that public culture is emasculated (Sykes) and made risk averse (Furedi) by a post–civil rights victim consciousness. They suggest that individuals and political collectives deny their own freedoms to act through their desire to identify with being wounded (Brown), laying particular blame for such victim politics at the feet of feminists and their "victim feminism" (Wolf), and civil rights activism (Sykes). In this latter sense, to be a victim is to misrecognize and sacrifice one's power to act as a woman, or as someone identified with raced, classed, and queer identity politics. The power to act on the world, in this formulation, turns inward, becomes less and less of the world and more and more of the self, becoming mired in a self-wounding orientation to past harms (see W. Brown 1995). For some critics, then, the political ascendancy of victims and their representatives signifies the dominance of injury and recovery as the terms of political debate and the status of political subjectivity. In the process, such language and wounded identity politics are said to marginalize collective agency and stifle the possibilities for democratic social transformation as a political goal (see, e.g., Cloud 1998; Rapping 1996; Kaminer 1995).

This is the current orthodoxy of cultural criticism on victim politics in the United States. From here it appears to "go without saying because it comes without saying" (see Bourdieu 1977, 167) that victim is an undeserved experience which becomes in turn a political position that harms political culture in democratic societies. The category of victim is supposed to be avoided. For the antivictimists, theirs is a palpable expression of anger and hostility toward claims of victimization (and its psychological harms in particular) that aims crusading critiques against "victimism" in the U.S. in ways that quickly turn antivictim (see Cole 2006). If one should become a victim of crime, oppression, neglect, or accident in this way of thinking, one should then not come to identify as such or desire to identify as victim. Victim talk becomes an indexical sign that points to the injuries public culture and the democratic process suffer when victim becomes one of the more visible political subjectivities. Yet, as Pierre Bourdieu suggests, "if one accepts the equation made by Marx in *The German Ideology*, that 'language is real, practical consciousness,'" then the boundary between "the universe of . . . discourse and the universe of doxa, . . . of what goes without saying and what cannot be said for lack of an available discourse, represents the dividing line between the most radical form of misrecognition and the awakening of political consciousness" (1977, 170). From a Bourdieuan perspective, the antivictimists misrecognize the field of play and maneuver between what appears in the political representation of victims and what is possible to say, and by whom, in their political talk. They misrecognize and conflate the proxies for victims — the secondary victims — with depictions of victimization (the stories that make up the politics of crime in the United States) and deny the political work of representation both do.

As I argue, now more than ever there needs to be a public language of victimization precisely because of the attempts of political conservatives and numerous academic critics to make victimization unspeakable. Victimization is a powerful language for naming the harms and accumulated power of institutionalized oppressions. Victims' rights make this language more powerful than ever. The recognition of secondary victims as victims constitutes one space of maneuver between the universe of victim discourse and the political doxa of victimism. It recognizes the agents and the terms of debate within this field of play. It also recognizes that the political representation of secondary victims is a site of struggle and contestation over the politics of crime rather than a naturalized state of being and knowing that necessarily emerges from the social relations in which crimes occur. Culture in this perspective offers no fix to calls for victim recognition within victims' rights, for culture is the field of struggle, the site of its contestation. Culture "is always an instrument of vision and di-vision, at once a product, a weapon, and a stake of struggles for symbolic life and death — and for this reason it cannot be the means to resolve the running battle for access to recognized social existence that everywhere defines and ranks humanity" (Wacquant 2005, 21).

Instead, culture is a space of political struggle in which victims' rights activists work to represent the complexity of what it is and means to be a victim of crime and criminal justice, and the feelings of grief, rage, and collective identification that go with it. This collective grief work offers an avenue into the recognition of the unacknowledged and complex personhood at stake in relations of victimization. To be a victim is not to be a particular kind of person but to occupy and be placed by relations of power into a space of political, affective encounter with crime and the social and political systems that create, intensify, and purport to address it. According to Avery Gordon, the recognition of complex personhood treats power dynamics and consciousness "as more dense and delicate" than our categorical terms of social and textual analysis tend to allow (2008, 3). Power viewed as such reveals victimization to be a far more complicated set of institutional relations, affective economies, and forms of political subjectivity than most representations of crime and victims reveal.

My goal is not to get to the "truth" of victimization in the United States, nor do I seek to wage battle in a war of classification over who is and is not a real victim. This book instead accounts for how people come to occupy the political subject position of victim when they are the secondary victims of

crime. It examines the social and political conditions that create the subject
position of the secondarily victimized, and what constitutes and organizes
their public cultures of victim identification in the United States. To be
absolutely clear, I recognize that secondary victims *are* victims. I also recognize that they have as much claim to the truth and the practices of truth
telling around victimization as direct crime victims do. But what interests
me — and what matters most — is how the public culture of victims that
has formed around the representation of crime in the United States after
1964 articulates a broader expression of cultural truth claims about crime
and victimization whose politics remain contingent, and interestingly so,
despite the dominant law-and-order ideology of much of victims' rights
activism.

Outline of the Book

The book is divided into two parts. The first examines the genealogy of victims' rights through the emergence of the victims' rights movement and its
discourses. It does so through historical documentation, examination of
national communication networks, and application of other critical scholarly literatures that enable one to view the movement in retrospect (see,
e.g., Bumiller 2008, xiv). Chapter 1 examines the hegemonic law-and-order
orientation of victims' rights, where it came from, and how it shapes the
very language of victims' rights activism. Chapter 2 examines how the relationship between the victims' rights movement's dominant law-and-order
framework and its other political genealogies has been scripted into activist training texts' genealogy of the movement. Movement organizations'
narratives of the movement's national institutional building and increasing
professionalism marginalize other accounts of its political activism. This
chapter highlights some of the disagreements and debates over who and
what a victim is within the movement.

Part II analyzes the movement's mainstream media strategies, its appropriation by news and entertainment media, and activists' reappropria-
tion of those tactics. It traces how national organizations made a language
of victims' rights available to their own advocates and to media organizations. It then follows the effects these efforts had within journalism education, and the results of this victims' rights–oriented education in emergent
news genres that commemorate the lives of dead victims. In particular, I

examine the obituary format of the recent profile of life news genre to show how it produces and disseminates commemoration of victims alongside political action without itself becoming explicitly political. I also examine how victim advocates take up the work of commemorating killed victims in more explicitly politicized venues. These developments also illustrate a shift in the scale of victimization that media cover and are further enabled through the framework of second wounds—from murder and other interpersonal violent crimes to the larger scale of major crimes and terrorist attacks broadcast as major twenty-four-hour media events.

Drawing on a body of the movement's training documents, videos on the topic of crime victims in the media, and interviews with movement staff and victim advocates, chapter 3 discusses how crime victim movement organizations perceive news media and talk shows as victimizing agents that make victims, but also as agents of healing that enable victims to testify to their experiences of victimization to a large listening public. This chapter analyzes how movement organizations direct themselves to encounter the press and talk shows by perceiving those encounters as both harmful and potentially therapeutic. In the process, they train their advocates to think like reporters. Chapter 4 examines how victim advocates' media-oriented training mobilized some U.S. journalism schools to develop victim-centered curricular materials. These materials shift the emphasis from an explicit victims' rights framework to one that sees secondary victims as key sources on the traumas of victimization. Journalistic trauma training also marks a key shift in the scale of victimization around which journalism students are being trained to embody a victim orientation to news making—from interpersonal violent crime to major acts of mass victimization like the Oklahoma City bombing and the 9/11 terrorist attacks, among other events. Chapter 5 extends the analysis in chapter 4 to examine a news genre that has resulted from journalists' trauma training that commemorates the lives of people killed in major acts of mass victimization: the profile of life. The editor and reporters of the *Oklahoman*'s commemoration of the Oklahoma City bombing victims took the lessons they learned to journalism educators at the Dart Center for Journalism and Trauma and the University of Central Oklahoma, who then codified them into training texts. They are now systematically teaching journalism students how to profile the lives of victims killed in acts of mass violence. Chapter 6 analyzes the media encounter between victims' rights activism and anti–death penalty activism in the form of portrait-based commemorations to murder victims and death row inmates by Parents of Murdered Children and Benetton, respectively. The former used commemorative portraits of murder victims not unlike the profiles of life examined in chapter 5 to argue against the representation of death row inmates, while the latter drew upon death row portraiture to recognize the worthiness of the lives of men and women living on death row. In chapter 6 I show in far starker and more vivid terms the life-and-death struggles that occur through victims' rights discourse in the practice of profiling victims and convicted killers' lives.

The conclusion reflects further on the necessity of nurturing a language of victimization in the United States as one of the key means to talk about and politicize oppression. It turns its attention to some alternative articulations of victims' rights in the abolitionist work of murder victim families who have found common ground with the families of people on death row. These families put a face to the difficult work of finding commonality with each other in their experiences of criminal justice and in their opinions of the death penalty. They do this difficult work while also confronting a durable divide that has been drawn between criminals and victims by the criminal justice system and hardened by law-and-order activists. Through their shared struggle against the death penalty, I seek to tell a different political story about the visibility of victims and the public discourse of victims' rights.

I hope this book demonstrates that people's calls for rights to representation as victims can mobilize a powerful public language toward more socially just and less punitive responses to crime and mass violence in the name of victims. It is important to remember that the subjectivity of victim does not necessarily signify the desire to punish, nor is victims' rights necessarily, always, or only a punishing politics. Victims' rights is also a position from which demands for equality and social justice are amplified in ethical, politically progressive ways around the shared personhood and humanity of victims and offenders and the families who advocate on their behalf (e.g., Dubber 2002). This book is an attempt to hear those calls in the midst of the loud clamor for increasingly brutal forms of punishment in a media environment overwhelmingly populated with representations of victims.

part one

The Life and Times of Victims' Rights

The idea that there is a zero-sum contest between victims and offenders . . . is a key feature of the currently dominant politics of law and order. But it is not a universal feature of popular culture or political discourse.

ROBERT REINER, the author of *Law and Order*

one

Law and Order
The Dominant Ideology of Victims' Rights

This chapter focuses on the dominant law-and-order dimensions of victims' rights, its punishing politics and talk of defendants' rights and legal permissiveness against which the rights of victims would be defined. *Law and order* signifies a political ideology vis-à-vis crime that focuses on crime control and the containment and warehousing of those deemed criminal. Beginning in 1964 with Barry Goldwater's run for the U.S. presidency on a crime control platform, the law-and-order movement gained momentum over the 1970s as part of the right-wing movement's political ascendency (see Beckett 1997). By the 1980s, law-and-order policy became a central feature of federal politics in the United States under President Ronald Reagan, and in the United Kingdom under Prime Minister Margaret Thatcher. The term *law and order* crystallizes a number of specific meanings about criminal justice, "above all, that law could and should produce order, but failed to do so because of weak enforcement." The primary purpose of the law as law-and-order advocates see it is crime control, yet lawmakers were also the movement's greatest adversaries. Many advocates felt "shackled by excessive due process restraints that frustrated effective enforcement" of legal measures of crime control (Reiner 2007, 119).[1] In this context, in which calls for crime control were starting to be made in the name of victims, as Alyson Cole warns, "American discourse is dominated not by claims of victimization as much as by claims against victims" (2006, 2).

I want to probe the law-and-order movement's ventriloquism of crime victims as it defined the movement for victims' rights. The law-and-order movement was a key site for the production of the language of victims' rights. By the 1970s, victims' rights would replace law and order as a rallying cry for those who blamed prosecutorial leniency and constitutional rights protections for criminal defendants for the social problem of crime and its victims (Kaminer 1995). My analysis relies on evidence found in a collection of policy texts, task force reports, and political commentary identified with law-and-order perspectives on crime and criminal justice that constitute the dominant discourse of victims' rights. How law-and-order advocates imagined victims' rights and the victims it represents has had profound implications for criminal justice policy and the activities of victims' rights activists over the 1980s and 1990s, once the movement nationalized. Law-and-order conceptions of the victim of victims' rights redefined the issue of criminal justice away from crime toward the control and incapacitation of whole populations in the United States deemed dangerous and criminal by white ruling elites.

The story of the victims' rights movement really starts in the middle of its forty-year history in the United States. Its ascendancy was achieved in 1982, with the publication of the *Final Report of the President's Task Force on Victims of Crime*. From a movement perspective, the task force report of 1982 signaled the national arrival of victims' rights, evidence that its discourse and political practice were part and parcel of a national policy vision of victims. The report set the national policy agenda and political apparatus for victims' rights, presenting sixty-eight recommendations to "balance the scales of justice" by creating constitutional rights of participation for victims within the criminal justice system, while some of its authors simultaneously advanced assaults on defendants' rights in other venues (e.g.,

Task Force on Violent Crime 1981). Reagan had called for the task force in 1982 to help launch a federal law-and-order agenda defined around victims and their (lack of) rights. The task force held hearings around the United States, at which it heard testimony by crime victims, victim advocates, and people working in criminal justice as well as other social institutions, such as churches and hospitals. The portrayal it cast of victims' experiences of criminal justice called out for broad reform, specifically around the constitutional rights of victims.

According to the report, the hearings compiled a picture of "all crime victims in America." Its imagination of the social totality of crime victims in the United States took unique form in the case of a textual victim composite, a kind of worst-case scenario of institutional victimization that looked nothing at all like a typical crime victim. This was the point, for the report sought to identify all the possible forms of harm a victim could suffer after a crime and then defined these harms as kinds of victimization on a par with criminal victimization. Victims were created not by crime alone but also, more significantly, by their encounters with the criminal justice system. In its vision of victims, the report is a testament to the law-and-order focus of most victims' rights politics, with their emphasis on the criminal justice system as the main barrier facing victims and their search for justice (see Henderson 1985; Aynes 1983/84). It argues that this same system should be reformed to serve the needs of victims—needs understood to be in conflict with the rights of defendants. In the process, the composite victim distilled the worst-case scenario as a dominant rhetorical feature of national victims' rights texts. That the report made this point through a fictional chronicle of the travails of a composite figure rather than through a single victim testimonial also points to the authors' belief in the political power of compound fiction—the creation of a single fiction out of a multiplicity of testimonials.

There is much to be learned from the forms such policy documents take as well as from their content. As the anthropologist Annelise Riles argues, policy documents are "aesthetic objects with uses distinct from their qualities as 'texts,'" but they have often been treated as little more than "instruments of political or ideological control" in which the analyst uncovers the hidden work of norms within them (1998, 378). The norms of the task force report, however, "are not hidden but made quite explicit . . . [even] insistently posed and restated at every turn," and therefore the task of revelation is largely moot (see Riles, 378). From this perspective, the point instead is to understand how and under what conditions such claims about victims, who they are, and what their needs are could be made in the first place. Understanding these conditions also helps to reveal how the task force report could have the broad-reaching effects it had on the victims' rights policy agenda. Through its imagination of the victim and its status as the document that nationalized victims' rights, the task force report is the primary artifact of its national story.

Legal Permissiveness and Defendants' Rights

Leading up to 1982, the place of victims' rights discourse in the law-and-order movement rested in part on the assaults its leaders made on U.S. Supreme Court decisions from the 1960s that protected the rights of defendants to fair and due process. Mobilizing during the late 1960s and early 1970s, after several state and U.S. riot commissions had processed the social rebellions of African American citizens in cities across the country as signs of black "crime in the streets"[2] (Scheingold 1991, 1995; M. Lee 2007; M. Davis 1990; Kennedy and Sacco 1998), several key Supreme Court decisions established the constitutional rights of criminal defendants and abolished the death penalty. Law-and-order politicians and activists fought these decisions and in the process defined the prevailing discursive terrain of victims' rights in terms that cast crime as racial, class-based, and urban.

Law-and-order advocates of the 1960s and 1970s depicted street crime as the work of African American outlaws who profited from a permissive legal system. Constitutional protections of defendants' rights, they argued, let criminals off on legal technicalities and undue concern for fair investigative and prosecutorial procedures. Law-and-order advocates further challenged these landmark constitutional decisions by portraying the criminal justice system as a perpetrator against a vulnerable public besieged by inner-city criminal classes whose rights protections as defendants accounted for the increasing problem of street crime. From this law-and-order perspective, the criminal justice system created its own victims through the overprotection of defendants' rights.

The Supreme Court decision in *Mapp v. Ohio* (1961) established the exclusionary rule, which meant that evidence of an accused person's guilt would not be admissible in court if it had been obtained in the course of, or resulted from, an illegal search and seizure. *Gideon v. Wainwright* (1963) required courts to provide indigent defendants with legal counsel in felony cases. The *Escobedo v. Illinois* case from 1964 established defendants' right to counsel and also established that the right to not speak to the police arises at a certain point in police questioning. *Miranda v. Arizona* (1966) established that police must advise a person of their rights against self-incrimination prior to interrogation, and if such advice is not given no statement made by a suspect can be admissible in court. *Chimel v. California* (1969) established that warrantless police searches incidental to a lawful arrest could encompass only areas within the arrestee's immediate control. Each of these rulings formally codified into constitutional law that defendants are not guilty until proven so through fair and just procedures of search, seizure, arrest, and counsel.

These decisions proved to be major targets for the forces of law and order, which launched attacks on the constitutional rights of defendants that continue to the present. Defendants' rights, they argued, trumped the rights of victims in the criminal justice system; protecting defendants was anathema to protecting the rights of victims. For law-and-order politicians and the New Right activists of the 1970s, speaking in the name of crime victims became one of their primary discursive strategies for responding to social movements of the sixties that claimed victimization as the grounds of the individual and collective activism: for women's rights, civil rights, gay and lesbian liberation, and antiwar activism (Cole 2006, 40). The politics of victimization in the 1960s, Alyson Cole suggests, were so "resonant with the experiences of whole groups that it had to be blunted by ideological enemies" (2006, 40). Whether it *had* to be is a matter of interpretation, but the political right certainly used its ventriloquism of victims against major civil rights victories of the 1960s.

In each of these Supreme Court decisions, the state protects defendants from unwarranted state intrusion and retributive acts. Attacks on these decisions became central to the development of victims' rights as a political position, whereby a law-and-order perspective on crime meant challenging the rights protections guaranteed to criminal defendants as assaults on victims by the state. Victims' rights perspectives on crime treat the state as a coconspirator of defendants against victims. The formal protections of defendants' rights in these Supreme Court decisions and the *Furman v. Georgia* decision in 1972 holding the death penalty to be cruel and unusual punishment signaled to law-and-order advocates that the state protected the defendant at the expense of the victim. The law-and-order criticism of these decisions suggests that the state should act more concertedly as a legal surrogate for victims in order to reap more punishment and retribution in the name of crime control. Yet while it should amplify the voice of the victim in law to this end, law-and-order advocates did not think the state necessarily needed to surrender this voice to victims.

Law-and-order activists questioned the very presumption that defendants should be treated as innocent until proven guilty, that their rights should trump their possible guilt. To them it was the relationship between defendant and victim before the law, not that between the state and the defendant, that represented the primary inequality. Police particularly attacked the *Miranda* decision as an imposition on their ability to do their jobs. Their criticisms helped create a backlash against the rights of the accused, making it appear as if criminals' rights took precedence over issues of guilt or innocence (see Weed 1995, 6) and presuming further that defendants are innocent only if proven not guilty.

Frank Carrington was one of the principal law-and-order advocates who linked assaults on defendants' rights with the struggle for victims' rights. A right-wing movement regular, Carrington brought the issue of victims' rights to Reagan as a New Right comrade in the late 1970s. At the time, Carrington headed Americans for Effective Law Enforcement (AELE), a small think tank that responded to criticism of the notions of expanding law enforcement powers and widening punitive crime control practices. In 1979, Carrington left AELE because he reportedly could make more money fundraising for victims than for law enforcement. According to the present executive director of AELE, Wayne Schmidt, Carrington cared much more about advocating for the rights of victims than for law enforcement (interview with author, 28 October 1999). Carrington founded the Victims' Assistance Legal Organization (VALOR) in 1979 to help lead the effort by a coalition of groups to pass a constitutional amendment to secure victims' rights. Currently, VALOR helps run the National Victim Assistance Academy, a credentialing academy for professional victim advocates and service providers located at California State University, Fresno, as well as the National Crime Victims Research and Treatment Center at the Medical University of South Carolina, in conjunction with the federal Office for Victims of Crime.

In many ways Carrington served as a charismatic single-person node in the network between victim advocacy organizations, right-wing leaders, and the presidency.[3] According to Schmidt, Carrington knew a number of wealthy socialites and was aligned with several conservative organizations, which meant that he had a number of personal connections to right-wing political elites (author interview with Wayne Schmidt, 28 October 1999). Through these political connections Carrington lobbied for victims' rights with Reagan and the U.S. Congress. Additionally, through his association with the Heritage Foundation he published several books on crime and its victims, including *Neither Cruel nor Unusual: The Case for Capital Punishment* (1978) and *The Victims* (1975).

In an article from 1970 entitled "Speaking for the Police," Carrington made an impassioned call for the professional policeman to find his political voice so that he might speak out against the Supreme Court decisions "restricting the police and enlarging the rights of criminal defendants and suspects." Citing a national Gallup poll of 16 February 1969, on public attitudes toward the Supreme Court's leniency on criminal defendants (246–47), he declared that the Court was "undeniably the leader in the atmosphere of permissiveness and leniency that has so irked the public." In a line of argument that demonstrates how central the figure of the armed rioter was to law-and-order assaults on the constitutional protections of defendants' rights in the 1960s, Carrington's article further criticized the *Chimel v. California* decision for the ways in which it restricted police seeking to make arrests "under the stress of riot conditions" in the following hypothetical situation: "Officers under fire on the street pinpoint a suspected window from which shots are being fired. They enter and arrest the lone occupant of the apartment from which the shots emanated. They seize a rifle from him. Now, how much further do they go? . . . What about a careful search of the apartment for a cache of weapons and ammunition? . . . What if a carefully concealed cache of arms and ammunition *is* discovered in a closet in a room other than that in which the suspect was arrested? Ought this evidence be suppressed because the warrantless search violated *Chimel's* mandate?" (253). Carrington also filed an amicus brief written by James R. Thompson of Northwestern University Law School on behalf of AELE to illustrate an effective act of speaking for police against the National Association for the Advancement of Colored People (NAACP) Legal Defense and Education Fund's own brief in *Terry v. Ohio*, in which the Supreme Court granted police the right to stop and frisk individuals who appear to be in the process of committing, or about to commit, a crime. Thompson's brief makes its point by imagining the police withdrawing from the ghettoes of American cities:

> The police could, of course, withdraw from the ghetto and end all police-citizen conflicts. This alternative might be somewhat tolerable, if only criminals lived in the ghetto; at least *their* interferences with human liberty in the form of murder, robbery, rape and other crimes, would be practiced only on each other. But, others live in the ghetto as well— innocent, law-abiding American citizens; by far the overwhelming majority. They are entitled under the same Constitution that the *amicus* says compels the rejection of stop and frisk to live their lives and experience the safety of their homes and their streets without fear of criminal marauders. They have suffered enough—discrimination, poverty, lack of education, appalling conditions of housing, and community alienation. Must they also be deprived of their right to the protection of the laws as well? (quoted in Carrington 1970, 263)

Thompson's AELE amicus brief does not recognize the police brutality and racial profiling on which the NAACP made its criticism of police stop-and-frisk procedures and instead identifies the police and its powers with the plight of potential victims living in the ghetto. Police profiling and unwarranted stop-and-frisk police action, then, are warranted because they are carried out in order to protect the African American victims against whom "ghetto criminals" commit crime. Police violation of the right not to be stopped and searched by the police without warrant, according to Thompson, trumps one's civil liberty protections because it protects potential victims from the criminal threats of other African Americans, thus legitimating police profiling and illegal stops in the name of victim protection. In their article "The Victims' Movement" (1984), Carrington and his coauthor George Nicholson compare the birth of the victims' rights movement to "the causes of racial minorities, women, prisoners, and others *who perceive themselves, or are perceived, as being disadvantaged within our socio-political legal systems*," people "*discontented* with their treatment by the system" (4, emphasis added). In a careful attempt not to speak of social oppression but instead of "perceptions of disadvantage," Carrington and Nicholson compare the victims' rights movement to other civil rights movements while also denying the existence of the structural forms of oppression that cause systemic discrimination based upon class, race, sexuality, and gender. To perceive disadvantage, according to Carrington and Nicholson, is to be disadvantaged; oppression appears as a state of mind rather than as a structural state of social life enacted and exacerbated by histories of police abuse against African Americans.

Another major constitutional decision raised the ire of law-and-order advocates in the early 1970s: in *Furman v. Georgia* (1972) the Supreme Court rendered the death penalty unconstitutional in thirty-four states. Carrington stated in *The Victims* that "no other issue brings into focus the current permissiveness toward criminals. No others more clearly display an utter disregard for the victims of crime than the advocates of the abolition of the death penalty" for the "abolitionists speak for the killer" while the "pro–death penalty forces speak for the victims. The lines are drawn" (1975, 182). The issue for Carrington was the denial of the desire of some victims' families that the state mete out capital punishment on behalf of murder victims; but nowhere does he give space to the families of murder victims who, by conscience or creed, oppose the death penalty and advocate on behalf of the rights of death row inmates.

The Supreme Court in the 1980s, under Chief Justice Warren Burger, was receptive to law-and-order assaults on defendant's constitutional rights protections, but not to the extent that subsequent courts were. At this time, the Court started to change its view of criminal cases as a relationship between the state and the defendant to one between victims and criminals. Criminal cases began to be treated more like battles between those who follow the law (coded as victims) and those who break the law (coded as criminals). Yet cases before the Supreme Court in which lawyers attempted to permit victim impact statements in trials involving the death penalty—in which the defendant is often a nonwhite person of color while the victim is generally light skinned—were still being decided in favor of the defendant. The court ruled in *Booth v. Maryland* (1987) and *South Carolina v. Gathers* (1989) that victim impact statements in death penalty cases would lead to the arbitrary imposition of this punishment. A reconstituted Supreme Court reversed these decisions in 1991 in *Payne v. Tennessee*. In this case, the grandmother of a young boy who had witnessed the murders of his mother and sister wished to testify about the effects the murders had on her grandson. The court ruled in the grandmother's favor. Chief Justice

William Rehnquist argued that "victim impact evidence is simply another form or method of informing the sentencing authority about the specific harm caused by the crime," linking victim impact evidence of harm to the decision about what kind and length of punishment the judge should impose (see *CQ Researcher*, 22 July 1994, 635–37; see also Wood 1999). U.S. Attorney General Dick Thornburgh testified before the Supreme Court, arguing that the jury should "be given the full picture of the nature and extent of the harm that's been caused to the family" (*CQ Researcher*, 637). When the nation's top law enforcement agent speaks in favor of victim impact statements in capital punishment cases, victims' rights has become a central discursive and legislative strategy of the criminal justice system.

In 1981, the Task Force on Violent Crime, created by Attorney General William French Smith, issued a report that offered several proposals for reversing the "permissive" Supreme Court decisions of the 1960s and early 1970s. Carrington was a member of this task force, and through him victims' rights became a visible and audible perspective in the decision-making processes of the task force. The stated purpose of the task force was to identify ways to toughen the criminal justice system's response to violent crime, and it did so through an explicit victims' rights perspective. The report offers the argument that to balance the scales of justice between victims and defendants, victims need to have the same, if not more, rights to participation in prosecution as defendants. The balancing of the scales of justice through a battle over victims' and defendants' rights operates through zero-sum logic: victims must have the same number of rights and the same state protections as defendants, codified in law, in order for the criminal justice system to be just. Yet, among other things, the task force sought to limit defendants' rights, so it did not seek to increase the rights of victims on a par with defendants; it advised instead that defendants' rights protections be weakened. It focused on ways to limit due process for accused defendants, deny bail on the presumption that a defendant is a danger to the community (which means that more poor people with little access to representation would remain in jail before trial and have even more limited access to public defenders), loosen the exclusionary rule on search and seizure, and limit defendants' rights to appeal (49–60). It also suggested an amendment to the Freedom of Information Act of 1966 because "it has served to protect the criminally inclined" by allowing people to request information on law enforcement procedures (40). The task force's capstone recommendation was to build more prisons and rebuild existing ones; a two-billion-dollar budget was recommended. Combined, the task forces of 1981 and 1982 and the Burger Court set the stage for battle between victims' rights and what law-and-order advocates saw as a permissive legal system; the victims now had more powerful voices officiating on their behalf than defendants did.

Recommendation 13 of the *Final Report of the Task Force on Violent Crime* states, "The Attorney General should take a leadership role in ensuring that the victims of crime are accorded proper status by the criminal justice system" (22).

> In the past several years, the realization has grown that victims of violent crime all too frequently are twice victimized: first, by the perpetrator of the violent criminal act and, second, by a criminal justice system unresponsive to the needs of violent crime victims. . . . Victims of violent crime are particularly vulnerable because of the physical, emotional and financial stresses they are subject to as a result of their unique status in the criminal justice system. . . . Both victims and witnesses play a crucial role in the criminal justice system, and neither victims nor witnesses should have to suffer as a result of their contribution to the cause of justice in America. (1981, 22)

Similarly, Recommendation 62 suggests that the Department of Justice establish "Federal Standards for the Fair Treatment of Victims of Serious Crime." The report lists the rights most victims seek in relation to their participation in the criminal justice system.

The task force document of 1981 presents the idea that victims suffer harm from their participation in the criminal justice system. By 1982, victims' rights to participation and representation in the criminal justice system were a central organizing discourse on crime in the Reagan administration. The concept of secondary victimization—the idea that victims are victimized twice, first by crime and second by their mistreatment at the hands of the criminal justice system or by the ignorance of that system—and the definition of the criminal justice system as a perpetrator against victims appeared as one of the highest priorities of criminal justice policy, precisely when victims' rights crystallized as a national discourse for the crime victim movement in the early 1980s.

Furthermore, the language of the task force suggests how central the

notion of victims' rights is to victim participation within the criminal justice system. The report of 1981 explicitly describes victims as necessary
players in the conviction of violent felons: "If victims and witnesses co-
operate fully with the criminal justice system, it will be much easier to bring
to justice and punish those responsible for breaking the law. Our society
will thus become much safer" (88). Reagan would echo this sentiment in
announcing his Task Force on Victims of Crime a year later. The report of
1982 describes how victims "learn that somewhere along the way the system has lost track of the simple truth that it is supposed to be fair and to
protect those who obey the law while punishing those who break it," reminding readers that "without the cooperation of victims and witnesses
in reporting and testifying about crime, it is impossible in a free society
to hold criminals accountable" (iv). Both reports frame their analysis of
the criminal justice system through the perspective of victims as central to
prosecutions, but also neglected and harassed in that role by investigators
and lawyers, precisely because they occupy such a necessary, if still largely
nonparticipatory, role in criminal justice.

The Task Force Report of 1982: Victim Composites and
the Typification of the Twice-Wounded Victim

During his presidential campaign in 1980, Reagan created an Advisory Task
Force on Victim's Rights, signaling that victims' rights would be a central
strategy of his campaign (*Final Report*, Attorney General's Task Force on
Violent Crime 1981, 88). In a ceremony in the Rose Garden in 1982 announcing the formation of the task force he declared, "The innocent victims of crime have frequently been overlooked by our criminal justice system. Too often their pleas have gone unheeded and the wounds—personal,
emotional, and financial—have gone unattended. They are entitled to
better treatment, and it is time to do something about it" (Office of Victims of Crime, 1990 *Report to Congress*, 2; cited in *CQ Researcher*, 22 July
1994, 634).

The task force of 1982 represented the culmination of victims' rights
as a dominant discourse of victimization in the United States. The ideal
solution to the problem of crime, reimagined as a problem of the criminal
justice system's treatment of victims, was constitutional rights for crime
victims. The task force took the victim rights' perspective on violent crime

contained in the earlier task force report and applied it to the investigation of victim-based policy and the experiential dimensions of being a crime victim. Carrington was a member of both task forces. In December of that year, the final report of the task force was published, setting forth sixty-eight recommendations for changing the ways in which victims are handled by public and private institutions and emboldened to participate in the criminal justice system. Among other things, the report stated that "The victims of crime have been transformed into a group oppressively burdened by a system designed to protect them (1982, 114).

The report of 1982 reads in part like a witnessing text, in Paul Frosh's definition (2006), a text that portrays the testimonials of others and circulates them widely. It is, nonetheless, a very bureaucratic document, not a media text to be read or watched by media audiences. It is more similar in form to a United Nations report than to the nightly news, circulating in those middle-range discursive spaces of policy institutions and victim advocacy organizations where it is well known and well regarded. The report is widely referenced in victims' rights activism and serves as an index within the history of victims' rights—as a signpost of the movement's federalization through the Reagan administration, and a soon-to-be convention of victims' rights claims making.[4] Fifteen years after its original publication, an updated report called *New Directions from the Field: Victims' Rights and Services in the 21st Century* was published; this document evidences the abilities of the original one to shape the national, state, and local policy agenda for victims' rights. While the original report purported to represent the voice of crime victims and their need for rights protections, the report of 1998 could presume that that need had been met. It represented the voice of professionalized victim advocacy—a shift from the voice of victims to that of victim advocates at the center of the movement.

Instead of being headed by right-wing movement regulars, as the task force of 1982 was, a group of well-known victim advocacy professionals constituted the authorial voice and direction of the document from 1998, including, among others, Anne Seymour; John Stein, now the former deputy director of NOVA; Marlene Young, now the former executive director of NOVA; Susan Herman, the former executive director of NCVC; Lucy Friedman, the former executive director of the largest victim service organization, Victim Services (now Safe Horizons) in New York City; and Janice Harris Lord, formerly of Mothers Against Drunk Driving. In content, it is also quite unlike the earlier document, for it represents the now-established professional orientation of victim advocacy. Called *New Directions from the Field*, the text reflects upon the best practices in the victim service profession in ways the earlier document simply could not. At the time, victim services had yet to be fully established as a profession. Instead of representing the voices of victims, as the earlier document claimed to do, *New Directions* amplified the voices of victim advocates. In the margins of the text, victim advocacy professionals are quoted on the task of victim service, casting in terms of client and provider the needs of victims that can be met through better victim service arrangements.

The report of 1982 also made its case for victims' rights through the very aesthetic form the document took alongside its claims making. Its ideological purchase came in part through marginalia that testifies to the experiences of secondary victimization on which victims' rights claims making is based. The report interweaves victims' statements that were gathered at six public hearings across the United States not only in the chapter that presents its compound fiction of the victim composite, but also alongside each of its policy recommendations. The marginalia bear their truth-telling function, for each quote constitutes a form of testimony that represents the "crime victim experience" in the United States. The conceptual force of the text lies in this feature. Quote after quote speaks to victims' experiences of secondary victimization, particularly the encounters through which they were made victim of the criminal justice system.

The report tells its readers that to understand its proposals for victims' rights reforms, they must put themselves in the position of the crime victim: "You must know what it is to have your life wrenched and broken, to realize that you will never really be the same. Then you must experience what it means to survive, only to be blamed and used and ignored by those you thought were there to help you" (1982, v). Next to the task force's recommendation for a constitutional amendment, a nameless victim states, "They explained the defendant's constitutional rights to the nth degree. They couldn't do this and they couldn't do that because of his constitutional rights. And I wondered what mine were. And they told me I haven't got any" (114). The marginalia and chapter-long victim composite facilitate this empathic reader identification.

The report's composite is unbelievable as a common, or average, account of crime victim experience within the criminal justice system. One legal scholar called it "a particularly apocryphal story" and "insulting to judges, prosecutors, defense attorneys, and law enforcement officers" (Henderson 1985, 967–68). The composite is not any one particular victim's story, but a hypothetical individual account supposedly compiled from victim reports made at the task force's public hearings. It is meant to portray "a victim of crime in America today. *This victim is every victim*; she could be you or related to you" (1982, 3, emphasis added). Like the nineteenth-century composite portraits by Francis Galton of criminals, the mentally ill, and racial types, the report presents the composite as a "generalized picture; one that represents no man in particular, but portrays an imaginary figure possessing the average features of any given group of men" (Galton 1879, 132).[5]

The composite itself is set against an "ideal criminal process, one that more closely resembles a model produced by crime control ideology than by supporters of a program designed to spare victims unnecessary trauma" (Henderson 1985, 968). The account begins with the words "You are a 50-year-old woman living alone" (1982, 3). The composite victim is a widowed rape and robbery victim; she does not speak for herself but is instead spoken of and to in a shifting second- and third-person account—a mode of address that makes it stand out from the first-person testimonials in the text's margins.[6] The account of secondary victimization it tells is also extraordinary. It does not represent a typical victim experience, but the very worst possible scenario in which the typified victim is repeatedly revictimized by multiple institutions and people—her rapist robber (who later tracks her down after being released by the court, an action about which the victim had not been notified), her employer, the police, staring passersby, a medical intern, a nurse, the press, the suspect's lawyer, and the prosecutor.

There is a stark difference between the report's victim composite and a chronicle of an actual case. For what is at stake here in the report, presumably, is a kind of truth-telling operation based on the facts of real victims' experiences. After all, the text tells its readers that it needs to understand the victim experience in order to comprehend the significance of its recommended reforms. Yet it is striking how exaggerated and spectacularly unreal the account is, blurring the supposed average or "generalized picture" the composite says it provides with the markedly atypical nature of the account (see Ginzburg 2004). It is not a generalized picture, but a manufactured worst-case scenario of repeated secondary victimization. This stands in stark contrast to a composite of death row inmates from 1969 that I discuss in chapter 6, in which two sociologists examined the common statistical features of the lives and circumstances of men living on death row over a thirty-year period. This composite follows a scientific approach to the life status of men to be punished by state death, creating a generalized picture whose goal was to capture the average *bios* through a composite man living on death row. The victim composite, on the other hand, does not integrate average or common features of crime victims; it offers an additive approach that portrays each distinct form of harm enacted against victims as if it is a general feature of the typical victim experience. It does the opposite of producing an average or general picture of crime victims.

The marginalia, on the other hand, is where the burden of credulity for the report's policy recommendations is borne. Their testimonials provide a kind of reality quotient to the political imaginary of the composite. Victims speak of being blamed for the crimes they suffered, of facing a wall of silence when they wished to speak to others of their sons' or daughters' murder, of feeling fear of reprisal from their assailants after the assault, of being forced to place their children in traumatizing situations when they were asked to identify their molester in court, and of feeling betrayed and abused by the criminal justice system. As first-person accounts, they carry the moral weight of testimonials, of people who have been there and become victims of the system. Yet, while the marginalia offer first-person testimonial as evidence of the kinds of unexpected harms committed by the criminal justice system against victims who have little prior experience of it, they are so brief that they cannot function as any kind of chronicle. They instead offer episodic snapshots of survivors, witnesses, and crime victim advocates who recount the primarily emotional burdens of secondary victimization. They are not accounts of the crimes committed against them or their loved ones per se; they are descriptions of the emotional aftermath of feeling wounded again by the system.

If Galton's photographic composite portraits were meant to represent "not the criminal, but the man who is liable to fall into crime" (1879, 135), the report of 1982 portrays the typicality of the potential of the criminal justice system to make its own victims when it denies victims their rights to participation and representation. One rape victim is quoted as saying, "I will never forget being raped, kidnapped and robbed at gunpoint. However, my sense of disillusionment of the judicial system is many times more painful. I could not in good faith urge anyone to participate in this hellish process" (5). Another speaker identified by name, Robert Grayson, states, "To be a victim at the hands of the criminal is an unforgettable nightmare. But to then become a victim at the hands of the criminal justice system is an unforgivable travesty. It makes the criminal justice system partners in crime" (1982, 9).

Accounts like the one manufactured as a composite in the report of 1982 speak as policy surrogates for victims for the purpose of strengthening criminal justice, despite, I would suggest, their failures of credulity. As the victimologists J. Holstein and G. Miller argue, "Descriptions — as when we describe someone as a 'victim' — are not disembodied commentaries on ostensibly real states of affairs. . . . [T]hey are reality *projects* — acts of constructing the world" from a victim-identified perspective (1990, 105). Viewed from another perspective, the composite might be seen not as a clear typecasting, but as a role-play scenario. As the text tells its readers, insistently in the second person, you have to imagine yourself in the position of victim in order to understand the stakes of its policy suggestions. Despite the fact that the report calls its account in chapter 2 a victim composite, it much more clearly resembles the staging of a theatrical role-play, replete with scene setting, voice-over, and the narrative chronology of a one-woman show.

The composite, then, is not a compilation of the testimonials in the report's marginalia, but a "made up person" in Ian Hacking's sense, one whose typecast constitution compiles a picture of law-and-order advocates' ideal victim — not only twice wounded, but multiply wounded, not by crimes or social oppressions, but by the very systems set up to serve and protect her. It represents not the personhood of an injured victim, but the encounter between individual and the criminal justice system, between person and law, as itself injurious. The composite is not of the victim as a person or individual, but of the victimizing potential of victims' encounters with criminal justice. In a rather paradoxical way, it is both a desubjectified portrayal of victimization as the encounter between subject and institution, and a desubjectified portrait of an unreal rape victim. In this way, the composite does not reveal the sameness or commonality of experience victims might share. It instead illustrates the similarities in their constitution as victims from their encounters with the criminal justice system. As such, the composite attempts to signify a victim type, yet the type is not a kind of person but a kind of encounter with the criminal justice system coded as victimization.

The choice to portray secondary victimization through a rape victim is also no coincidence, for the implicit critique of law and criminal justice the composite makes is indebted to histories of feminist organizing against rape and domestic abuse. Yet, unlike this report, feminists framed their criticisms in light of a larger critique that law and the criminal justice system played in men's perpetration of violence against women. This report, like many others in victims' rights, draws from the language of "the second rape" through which feminists politicized the social blame criminal justice institutions and prosecutors cast upon rape victims for their victimization. In doing so, however, it generalizes from the feminist critique of the systemic structures of sexual violence and its production of victims and perpetrators to say that all victims are revictimized in similar ways. Rape becomes a metaphor of generalized victimization, much as Susan Jeffords (1991) argued it was used to justify U.S. military intervention in Iraq in 1991 after Iraq's "rape of Kuwait." The report suggests that the second rape is not specific to the experience of rape and sexual assault victims, but is a general feature of being victimized by the state. And yet it chose to depict its typified composite victim as a victim of rape. This choice might rest as well on the construction of rape as a form of violence that transforms the victim's essential self, in which victimization can be portrayed as an experience that profoundly changes who you are, except that in this case the rape is committed not by a rapist but by the system.

The story many organizations in the victims' rights movement tell is that victim activism emerges from the "traumas of a 'second victimization' at the hands of the judicial system," rather than the experience of having suffered a violent crime (see Smith and Huff 1992, 202; interview with Diane Alexander, June 14, 2000; *From Pain to Power* 1998). If one thinks of the authors of the report as producers trained to raise the stakes of discourse in order to make policy change, then drawing on certain feminist constructions of rape as a traumatizing event so powerful that it changes one's very being amplifies the stakes of victimization. That is to say, the composite is not a compilation of rape victim experiences (in fact, only one of the victim testimonials in the chapter's margins is from a rape victim). The composite's portrayal through the figure of a rape victim signifies the high

stakes of victimization by appropriating the construction of rape as transformative of its victim's essential being. The composite is a not a real person. The fact of her rape is, more importantly than her fictive character, unreal. There is nothing specific to the woman in the composite's rape except
insofar as it made her a crime victim; that is why she matters to the rest of
the account.

Here's where the problem lies, for without a feminist critique of rape,
without a generalized picture of rape as a multiply signifying form of institutionalized sexual, heteronormative, racist, and often nationalist violence
(see, e.g., Enloe 2000), then the fact that the composite is a rape victim
means that the report uses women and abuses feminism for its own political priorities. The concept of the second rape is itself a contested term, and
rightly so, for it too conflates institutional neglect with sexual violence.
Troubled and troubling as it is, the term *second rape* was an attempt to name
the particularly durable, institutionalized forms of denial and blame cast on
women for men's rape of them (see Cole 2006, 120–23). Feminists began,
in turn, to adopt the language of secondary victimization rather than rape
to avoid just this reduction of rape to a metaphor. As two early researchers
on secondary victimization warned, "the victim must . . . defend herself
against public attitudes that assault her a second time," including the very
language of rape (Williams and Holmes 1981, xii).

If, as the historian Carlo Ginzburg suggests, nineteenth-century composite portraiture "helped articulate a new notion of the individual: flexible, blurred, open-ended" (2004, 549), what sense can one make of the
report's composite of a rape victim? How should one understand the connections it draws between certain feminist frameworks for depicting the
social blame women face for the rapes they suffer as a secondary form of
rape with a victims' rights model of secondary victimization conceived as a
series of assaults committed by the criminal justice system upon individuals already cast as crime victims? Assistant Attorney General Lois Haight
Harrington could open the *Final Report of the President's Task Force on Victims of Crime* with the statement that the nation is a victim of crime because in many ways the report was not really concerned with taking full
account of victims. Instead, it generalized a representation of victims' secondary victimization as an experience shared, potentially, by all. And in its
depiction of a composite form, the document collapses a construction of

victim experience into a fictive national rape victim repeatedly harmed by the criminal justice system, without any mention of feminists' systemic critiques of criminal justice on behalf of rape victims.

The authors of the report of 1982 were not social scientists or composite portrait artists; they were bureaucrats and right-wing movement regulars. Several were lawyers and attorney generals. None of them had the training to make a carefully analyzed general picture of victimization, and none of them were feminists. They were cultural producers of a key political discourse—that of secondary victimization in a law-and-order framework—and they chose to use a victim composite in order to typify their case. That their composite is not an average but an atypical case is precisely the point. The victim composite signifies a collection of attributes the report's authors sought to politicize as markers of a series of possible, harmful, and victimizing encounters individuals who are already coded as crime victims can have; in the process they become system victims. The authors may not be composite artists, but they were trained in how to raise the stakes of political discourse. In the process, they appropriated feminist frameworks already tested at the grass-roots level and part of public discourse on sexual violence, but they ignored feminist analysis of the very construction of the second rape.

The victim composite, then, is a gesture of cultural production against which there is no standard to be held, a political prototype, a kind of discursive portal through which secondary victimization, no matter how extraordinary, could be imagined in the starkest of terms. Its political meanings cleave around the two senses of representation Karl Marx discussed in *The 18th Brumaire of Louis Bonaparte*, that of *vertretrung* (representation in the political sense; e.g., to speak for) and *darstellung* (representation in the sense of depiction, writing, signification). The implied victim of this national victims' rights policy artifact is a bodily text to be interpreted around what can be said about victimization in a particular place and time, and who is able to speak it there—between law-and-order proxies for victims and the largely fictive depictions of victims that made secondary victimization visible. In representing secondary victimization through the particular portrait of a composite rape victim, multiply victimized beyond the criminal act of rape and robbery she is said to have suffered, secondary victimization is both a general set of conditions that create victims and a particular victimization experience tied to rape and individual rape victims. *Rape* stands in for a general state of being victimized, being raped by institutions, and a particular crime that produces a particular kind of victim delegated through the report to stand in for all victims. Such arrangements for speaking about the conditions of victimization powerfully reconstitute victimization as a political reality and political discourse of secondary wounds.

This chapter's history of U.S. victims' rights in law-and-order discourse demonstrates how central the notions of secondary victimization, legal permissiveness, and defendants' rights were to the victims' rights movement and where they originated. There are real stakes to this account, for the conceptions of victimization on which law-and-order activists articulated victims' rights lent further legitimation to punitive responses to crime—particularly around the reinstatement of the death penalty in the United States—all in the name of victims imagined through the construct of rape. In this context, the question who is the victim? is never an innocent one (Quinney 1972, 319). All policy decisions based on victims' rights code within them an imagination of who the victim is, and the harms that constitute victimization.

Victims' rights offered a fix to the problem of crime, according to law-and-order advocates. According to their logic, there would be less crime and fewer victims if the Constitution protected victims' rights as much as, if not more than, those of defendants. In the logic of law-and-order claims making, the police and the courts can presumably prevent crime by denying suspected offenders their constitutional rights. As Markus Dirk Dubber has suggested, "The victims' rights movement provided a convenient cover for [a] mass incapacitation campaign. . . . In order to cover the state's expansion of its system of criminal administration, the victims' rights movement had to operate with a very narrow concept of criminal law. In order to shield the state's apersonal system of hazard management through ever vaguer, wider and harsher incapacitative directives from public scrutiny, the victims' rights movement had to portray the criminal law as the state's response to serious interpersonal crime" (2002, 3–4). In this articulation, victims' rights function as a political signpost for a variety of law-and-order policies, political positions, and public emotions directed toward building a more openly punitive and incapacitating model of criminal justice. As a movement whose struggle is to define victims as rights-bearing subjects who can assert ownership over crime and its representation over that of rights-bearing criminal defendants, the victims' rights movement heritage rests in the law-and-order politics of the 1960s and 1970s, but it cannot fully be explained by it. As Dubber (2002) suggests, there is a "legitimate core to victims' rights" that reasserts a law of personhood in the otherwise inhumane and apersonal practices of criminal law and punishment.

The rest of the book demonstrates some of the other political histories of victims' rights and its struggles with the dominant law-and-order framework of victims' rights advocacy. While this chapter has illustrated how central law-and-order politics were, and are, to the language and political practice of the victims' rights movement, in the hands of victim activists and advocates, the victims' rights framework on crime and criminal justice does different kinds of political work.

two

An Activist History of
Victims' Rights

The antidefendant, propunishment victims' rights advocate has become one of the dominant faces of victims' rights, and for good reason, but "crime victims and crime victim advocacy have not been inevitable or uniform sources of punitiveness" (Barker 2007, 623). Instead they constitute historically and politically contingent links between different forms of victim advocacy and different political orientations to calls for punishment and vengeance that have been constitutive features of the movement for victims' rights. While many critics of victims' rights attend to its dominant law-and-order orientation (Shapiro 1997; Henderson 1985; Elias 1990; Wood 1999), victims' rights is a space of political and conceptual struggle between its dominant law-and-order ideas and practitioners, feminist antiviolence advocates, a victim service orientation toward the assistance of victims postcrime, and, in its most radical incarnations, an abolitionist stance against the death penalty.

While law-and-order policy initiatives of the 1960s through the 1980s established the policy framework and political discourse of victims' rights in the United States, the movement for victims' rights developed its own political capacities from a "coalition of 'strange' bedfellows of liberals and conservatives" that constituted its activist core (Elias 1990, 245; see also Hochschild 1989). Their relations are neither strange nor inscrutable, but are instead indicative of the particular issue orientation of the movement around the production of secondary victims and the movement's status as always already governmental in its language and orientation and in its funding. Rather than focus on the presumed oddity of the political differences gathered under the sign of victims' rights, this chapter offers an activist history of how and why the movement developed as it did, taking into account its political and organizational differences in the United States.

Alongside the dominant policy and discursive apparatus of law-and-order approaches to crime there developed a trauma and victim services framework that sought to assist victims from the perspective of their personal and collective experiences of harm from crime and the radiant traumas that affected them and their close friends and family. With the increasing interest of crime victim advocates in issues of victim trauma and recovery throughout the 1980s, and "as survivors of trauma began to tell their stories in more detail, service providers began to realize that not only were direct victims of crime affected by criminal attack, but so were many of their friends and family members — indeed whole communities could experience crisis" around the problem of crime (M. Young 1997, 200; see also J. Davis 2005).

The concept of victim in victim's rights emphasized a shared experience of victimization by the criminal justice system rather than the experiential particularities of certain crimes or their unique social sources. By the late 1980s, psychiatric definitions of victimization used measures of emotional and psychological distress to define victimization rather than the occurrence of a criminal event, shifting the emphasis from the facticity of crime and its production of victims to the experiential dimensions of being subject to, and in potential proximity to, experiences of victimization postcrime (Riggs and Kilpatrick 1990, 120–38). According to this model of victimization, a victim is described through the codification of *affec-*

tive and *psychological* responses to victimizing events — whether they are crimes or the practices of criminal justice. And while some organizations, like Mothers Against Drunk Driving (MADD), organized around particular crime victims, victims' rights claims often collapse distinctions between kinds of crime victims to assert a concept of victim that is shared by all of crime's victims, one in which the crime itself is secondary, if not tertiary, to the understanding of what constitutes a victim. Victims' rights discourse merged a conception of the crime victim with that of the trauma victim through the figure of the secondary victim and the harms she suffered from the criminal justice system. Or, to put it differently, victims' rights took the crime out of victimization while it made the encounter with criminal justice the victimizing agent. Such an approach to victimization marginalized crime in the definition of victimization while amplifying the work of criminalization in criminal justice.

The history of victims' rights is a history of the shifting models for conceiving of and talking about victimization and victims in terms that are analogous to the institutionalization of the movement around the focus on victims' services and legislative reform. The particular movement grammar of victims' rights picked up concepts and language that drew from, on the one hand, the law-and-order language of legal permissiveness and defendants' rights examined in chapter 1, discourses directed at lessening the constitutional prohibitions against state incursions against defendants. On the other, it helped articulate a language of secondary victimization by drawing on the therapeutic construct of post-traumatic stress disorder. This shift becomes especially visible in the media training texts produced by victims' rights advocates over the 1980s and 1990s and in the journalistic trauma training they helped codify over the 1990s (see chapters 3 and 4).

This chapter examines the movement genealogy in which the law-and-order language of victims' rights and the discourse of secondary victimization were combined. It looks to the history of the movement told in the training manual of the National Victim Assistance Academy (NVAA) directed at victim service professionals. In the manual, the history of the victims' rights movement appears as a tale of progress toward the professionalization of victim advocacy, progress marked by changing orientations within the field from responding to crime to treating and serving the traumatized victims of criminal justice. Through this training text, victim service personnel learn the history of victims' rights in an explicitly pedagogic framework. It is a useful history in that the students who study it learn how to see and speak about victimization within a narrative of the movement's own shifting language from victims of crime to victims of criminal justice.

The Advocates' Genealogy

Several organizations and scholars have attempted to historicize victims' rights as a movement. One of the most interesting attempts to narrate its histories and struggles through its political complexities is that of the NVAA, a training academy for professional staff in victim services associated with academic departments of victimology, including California State University, Fresno. NVAA published its first training manual in 1995. It included one of the initial comprehensive attempts to account for the history of the movement from a perspective aimed at training advocates working in victim services. Its history sought to be practicable within victim advocacy, mirroring a shift that occurred in the *Final Report of the President's Task Force on Victims of Crime* (1982) and its focus on victims' experiences to the *New Directions from the Field* (1998) policy text and its focus on victim advocates as a professional class. The NVAA manual presents a bullet-point chronological listing of the diverse practices that came together to create a social movement for crime victims. The history highlights central events across a four-period era of victims' rights in which groups of events come to signify the features of certain short periods in victims' rights development. Each period also highlights the emergence of key concepts in victims' rights advocacy, concepts that come to matter quite strategically as elements of the NVAA's training. Contextualized with the training manual, each strand of victims' rights history does not so much weave together into a unified pattern of movement development as much as list distinct events and patterns of funding and policy building that make up what NVAA sees as the significant parts of its history for the professional training of victim advocates.

As such, the NVAA periodization of the movement's history carries the major burden of its storytelling power, marked as a narrative of progress from political infighting and governmental underfunding to increasingly nationalized, institutionalized, and better-funded victims' rights advocacy geared toward the professional management of the field of victim services. While the history admits to the political disagreements and uneven developments that marked its emergence, it does so within a historical framework that offers increasing professionalism and movement/government integration as solutions to the mistakes of the past.

I use the NVAA training manual's division of the movement into four stages to analyze how its own telling of the history of victims' rights sets out the political differences and disagreements that still powerfully mark the movement, its interesting political alliances, its internal struggles, and the reach of victims' rights discourse beyond its perceived borders. I gesture to another kind of movement history that attends to the political resonances and modes of argument that extend from the past into the present in ways that challenge NVAA's political characterization of the movement's distinct eras.

The NVAA's history is a pedagogical one; it is meant to be useful to advocates who already labor in the movement and to those who seek to. In providing advocates with a language for how to talk about the movement's past in terms of political progress from uneven development and political disagreement to increasingly professionalized service provision that eschews the movement's political differences, NVAA's history becomes part of the credentialing and credentialed language of victim advocacy. Viewed in this light, the NVAA's narration of the shift from an openly politicized crime framework on victimization to a more professional, service-oriented trauma framework appears far less clear-cut and seamless than the realities of the political differences in the movement made visible, for example, around key constitutional and public debates.

Each stage of the movement's history is marked by legislative changes and by changes in victim services and in victim activism, three features that centrally define victim advocacy as a service- and reform-oriented profession. The manual frames this history as an efficient encapsulation of the many threads wrapped in the movement's skein and an easy-to-digest, patterned depiction of its key events.[1] I pay more attention to the first and third stages of the history. The first stage sets the terms for later disagreements over the constitutional amendment campaign for victims' rights. In the third, it becomes clear how the emergence of a trauma framework of victimization could better serve the political interests at the center of the movement — specifically, their interests in publicizing the plight of victims' harm by criminal justice and the media in the service of enabling and increasing victims' participation therein. While my discussion is structured around the chronology and historical characterization NVAA set, my closer attention to stages 1 and 3 purposefully interrupts their narrative of political overcoming by probing those moments when definitional crisis appears to complicate the story of political progress—particularly around what constitutes the victim of victims' rights.

Stage One: "The Response to Crime" (1972–1976)

Stage One of the NVAA's history marks the central role official criminal justice policy played in building the crime victim movement. Its beginnings here mark the centrality of a victims' rights perspective within the federal criminal justice administration to the very possibility of the movement. This stage covers the important players and events that mark the early articulations of the movement in the 1960s and its relationship to the criminal justice system, including the institutionalization of state victim compensation programs, the development of what by 1981 would become repeatable publicity events (such as National Crime Victims' Rights Week), a grass-roots victim activist constituency, and the institutionalization of the academic and professional field of victimology. Together, these developments shaped the concept of secondary victimization as the wounded or injured property of the self created through encounters with criminal justice.

At this early stage in crime victim activism—the early to mid-1970s—federal law enforcement agencies saw both law enforcement and victims' needs as contiguous: both could ideally be served, from their perspective, by improving law enforcement's abilities to control crime and apprehend offenders and by increasing victims' abilities to participate in the criminal justice system by redressing some of its harms. At the same time, a number of organizations began to advocate for and publicize the experiences of victims whose victimization was not redressed by the criminal justice system, such as victims of child abuse, child abduction, sexual assault, domestic violence, and drunk driving. Notably, these crimes had traditionally received little sustained attention from police and prosecutors and often were not considered crimes until the women's liberation movement, movements for child survivors of sexual abuse, and drunk driving victims forcefully asserted the need for the criminal justice system to recognize them as crimes and prosecute their offenders in turn (see J. Davis 2005; Herman 1992; Jenkins 1998; Warshaw 1988). Grass-roots organizing for victims thus developed alongside the criminal justice system–supported crime victim movement but often at cross-purposes or for different reasons. While law-and-order advocates were developing a language of victims' rights to support increasing social control and more punitive responses to crime in the 1960s and early 1970s, movements for women's rights and child protection politicized the ways in which victimization against women and children continued, unabated by law-and-order reformers who still refused to see them as crimes.

In spite of federal intransigence and even hostility against taking crimes against women and children seriously, the infrastructure of the developing movement for victims' rights benefited from federal assistance. Between 1972 and 1976, the federal government funded the development of several national victim advocacy conferences that brought together disparate advocates and improved conditions for strengthening national victim organizations and coalitions. The National Organization for Victim Assistance (NOVA) and the national coalitions against sexual assault and domestic violence were all formed out of these meetings funded by the Law Enforcement Assistance Administration (LEAA). The National Coalition Against Sexual Assault (NCASA) was formed when sexual assault program representatives at the NOVA national conference in 1978 voted to establish a separate national organization (see Weed 1995, 1–27; M. Young 1988, 324). The National Coalition Against Domestic Violence (NCADV) also formed that year. Marlene Young, the executive director of NOVA, explains NCASA's decision to break away from NOVA as an example of the divisiveness of the burgeoning crime victim movement. As she describes it, "The diversity of the movement was a phenomenon not highly prized by its members" (M. Young 1988, 324). NCASA sought to address the particular needs of sexual assault victims more directly and began to work as an umbrella organization for state-based and nongovernmental sexual assault services. At this point in the movement's history, advocates were articulating different political visions of the movement—precisely when some feminist victim advocates were breaking away from NOVA.

Most histories of the movement mark California's victim compensation program of 1965 as the first victim-centric governmental initiative around which the movement would develop. Victim compensation programs provided official assistance to victims of crime as victims deserving compensation for their harms. Yet, according to the criminologist Robert Elias, compensation programs have often failed to offer substantial financial support to victims of crime and function instead as primarily "symbolic, political or psychological gestures" (1983, 214). Such compensation programs have been closely associated with law-and-order approaches to law enforcement. Elias writes, "Promoting victim assistance programs such as victim compensation indicated the concern of law enforcers and legislators for the general public as potential victims, and in return, the public was willing to support tremendously strengthened police departments" (1983, 214). While compensation programs appeared as "a sign that we are finally doing something for victims" (Elias 1983, 213), they were adopted in a sociopolitical context that also saw law enforcement powers greatly increase in light of major urban riots across the United States. They were not only new forms of criminal justice policy, but, according to Elias, "a kind of social control policy" aimed at the pacification of antistate and antipolice dissent being mobilized by movements against the Vietnam War and for civil rights (1983, 215).[2]

Moreover, victim compensation programs powerfully redefined victim harm by conceptualizing the effects of crime as forms of emotional and physically traumatized property. They legitimated the idea that victimization could be defined through the loss of victims' emotional and physical property and further enabled the quantification of victim harm according to the kinds of costs and loss of property value it has on victims: medical, psychological, and financial. Victim compensation's redefinition of victimization as a loss of the property of the self became a central feature of victims' rights claims making. The development of state-based victim compensation programs would define the victim as a person without rights to private redress, yoking victims' interests in private redress from crimes committed against them to the processes of law enforcement and state ownership of crime (Quinney 1972, 319).

Victimization, in other words, came to signify a loss of well-being that "can become a claim against society to help restore the person, thus creating in society's legal framework an *emotional property right*." In this way of thinking, "individuals have emotional well-being, which is taken away from them, like property, by the criminal; as a victim, the person can claim due consideration and even restoration for the harm done" (Weed 1995, 46). Victim compensation programs both turn the victim into a form of devalued property in order to make the case for victim harm and also create the opportunity to challenge the very reduction of victims to a form of state-owned property.

In victim compensation law, or what Markus Dirk Dubber (2002) calls "the law of victimhood," emotional well-being is translated into a kind of devalued property of the self after victimization. From the perspective of the crime victim movement, the state "'steal[s]' crime from those who suffer it" (Comaroff and Comaroff 2006, 226). This critique perhaps indicates most directly the political liberalism that lies at the heart of victims' rights, for it states that victims have rights to selfhood that are impinged upon and damaged, as forms of property, by crimes committed against them (see, e.g., Dubber 2002; P. Williams 1991). Compensation laws reframed violent crime in terms of victims' loss of property—of the self, of the capacity to earn a wage, of well-being. The claim to victims' rights became a claim to the property of the self, claims that take quantified form through victim compensation programs (wherein the state takes responsibility for the loss of property one suffers as a result of violent crime or, for instance, fraud).

Victim compensation programs made it possible for advocates to assert, in quantifiable terms, that victims can make ownership claims to the crimes committed against them as a form of property right. Reconfigured as propertied participants in criminal justice, victims appear as deserving of rights to participation as propertied legal subjects empowered to speak. As one legal scholar of provictims' rights put it, in terms that link victims' property claims to their victimization with the interests of the prosecution to prosecute the offender:

> Consider the judicial process from the victim's perspective: Victims are introduced to a system grounded on the legal fiction that victims are not the injured party. Victims soon learn they have no standing in court, no right to counsel, no control over the prosecution of their case, and no voice in its disposition. In an attempt to alleviate these problems, programs have been developed to educate witnesses as to their role in the criminal justice process, reduce their confusion, and thereby minimize the prosecutors' problems with witness non-cooperation. The theory was that if the state helped victims, victims would in turn help the police to apprehend and the prosecutors to convict offenders. (D. Kelly 1983/84, 16)

Deborah Kelly explains the logic behind victims' rights calls for participation and representation in the criminal justice system around the state's function as the proxy for the injured party in crimes—that slippage between the harmed individual and the harmed social order on which the definition of violence as crime depends. As the criminologist Nils Christie (1981) has argued, the criminal justice system treats crime as a conflict between the accused and the state, while the adjudication of crime in the courts serves as a battle over the property of conflict. Early victim compensation programs articulated the propertied nature of the criminal court battle in terms that, rhetorically at least, sought to wrest from the state the property of harm for the victimized party. For most compensation programs, however, the payout for victims was and still is largely symbolic.

Diagnoses of psychological trauma from victimization and data from national victimization surveys that started to be gathered in 1967 also became important evidence for seeing the emotional and economic tolls of victimization in more quantifiable terms.[3] To credibly prove victimization as a propertied form of harm, its effects have to be quantified. Human well-being has to be transfigured not only into an individual possession that can be stolen and destroyed, but whose theft and destruction can also be said to harm the social order. According to one well-known national victim advocate, the restoration of emotional well-being becomes so important in court cases because it is the longest lasting and most neglected injury with which the families of victims must deal (M. Young 1991, 32–40). One of the battles being waged for victims' rights and enabled by early victim compensation programs was to turn experiences of crime and victimization into measurable quantities—victim "quantifacts" (see, e.g., Comaroff and Comaroff 2006). These measures qualify the emotional and economic dimensions of victim harm as forms of subjective (e.g., emotional) and objective (e.g., financial) property.

Victim compensation reimagined the victim as a kind of wounded property, requiring a different way of thinking about and measuring victimization through its psychological harms. With this came the need to publicize the problem of victimization in terms of compensation and to inform possible beneficiaries of program benefits. Publicity for such programs and other victim services quickly defined the terrain on which the movement and its public face would develop. Its publicity orientation was codified, in one way, through the annual commemorative event called National Crime Victims' Rights Week. In 1975, publicity for the first local Victims' Rights Week was begun in Philadelphia by the district attorney's victim and witness unit (NOVA, 1983). At the time, Philadelphia was the only city with such a publicity initiative directed at crime victims. Within six years, Victims' Rights Week went from being a local program sponsored by the district attorney of Philadelphia to a national publicity campaign. In 1981, Reagan declared a national Crime Victims' Rights Week to be held annually every April, providing official publicity opportunities for the victims' rights movement. This national event illustrates how the perceived publicity needs of a prosecutor in Philadelphia helped set the publicity orientation of the victims' rights movement before it even existed as a movement. It is now a weeklong advocacy event held across the United States.

In the mid-1970s, the LEAA also played a key role in publicizing a victim perspective on crime through the media manufacture of crime waves against the elderly in New York City and of Chicano gang violence in Phoenix (see Fishman 1978; Katz 1987, cited in Weed 1995, 37–38). Mark Fishman's article "Crime Waves as Ideology" (1978) analyzed one such LEAA-supported media initiative around a New York City task force on crimes against the elderly. According to Fishman, the LEAA's funding enabled the task force to spin a series of news reports on crimes against older residents of the city, resulting in the media-manufacture of what appeared to be, but was not, a new wave of crime. While according to police reports crimes against the elderly had not actually increased, the number of news stories on the topic had. In effect, the LEAA helped publicize the crime problem by funding a task force that constructed the concept of crimes against the elderly for the news media.

The mid-1970s also saw the emergence of the field of victimology, a subfield of criminology that sought to examine and produce knowledge on the victim side of the criminal/victim relationship. As a field, victimology provides the research and training for the professionalization of victim assistance, representing what became part of the research wing of the emergent victims' rights movement. Victimology represented changing ways of thinking about crime from a victim perspective. The originary text in the field, Hans von Hentig's book *The Criminal and His Victim* (1948), argued that crime had to be understood as a relationship between criminal and victim. The psychological interaction between criminal and victim, von Hentig argued, went far beyond that which the mechanical and rough distinctions of criminal law could handle, and he openly treated victims as partially culpable for their victimization (Schafer 1968/1974, 17).

Von Hentig and another early victimologist, Beniamin Mendelsohn, invented victim typologies that distinguished victims according to varying levels of culpability and innocence (Schafer 1968/1974, 19).[4] Over the 1970s, however, victimologists politicized by the antiwar, women's, and civil rights movements deemed von Hentig's, Mendelsohn's, and others' studies of victim culpability to be victim blaming (e.g., Cole 2006). Under the rubric of radical victimology, scholars developed more critical perspectives on the relationship between the production of victims and histories of institutional oppression. In the early 1970s, when these debates occurred between victimologists, the field began to be institutionalized within stand-alone academic departments and started publishing its own journal, *Victimology*, around the burgeoning amounts of empirical data on victims and their attitudes made possible through national victimization surveys (Glaser 1970/1974).

Von Hentig and other early victimologists treated crime as a mutual relationship between criminal and victim; they also argued, however, that the distinctions between the two blurred in some cases, presaging some of the disagreements anti–domestic violence advocates would have with the U.S. constitutional amendment campaign in 1997 for victims' rights around its definition of victims and defendants as different kinds of people. A victimological framework on crime opened up a key terrain of ideological debate within the movement over the distinctions and similarities between the subjects of criminal and victim, a debate that continues today. The political relations that make up victims' rights have been hotly contested over such central terms as who and what constitutes a victim and a defendant — a battle fought in and through a language of victims' rights made possible, in part, by early victimologists' recognition of the victim as having a distinct (by and large unchosen or involuntary) role in the criminal event. Disagreements over the fundamental categories in the construction of crime's subjects — criminals and victims — mark out the ideological divisions and contrasting missions that shape the political terrain of victims' rights activism and their politics of representation.

In 1997, anti–domestic violence advocates withdrew their support from a federal bill for a U.S. constitutional amendment for victims' rights. They did so on the grounds that the bill collapsed the distinction between victim and defendant in a way that would prevent victims of domestic violence from claiming status as victims. The National Clearinghouse for the Defense of Battered Women and the National Network to End Domestic Violence both produced official position statements against the congressional bill on the grounds that battered women would be denied rights as victims. Battered women who are criminally charged after physically defending themselves from their abusers would not have been recognized in the victims' rights amendment as both victims and defendants (see National Network to End Domestic Violence, 27 March 1997, 2; National Clearinghouse for the Defense of Battered Women, 21 April 1997, 1).

In its position paper, the National Clearinghouse called into question the very categories of victim and defendant by asking, "Do these women lose their 'victim' status once they have defended their lives and become defendants? And, once battered women defend themselves against their abusers' violence, do these batterers who terrorized and victimized their partners deserve the exalted constitutional status of 'victims'?" (1997, 1). Challenging the proposed amendment's definition of victim as solely the designation of someone who becomes victim by virtue of the fact that another person has been charged with a crime, the National Clearinghouse called out the amendment's absolutist position "that the defendant is the perpetrator and the complaining witness is the victim" (1997, 1). According to the authors of the statement by the National Network to End Domestic Violence, "There could be but a day's difference between the battered woman 'victim' and the battered woman 'defendant.' . . . The categories 'victims' and 'accused' perpetrators of violent crimes . . . are not mutually exclusive" (1997, 2, 4). The message from both organizations was that "it is essential to the interests of victims of domestic violence that all criminal defendants retain their constitutional protections" because battered women become both victim and defendant (National Network to End Domestic Violence 1997, 4). To be against defendants' rights protections, in this perspective, is to be against the rights of domestic violence survivors as victims. As these letters suggest, victims are not a kind of person, nor are they a position occupied distinctly from that of criminal defendants—

often they are one and the same. In 1998, the National Center for Victims of Crime (NCVC) also retracted their support for the federal constitutional amendment after the language of the bill was amended to exclude victims of nonviolent crimes (National Center for Victims of Crime 1999).

Strident law-and-order advocates, on the other hand, seek to draw hard and fast distinctions between criminal defendants and victims as not only different kinds of people, but as the central distinction on which disparate kinds of politics on victims' rights hinge. In his book published by the Heritage Foundation, *Crime and Justice: A Conservative Strategy* (1983), Frank Carrington put it this way: "In matters of justice, the liberals' clientele is the criminal; the ACLU and other liberally inclined organizations devote their efforts to protecting the criminal. Conservatives have a different clientele: crime's victims" (41). Carrington not only attributed victims' rights to conservatism while denying its roots in liberalism and progressive politics, but also insisted on a distinction between victims and criminals that other victim advocates directly challenge.

I came across Carrington's book in the library of the NCVC while on one of my research trips to their former headquarters in Arlington, Virginia. The library itself is a telling archive of the movement's mixed political orientations, with its inclusion of Carrington's right-wing missives on victims' rights shelved alongside anti–domestic violence reports and federal corrections' reports on the uses of prison labor as a way to channel money into victim restitution funds. As a political archive, the NCVC, which was formed in 1986, lays bare the political conjunctures and unexpected political differences that are at the heart of victims' rights. Carrington's autograph on the title page of *Crime and Justice* captures a small piece of this complexity: "To the Sunny von Bulow National Victims' Rights Center, with best personal and professional regards," signed on 12 June 1986; the center originally named after the heiress Sunny von Bulow never included *Rights* in its name.[5] The center, now called the National Center for Victims of Crime and headquartered in Washington, D.C., has never been an organization solely for victims' rights, nor has its name included the term. While much of its policy and media work has been done in the name of and in support of victims' rights, this work has occurred alongside other conceptual and political frameworks for responding to victimization (see below).

Stage Two: "Polarization and Unstable Funding" (1977–1981)
Stage Two in NVAA's movement history marks a time of unstable funding in the burgeoning movement that, despite shifts in financing, catalyzed the movement's nationalization at the state level. Between 1968 and 1980, the LEAA awarded $7.5 billion in criminal justice grants, but only 1 percent of these monies (approximately $50 million) was disbursed to help victims of crime (Austern 1987, 23). In 1974 the LEAA spent $3 million setting up nineteen victim assistance centers. By 1979 the federal government had begun to defund the LEAA because of its largely decentralized and poorly focused mandate over how to implement the Omnibus Crime Control and Safe Streets Act of 1968. Leadership in the LEAA changed almost yearly, and each new administrator brought new priorities for the administration's discretionary funds. Beyond the purchase of expensive riot gear (see Feeley and Sarat in Scheingold 1984, 85), the LEAA had little effect on local law enforcement's crime control abilities (Weed, 1995). As a last act, the LEAA infused $1 million into their prior funding commitments, including victim services, to last through 1981. This funding helped launch a broader, deeper crime victim movement.

Precisely as the federal government defunded the LEAA, a victims' rights approach to crime within victim advocacy and victim service organizations became ascendant: "At a time when future support for crime victim services was in doubt, the state legislatures were being lobbied to recognize a new category of citizens—crime victims—for special consideration and treatment by the state" (Weed 1995, 22–23). The movement's funding shifted, as a result, from federal law enforcement monies coming from the LEAA and other sources toward state funding. After the publication of the *Final Report of the President's Task Force on Victims of Crime* in 1982, the national crime victim movement began lobbying states for crime victims' bills of rights and statutes that would provide victim compensation and other services. Many states also began to establish their own crime victim funds, since the federal victim fund's compensation is reserved for victims of federal crimes. But without LEAA and other reliable forms of funding, victim service organizations had to retool themselves to meet the needs of the criminal justice system in order to secure federal and state funding. Many became publicity mechanisms for the criminal justice system through the research they conducted on victimization, research that was useful to law enforcement and criminal justice.

Competition for a relatively scarce number of federal seed grants during the mid- and late 1970s fractured an already contentious and disagreeable network of state and nonprofit prosecutorial and victim service initiatives (see Matthews 1994; Weed 1995; M. Young 1988). There was a lot of competition in the field of victim advocacy for very little funding; battles over limited funds and philosophical and political differences defined the crime victim movement from its early days. Many of these battles were the result of government attempts to take over victim service provision from feminist, civil rights, and child advocate organizations. The more politicized by a leftist and feminist agenda a victim advocacy group appeared to be, the harder it was and has been to get government funding. Most of the growth in victim activism at this time happened to be among surviving family members of homicide victims, including vehicular homicide, which groups such as MADD advocated as the term for being killed by a drunk driver. Amidst political and financial contention, activists who were supportive of the criminal justice system and who did not challenge the basic tenets of traditional familial and gender relations directed the field to build a more effective and victim-sensitive criminal justice system. Additional tensions emerged when states began to form their own agencies to provide services for victims, often in direct competition with nongovernmental providers of victims' services.

By the 1980s the crime victim movement had gone through a series of reorganizations that eventually institutionalized a rather loosely organized, decentralized core of the movement under the rubric of victims' rights. The policy changes set in place during the 1980s under the Reagan administration would nurture some and starve other political institutions responding to victimization, remapping the landscape of victim activism and further investing it in the needs of law enforcement and criminal prosecution through a reframing of victimization as an experience of trauma.

Stage Three: "Public Awareness" (1982–1986)
As Robert Elias argues, "In 1981, the victim movement got a national spokesman in Ronald Reagan" (1990, 246). Reagan's federal victim-centered policy initiatives of the early 1980s helped consolidate a law-and-order focus within the crime victim movement and framed the movement's struggle as a legal battle between victims' rights and defendants' rights. Victim advocacy during this time became more and more directed toward

federal criminal justice issues and legislation. Increased federal funding was central to this development (Viano 1990), enabling the movement to develop communication networks among law enforcement, criminal justice, and victim service agencies through which the crime victim movement as a whole could be organized. By the early 1980s, there was also an explosion of victim advocacy organizations—some that delivered services to victims and others that worked to increase public awareness of particular crimes and publicize the experiences of victims and their families (see Weed 1995, 19). Some of these victim organizations and coalitions formed at the national level through the LEAA's earlier resource allocation. The burgeoning state-based provision of victim services in the 1980s was possible only because of the simultaneous expansion of law enforcement powers, replete with harsher sentencing standards and increased imprisonment rates, on which victim service funding depends.

The Victims of Crime Act of 1984 established an Office for Victims of Crime in the Department of Justice that administers federal funding for victim services. Its funds feed state-based victim service providers and non-profit victim advocacy organizations, many of which rely on sustained access to this funding source. This fund comes from monies collected through the federal court system, in the form of restitution, forfeited bail bonds, and criminal fines and fees. By 1996, the fund contained just over $528 million. Most of the money has gone to state victim compensation programs and state victim assistance programs. Ten million dollars went toward the investigation and prosecution of child abuse cases. The remaining money (3 percent) funded demonstration projects, training, and other assistance to improve delivery of services to federal crime victims. States competitively awarded the money they received from the fund to local community-based organizations that deliver services directly to victims.[6] The point here, ultimately, is that the federal funding on which the states depend to fund some of their governmental victim service agencies relies upon federal criminal prosecution. The more people are arrested, charged, and prosecuted through the federal judicial system, the more money ends up in the federal Crime Victims Fund. This means that the material resources for victim services issue directly from the more powerful criminal justice system achieved in part through victims' rights policy victories in the 1980s.

In the NVAA's history, Stage Three therefore marks a shift to group-level national politics, financed and otherwise supported by the federal government. After the publication of the *Final Report of the President's Task Force on Victims of Crime* in 1982, which signaled the federal institutionalization of victims' rights and set the policy course for victims' rights legislative advocacy, other major milestones included the passage of the Victim Witness Protection Act in 1982 and the Victims of Crime Act in 1984. Each carved out space within the legal system and policy circles for victims' rights advocacy. They also mobilized federal resources and money for victims' rights-based advocacy and legislation. During this period, MADD and other groups formed the National Victims' Constitutional Amendment Network to direct an organizing drive for a U.S. constitutional amendment campaign for victims' rights.

Some of the core theoretical concepts within the movement also emerged during this period. Movement activists began to speak more explicitly through concepts like secondary victimization and post-traumatic stress disorder because of their deepening relationships with people working in psychology and mental health counseling. Once these concepts began to circulate within the movement, the mission statements of movement organizations also began to reflect the psychological dimensions of victims' treatment needs. The movement's vision of political action became more and more defined by the perceived need to heal the trauma of victimization by creating procedures and educational campaigns geared toward the law enforcement officers, emergency responders, and court personnel whom victims encounter postcrime to help prevent and redress their secondary victimization by such personnel.

Major national victim advocacy organizations were founded at this time—such as the NCVC and MADD—and several victim activists began to occupy high profile positions vis-à-vis the mass media. In addition to the parents of murder victims who became visible media activists, celebrities like the fashion model Marla Hanson and the actress Theresa Saldana, both of whom suffered assaults by knife-wielding attackers, used their media status to advocate for victims' rights. Saldana, for example, formed a victim advocacy organization called Victims for Victims, as a result of her experiences recuperating from her assault. The growth of victim advocacy organizations during this period corresponded with funding that became available from some wealthy patrons who were victimized and became "media victims" as a result of the media coverage of their cases. The children of Sunny von Bulow formed the NCVC with the help of a core group of victim advocates who were looking to form their own organization. Von Bulow's son specifically wanted to fund an organization that could help victims respond to media coverage that portrayed victims in a negative light. Examples such as these demonstrate a general tendency within the movement at this time to organize around and through the victimization of wealthy social elites. This might also explain in part why the movement targeted the criminal justice system and the news media for not acting on behalf of victims, for the wealthy social elites around whom the movement was first organized were used to being better served, or at least attended to, by these institutions. For people whose lives and histories have been defined by a lack of access to the criminal justice system and the news media as victims, particularly, in the United States, poor and nonwhite victims (see, e.g., Stabile 2006), the most pressing issue tends to be repeat victimization more than a lack of rights as participants in the criminal justice system. Wealthy socialites and celebrities expect to be served by social institutions and the media; as crime victims, they felt their relationship to each change.

The NCVC is an especially significant organization to consider from the perspective of publicity on victimization. The family of Sunny von Bulow formed the center after her husband, Claus, apparently tried to kill her with an overdose of insulin. As is typical of most high-profile criminal trials (von Bulow won his criminal case and was then tried in civil court, where he won again), the media coverage of the case tended to focus on the life of the presumed perpetrator, Claus von Bulow. During one of his trials von Bulow posed in black leather alongside his mistress for a photograph in *Vanity Fair*. Meanwhile, the press presented Sunny von Bulow as a "pill-popping, sugar-craving drunk who brought her coma on herself" (F. Rose 1989, 40). According to her children, the media and the prosecution treated von Bulow and her family as if they were the ones on trial, not allowing any of them into the courtroom during Claus von Bulow's prosecution. As the reporter Frank Rose describes her adult children's response to the trial, "Watching the proceedings on TV—gavel-to-gavel coverage was provided by Cable News Network—they began to feel like other people who've met the cold arm of the law: They felt victimized all over again" (1989, 40).

Sunny von Bulow's children, Annie-Laurie Isham and Alex von Auersperg (both from a former marriage), were enraged by the treatment of Claus von Bulow's trial by the news media and the criminal justice system. During his civil trial for attempted murder, Sunny von Bulow's mother died, which resulted in the establishment of a sixty-million-dollar trust for her grandchildren. Morris Gurley, the von Bulow family trust adviser, and von Auersperg decided to invest money from the trust into an existing victim advocacy organization to help other victims' families deal with news media coverage of trials. In early 1985, Gurley and von Auersperg were unable to find an organization that suited their interests in victim advocacy (see Weed, 64–70).[7]

According to Frank Weed's history of the movement, in April 1985 Gurley and von Auersperg attended the NOVA and MADD SHARE (Self-Help Associations Relating Experiences) conference in search of possible organizations to fund. One of the workshops they attended, presented by Anne Seymour, who was the director of public affairs and the media and legislative specialist at MADD at the time, dealt with the issue of victims in the media. Today, Seymour is a well-known victims' advocate who works on media issues and consults nationally on this topic. At the conference, Gurley and von Auersperg also met with members of an ad hoc committee that had formed in 1983 to study the recommendations presented in the *Final Report of the President's Task Force on Victims of Crime* from 1982. Specifically, their aim was to figure out a way to implement a campaign to lobby for a constitutional amendment on victims' rights. Gene Patterson, director of chapter development for MADD, and Janice Harris Lord, who had just joined MADD as director of victims services, were part of this committee. Lord now consults nationally on news media coverage of high-profile court cases and victims' rights. According to Weed, the committee was trying to establish a regional center of NOVA in Texas to facilitate state constitutional amendment coalitions, but NOVA was not interested. The committee needed money to establish a center where they could develop training programs to educate advocates in coalition building and political action tactics. They found the funding they needed in Gurley and von Auersperg.

After the conference in 1985, Gurley and Seymour kept in touch about von Bulow's trial and the surrounding media coverage. After the trial, Seymour sent Gurley a copy of the proposal Patterson had written for the new center. Gurley and von Auersperg had been considering the need for a new victim's organization. According to Weed, Gurley liked the proposal but thought its vision was too limited (68). In August 1985 Gurley met with Patterson and Seymour in Fort Worth, where they decided to create a new victims' rights organization that would carry the name of Sunny von Bulow. The Annie-Laurie Aitken trust funded the center for three years at $1.7 million a year (69). Compared to the $3 million with which the LEAA funded nineteen victim organizations in the mid-1970s, this was a significant amount of money. In December 1985, five former MADD employees, including Patterson and Seymour, became the staff of the Sunny von Bulow National Victim Advocacy Center. As Weed suggests, the center worked its way into the middle of the crime victim movement's loose network of organizations by becoming a source of information and training expertise (1995, 70). The center changed names twice, first, to the National Center for Victims, and then, in 1998, to the National Center for Victims of Crime.

NOVA and NCVC were formed around the perceived need for activist publicity on victims' plight — specifically, for what they termed the secondary forms of harm caused by the criminal justice system and the media. While NOVA was formed through an LEAA conference on victim services in 1975, NCVC was formed by victims and advocates who wanted to deal more directly with news media coverage, high-profile trials, and the push for victims' rights legislation and constitutional amendments. This work would not have been possible without the previous work of NOVA and the President's Task Force on Victims of Crime of 1982. Both NOVA and the task force brought together advocates, the criminal justice system, and policymakers, all vital players in the movement for victims' rights. Marlene Young, the first executive director of NOVA, was also responsible for much of the victims' service orientation and language in the 1982 *Final Report* (see Stein 2007).

Stage Four: "Legislation and Professionalism" (1987–Present)
Stage Four represents the further integration of the movement into legislation, federal, and state criminal justice agencies and victim service providers. As the NVAA argues in its training manual, "Political efforts during this time were much more organized and presented a clear and cohesive agenda" (1995, 2–11). By 1995 twenty states had adopted constitutional amendments on crime victims' rights, and forty-eight had passed Victims' Bills of Rights. All states, including the District of Columbia, enacted crime victim compensation programs. In other legislative battles, activists

promoted what they called common-sense interpretations of defendants' rights that sought to impose limits on the constitutional protections defendants secured in the 1960s through Supreme Court decisions.

As told primarily by organizations responsible for the reproduction of victim advocacy organizations and the professionalization of victim advocates—organizations like the NVAA—this history points toward the increasing professionalism of advocates whose labors are directed at redressing the harms of secondary victimization. Today, a handful of university-based and national credentialing organizations exist to train victim advocates in order to reproduce the values and expertise of the field. In 1989 California State University, Fresno started the first Victim Services Institute to certify victim service professionals in other states. In 1991 this school offered the first undergraduate major in victimology, and in 1993 they produced their first graduating class (NVAA 1995, 2–13). The NVAA today functions as a standardized national curriculum for training victim service professionals.

Yet the professionalism of the movement's victim service providers is only part of the story of victims' rights activism in the years after 1987. The increasing professionalism of victim advocacy, for instance, does not explain the ways in which advocates working in grass-roots victims' organizations shape and extend victims' rights political discourse. Their genealogy does not explain or clarify how both pro–death penalty victim groups and anti–death penalty victim groups could use victims' rights discourse to articulate politically disparate visions of victim-centered criminal justice.

For instance, similar claims to victims' rights can be found among pro–death penalty victim organizations like Justice for All and among anti–death penalty murder victim family organizations such as Murder Victims' Families for Reconciliation (MVFR) and Murder Victims' Families for Human Rights (MVFHR). Justice for All and MVFR make their cases on the death penalty through their claims that they represent victims. The similarities in their claims to speak for and as victims become the very grounds for their political difference. As an organization aligned with the law-and-order orientation of so many victims' rights advocates, Justice for All is authorized by the state to speak through the voices of the murdered in support of the death penalty, while the abolitionist victims' rights advocates of MVFR give voice to the families, as both families and victims, from a position without the recognized authority to speak through the state on behalf of death row inmates, also using the movement grammar of victims' rights. The online murder victim commemoration site produced by Justice for All, murdervictims.com, speaks in the voice of murder victims seeking the death penalty. Who speaks from this voice of the dead, however, is unclear. On one page of the website, a murder victim named Elena Semander "speaks" of her murder by Coral Eugene Watts, his fifth victim. It is not she who literally speaks, for she is dead, yet the account is cast as if it is her voice that addresses visitors to the website. Above the account is a professional photograph of a smiling Semander in a V-neck sweater, her long brown hair parted in the middle and hanging in waves over her shoulders. She is strikingly beautiful, a point made all the more significant in light of the accompanying caption, which discloses that she was strangled to death on 7 February 1982.

In addition to describing her death and the discovery of her body, the victim voice relates the organization's call for Watts's continued imprisonment to the visitors of the website:

> I wish I could meet you in person, but I was murdered over 20 years ago by a man named Coral Eugene Watts. Back in 1982, Watts followed me to my friend's apartment complex where he strangled me with my shirt, hog-tied my body, and threw me into a nearby trash dumpster. I fought as hard as I could . . . but lost my life in the end. After the garbage man found me the next day, my family received the heartbreaking phone call from the Houston Police Department.
>
> Coral Eugene Watts would eventually lead police to 3 bodies and confess to 13 murders; I was his 5th victim. Although he was sentenced to 60 years, an old Texas law will require Watts to be released back into society after serving only 24 of those years. This unjust law was abolished in 1995, but cannot be made retroactive. His release date was scheduled for December of 2005. Please sign my petition to ask the Governor of Texas to review this case, and somehow prevent my killer's early release. **Thank you for giving me a voice**. (www.murdervictims.com/watts .htm, accessed on 10 June 2008)

Framed in terms that question a Texas law that releases prisoners after serving a minimum number of years on their sentence, the victim voice amplified here is inflected through a law-and-order framework of legal permissiveness. The significance of victims' rights to representation is presumed in the assertion that victims' voices, even if ventriloquized, not only deserve representation in the politics of capital punishment, but also become a key feature of those advocating for it.

MVFR also makes the claim that murder victims' voices should be heard in the case of capital punishment, but they link their claims to victims' rights to an abolitionist stance on the death penalty: "Our members challenge the assumption that all survivors of murder victims want and need the death penalty in order to heal" and that "opposing the death penalty is a struggle undertaken only on behalf of the offenders, the people on death row" (King and Hood 2003, n.p.). MVFR not only gives but also produces a voice for victims' families and death row inmates' families who oppose the death penalty. The act of giving voice to victims is also presented as the group's main site of struggle in this politics of victim representation, just as it is for Justice for All. MVFR argues against punishment in victims' names, while Justice for All repeatedly makes the case for offenders' punishment on behalf of victims.

The organization must also make the case that it has a right to make claims against capital punishment as victims, whereas Justice for All presumes the ability to speak for punishment in victims' names, an effect of the ways in which the dominant law-and-order history of victims' rights authorizes pro–death penalty groups to speak for murder victims. It has published an eighty-four-page book, *Not in Our Name: Murder Victims' Families Speak Out Against the Death Penalty* (King and Hood 2003), containing photos of murder victims and their families and family statements against the death penalty that commemorate their dead. They describe how they have to argue for the legitimacy of their claims against state execution on behalf of murder victims. Unlike Justice for All, they do not speak as the voices of the murdered; instead, it is their family member's killing that enables them to speak for themselves as familial survivors, without putting words into the mouths of the dead. In one account, Bill Babbitt of Elk Grove, Calif., an African American man, speaks of his pain at turning his brother Manny in to the police for a murder he committed, learning the hard way that the corrections system did not seek to give his brother the mental health counseling he needed but instead put him to death (King and Hood 2003, 2). Babbitt and the other family members who speak in *Not in Our Name* delink victims' rights and support for the death penalty.

In their book *Dignity Denied: The Experience of Murder Victims' Family Members Who Oppose the Death Penalty* (Cushing and Sheffer 2002), MVFR also makes the case for prison abolition from a victims' rights perspective, challenging how prosecutors use victims' rights as a strategy to win death penalty cases rather than giving voice to families who are opposed to capital punishment. A short essay by Renny Cushing, the organization's executive director, "Ain't *I* a Victim?," draws explicitly from Sojourner Truth's famous address to the Women's Convention in Akron, Ohio, in 1851 about the status of black women's womanhood and its recognition in the women's movement. Cushing's question, "Ain't *I* a Victim?," is addressed to pro-punishment victims' rights advocates who continue to presume that victims need and want the execution of their family member's murderer, that to heal from the grief and loss of murder means taking the life of the person who can be held responsible. As Cushing states, "Even though I oppose the death penalty and would not find resolution in another killing, am I not a victim as well, with a loss as piercing as the losses of victims who do support the death penalty?" (Cushing and Sheffer 2002, 7).

MVFR's report *Dignity Denied* advocates on behalf of victims' rights to speak as opponents of the death penalty.[8] The report includes a letter to Marlene Young of NOVA asking that the group recognize its own commitment to ensure dignity for all victims, including those who oppose the death penalty. The fact that MVFR must address itself to NOVA, of which it is a member organization, on these terms suggests just how strong the links between victims' rights and pro–death penalty activism are.

To summarize, this chapter illustrates the movement's political conjunctures and disjunctures. The most significant differences are revealed in the articulation of victims' rights to particular political positions on the death penalty and in the disagreements among victim advocates about who and what constitutes a victim and a defendant in the case of battered women arrested for defending themselves against their abusers. While law-and-order frameworks still powerfully define victims' rights and its political linkages, victims' rights discourse also gives activists a language through which they can challenge law-and-order assumptions about victims and their desires for punishment, denaturalizing what the elements of the movement identified with law-and-order have represented as victims' inevitable, or natural, will to punish. By attending to these other branches of victims' rights political genealogy and their relative marginalization within the national infrastructure of victims' rights organizing, different political orientations to victims' rights become more visible; they also become a more visible feature of the story of victims' rights in the United States. The political complexities of the movement become even clearer when viewed from the perspective of national victim advocacy organizations' own orientation toward media publicity.

part two

Opening and Closing the Second Wound
Representing Victims

Media attention is itself a political resource.
EDIE GOLDENBERG, *Making the Papers*

Meet the Press

Representing Victims' Rights

This chapter examines strategies for engaging the news media found in media training texts and advocacy manuals of the victims' rights movement. These texts tactically define and reorient movement organizations' relationship to the press. The increasing public visibility of symbolic crime victims and of victims' rights rhetoric in the news media is due in part to the specific strategies some victims' rights organizations developed to produce media coverage of crime that takes crime victims and their rights as victims as its reference point. For a great portion of the victims' rights movement, national publicity about the needs of crime victims has been mobilized not only as a key organizing principle for its activists, but also as a right owed to victims.

Movement-based media training texts offer hidden transcripts, or what the sociologist Stanley Cohen calls "the quiet constructions of professional and expert claims makers" (2002, xxiii), of the ways in which the language of victim harm and the politics of victims' rights made their way into the very conduct of victim advocacy. As movement documents, they express the advocacy positions and policy and service priorities of victims' organizations. Training texts are artifacts of organizational ways of thinking in the movement. They illustrate how activists think about and orient their practices toward the media. These texts also reveal the significance that advocates place on the role of information in their movement mobilization. As modern forms of documentation, these training texts "demand a response" (Riles 2006, 24). That demand is directed at changing the behaviors of those activists and organizational staff internal to the movement. According to the victims' rights media specialist Anne Seymour, "In a very real sense, *information is the key that allows access to victims' rights, recovery and respect.* Unless victims are made aware of their rights, as well as how and when to exercise them, such rights have no meaning or usefulness. Simply put, *information is the means to victim service providers' ends.* . . . How victim advocates are able to gather, synthesize, analyze, expand, distribute, and dispense this precious commodity has a direct impact on the success of the victims' rights movement" (1999a, 2). From this movement perspective, information is both the content and conduit of victims' rights advocacy.

Rather than analyze the news and talk show representations that result from victims' rights media advocacy, I draw attention to the behind-the-scenes planning and organizational forms of intervention and documentation that create the conditions for more explicitly victim-based news coverage of crime. With its "superstructure of writings" (see Rock 1998, 139) and national communication networks, the movement for victims' rights constructs victims and mobilizes their representation in order to tell a different story about crime from the perspective of its victims and survivors (see Weed 1995).

I analyze the documented talk that occurs between and by victims' rights advocates about their views of the media and their methods for organizing themselves to speak to, with, and as its representatives. The talk examined here is that which is contained in written manuals produced for the express purpose of training advocates how to think about and strategize their and their clients' encounters with media organizations. While these materials do not provide a complete picture of how the movement as a whole thinks about and addresses the media, they do locate—in par-

ticular organizations, parts of the movement, and parts of the media industry — sets of practices that have been collectively organized in order that
they might speak with more authority and force as movement voices on
the media.

Following Paul Rock's findings that "who victims were and the shape
they were to take were pragmatic, contingent constructions" of the British
victims' rights movement (2004, xvii), my analysis demonstrates that the
U.S. movement's media strategies were coconstitutive of a definition of
victim modeled on the covictim of murder and the concept of secondary
victimization. The concept of the victim as one who experiences victimization in proximal relation to its representational politics in criminal justice
and the media is contingent upon an understanding of representation itself
as wounding in a victims' rights framework. Victims' rights discourse combines an understanding of media as victimizers and producers of victims
with a definition of victim that is presumed to be, at heart, vicarious. How
this developed in the U.S. movement suggests some uniquely American dimensions to the victims' rights imagination of the media. The notion that
practices of representation create victims constitutes representation as a
relation of harm between reporters and those they represent. Through the
concept of secondary victimization, the movement makes a set of inter-
locking claims about the wounding capacity of representation within the
politics of crime and criminal justice.

The movement documents analyzed here were all published in the
United States between 1990 and 2008, after the U.S. movement had nationalized a discourse of victims' rights in its push for victims' rights state
and federal amendments. Their training texts link the political assertion of
victims' rights in the criminal justice system to that of victims' assertion of
rights to control the news process for making crime news and its representations of crime victims. These texts mobilize a particular definition of the
victim in victims' rights that seeks to control the storytelling power of news
media coverage of crime: the families of victims killed by murder and other
criminalized acts of violence causing death, such as car accidents.

In the organizations discussed in this chapter, the families of murder victims, car crashes, and victims of school shootings exist mostly as ventriloquized voices in training texts (see, e.g., Lamb 1999). It is not their organizations that speak here, but their unique status as parents of murdered (and
otherwise killed) children, whose proximity to murder's victims as mothers

and fathers grants them cultural and political authority to speak about the lives of the killed as their grieving witnesses. In the context of training texts directed at changing media behavior, they also stand in as the evidence of injurious encounters between the press and murder victims' families that provide the emotional subtext for media activism around victims' rights. In other words, the families of dead victims speak in their own words through media training documents, but they do not necessarily speak for themselves. The presence of victims' statements in training texts represents a particular movement approach to the media vis-à-vis its portrayal of victims, where that relationship is described primarily as an affective one, an injurious form of encounter between media representatives and the victim representatives being interviewed for news stories and videotaped for nightly news broadcasts. As some victims-turned-activists make clear, the advocacy framework of treating the media as harmful to victims is in stark contrast to some victims' desires to speak to the media without the aid of advocates.[1] Some also see their relationship with the media as potentially therapeutic and empathic.

The politics of representation advanced in victims' rights advocacy illustrate the movement's historical links to law-and-order campaigning, with its focus on finding, apprehending, and punishing criminal offenders. The movement offers a victim perspective on crime that is still largely analogous to crime news, only it seeks to add a "victim" view of crime and prosecution to the press orientation toward police and offenders. Victims' rights activism around the press focuses myopically on getting victims into the news so that they have the opportunity to describe their experiences of crime and the effects it has had on their lives. For some it provides an opportunity to advocate on behalf of the movement.

In the absence of a critique of the press's investment in crime news as a staple of its profitability, and of the police and court focus of crime reporting, however, victims' rights activism presumes that the media coverage of crime victims adds an otherwise missing dimension to victims' search for criminal justice. They do not approach the media as part of a broader collective attempt to prevent the social reproduction of violence, where news *could* represent violence and victimization differently. Instead activists seek to play a more active and visible role in news of crime victims, in ways that might also prevent some of the harms they see being produced by victims' encounters with the press.

Victims' Rights Media Advocacy: The Injuries of News Making

From the perspective of the victims' rights movement, the most unexpected and therefore damaging harms committed against survivors and families of crime victims are caused by the criminal justice system and the media system, not the individual offender or the criminal event. This is a key distinction the movement makes in its definition of victims, a definition based on the concepts of secondary victimization and secondary or co-victims. According to Diane Alexander, former director of library and field services at the National Center for Victims of Crime (NCVC), most victim activists first come to their activism either because they suffered a particularly heinous crime or because something went wrong in the police investigation or the prosecution or both. They may feel as if the police botched part of the investigation or mistreated them. They may have seen what they consider to be inconsistencies in their court case, felt mistreated by the prosecutor, or had to endure testimony from a witness that criticized the victim or placed blame on him or her. They may have also experienced rudeness, insensitivity, unethical behavior, or intrusiveness by the news media (author interview, 14 June 2000).

Victims' rights media advocacy specifically addresses itself to the victimizing practices and harms particular to the media, practices that movement advocates discuss as producing its own victims. Media victims are those people who "suddenly become the focus of unsought media attention" (Lull and Hinerman 1997, cited in Corner 2000, 37). They experience what John Corner (2000) refers to as involuntary revelations of the media process. While many victims do not choose to experience the media as its objects of inquiry, some do. Even when they have voluntarily chosen to participate in news interviews or talk shows, some people report feeling revictimized by the process.

Across the movement, stories of victims' interaction with news media are referred to as forms of secondary victimization, or the second wound, coding into linguistic form the notion that the media-victim relationship is one that causes additional harm to victims. In the news media, such wounding is said to revictimize the survivor in the representation of their experience and in the implied responsibility the news media can cast onto victims for their suffering. The crime victim movement sees the media as a perpetrator against subjects who are victims of crime, and who then also become victims of journalistic harm. One twenty-six-minute training video produced by the Victims' Assistance Legal Organization for the National Victim Assistance Academy (NVAA) in 1999, "The News Media's Coverage of Crime and Victimization," demonstrates how victims' rights advocates frame the media as a violator of victims' rights. The narrator opens the narration in a voice-over of video showing people with cameras running across the school lawn at Columbine High School: "It's been called a swarm, a gauntlet, and a crime victim's worst nightmare." The news media appear in the film not only as aggressors, but also as interventionist public servants who fight crime by covering it. A few minutes into the film the narrator reinforces the film's interventionist framing of crime news: "The media aren't likely to go away or stop covering crime," but "media coverage of crime and victimization . . . can serve as a valuable and necessary function for all parties."

The film represents crime coverage and its potential harms to crime victims as an industrial product produced to meet audience demand for crime news. According to the journalism professor Greg Luft, speaking in the film, "Reporters are not thinking in terms of how it's going to affect the victim. They're thinking about the need to get [the story], where they need to get it, and how they are going to get it to the audience, because the audience is very hungry for the information, especially during a breaking story." Luft makes audiences responsible for the news media's production of crime news and its aggressive behavior toward victims. In his perspective, if there were no news-audience demand for the news media to cover crime and its victims, the news media would not act so aggressively toward victims. The film suggests that it is not news coverage of crime per se that is the issue, but the ways in which journalists must conduct themselves as producers of news commodities that audiences demand.

Through Luft, the film frames the problem of journalists' insensitivity toward victims as the effect of a larger market for crime news, embodied by audiences rather than by the news industry and its advertising clientele. The public who views and reads the news bears the blame for intrusive journalistic conduct toward crime's victims. By portraying the limits of crime news as an effect of audience demand, the film conflates a rather simple political economic imagination of the news industry (one which ignores advertisers altogether) in which the industry supplies what the audience demands and a victims' rights imagination of what audience demand might indicate: a desire for empathic connection with crime victims and their stories. The very notion of audience demand articulated in "The News Media's Coverage of Crime and Victimization" takes on additional meaning in a victims' rights perspective. The vast majority of victims' rights advocates think about the audience as the site of demand for and receptivity to stories about crime victims.

Alongside their critique of the news media's capacity to harm the victims of crime and create its own victims, advocates seek to understand the routines of news production so that they can learn how to play by the established rules of journalism. For them, the source of the wounding power of representation rests in victims' and advocates' incapacities to control the form and content of victims' news representation and the dimensions of its circulation across time and space. Certain accounts of the media's ability to harm victims in the process of telling stories about crime and its victims circulate widely in training texts. The NCVC booklet *Crime Victims and the Media* (1990), written by Seymour, narrates some of the stories that are repeatedly cited in the movement as evidence of the media's ability to create its own victims through intrusive, insensitive behaviors. One story tells of the news media coverage of an Oregon medical examiner who, while on-air, picked up the skull of one of the victims of the Green River serial killings. The news video showed sand falling from the skull cavity. It aired on three Seattle stations, and the families of the victims who had purposefully chosen not to see the remains of their murdered family members were faced with dramatic video imagery of one victim's skull. As Seymour argues, "The media, upon airing this offensive video, took away the families' choice to refrain from seeing what their daughters had been reduced to" (1990, 3), indicting the media as a perpetrator against the abilities of victims' families to remember their daughters as they wanted to.

Advocates like Seymour object to the kinds of news media coverage of victims that Neil Websdale and Alexander Alvarez call "forensic journalism" and its "hyperfascination . . . with weapons, wounds and the last horrific moments before death" (1998, 140). In forensic journalism, the visual display of crime victims' bodies offers up physical evidence of the crime. Like crime scene investigation television programming, including the CBS program *CSI: Crime Scene Investigation* and its two spinoffs, *CSI: Miami* and *CSI: NY*, forensic journalism images the dead bodies of victims of violent crimes. As Websdale and Alvarez write, "Forensic journalism is imbued with an 'investigative motif' or an 'ethic of detection' that feeds off minute details such as the location of corpses" (1998, 134). According to their analysis of newspaper coverage of homicide–suicides in Arizona, news crime coverage routinizes reporting on the details of murder victims' bodies and the immediate situational dynamics of the crime itself, rather than on the lives of the victims and perpetrators and on the histories of (primarily) male violence and abuse, histories which would lead to a better understanding of the killing of women in the case of homicide-suicide (126). News stories "selectively reconstruct the persona of victims ... to evoke a sense of loss" (136), but not necessarily in ways that surviving family members wish to understand that loss or have it represented — such as through the visual display of the bodily remains of their killed family members.

Against the forensic focus on wounded victim bodies in much news production, advocates like Seymour assert that victims, their bodies, and images are not mute witnesses, but subjects who, with the oversight of the victims' rights movement, can be "coaxed into telling a story" (Hartley 1992, 30, cited in Jermyn 2004, 176). Coupled with stories like the one of the Oregon medical examiner and his display of a crime victim's skull on local television news, Seymour tells other stories about successful uses of the media in *Crime Victims and the Media*. The text hails advocates as protectors in a scenario where media are the victimizers and crime victims' families are its victims. As protectors, victim advocates are also situated as powerful spokespeople for crime victims. Seymour characterizes the role of media activism within the crime victim movement as one of "giv[ing] a face and voice to victims, who are traditionally faceless and voiceless. To show the devastating consequences crime has on individuals and communities. . . . To educate people on how people are victimized and stress ways people can deal with being victims themselves" (author interview, 1 November 2000).

The problem is that the codes for representing victims and the industrial structures of crime news prevent victims from claiming the control they seek to represent their stories of victimization on their own terms. Some victims describe their experience with the media in terms of a loss of control over the representation of their experience, of the repeatable broadcasts and circulation of their dead one's images, and of who has access to those experiences. Local television news and feature stories in the newspaper represent victims' experiences in a very narrow time frame. They are abstracted from a particular moment and circulated, not only in the news story for which it is gathered, but also across the media, particularly in television, where video images are often repeatedly looped across broadcasts and across networks (Manning 1998). This feature of recording and broadcasting holds out the promise, on the one hand, of witnessing from a distance, in that repetition implies broader circulation of representation not just in one medium but in many, through which more audiences might receive mediated witnessing texts. Part of the desire to tell the victim's story in victims' rights approaches to the press extends this promise of broadcasting: to move the victim's story of crime from the one (the victim; the witness) to the many—where the potential mass audience is a potential mass witness to crime victims' testimonials (see, e.g., Peters 1994). Mass media supply, as Paul Frosh and Amit Pinchevski assert, the very possibility to constitute the distant witness through the repetition of recording for broadcast (2008, 8, 13). Television networks, in particular, are not only "gatekeepers of the airwaves," but "guardians of the event's repeatability" (13).

Such is the status of media witnessing, according to Frosh and Pinchevski, "a perpetual, generalized apparatus that welds together singularity [e.g., of a particular murder] and its ceaseless representation, the exceptional and the routine, specialized communication bureaucracies and ordinary people with everyday gadgets" (2008, 14). Activists like Deborah Spungen and others describe this state of media witnessing around the recording of the singular event of homicide and its replication in representation as the technological, industrial afterlife of the dead over which victims' families have little control. In cases of murder, "the initial television footage— glimpses of the victim's body bag, bloodstains on the street or sidewalk, chalk marks outlining the body—may be replayed for years as the murder case progresses through the criminal justice system or as other events put the story back in the news" (Spungen 1998, 219). Brian Rohrbough, whose son Daniel was murdered in Dylan Klebold's and Eric Harris's shooting spree at Columbine High School, reported to USA Today on 20 March 2000, "I can tell you from a victim's family perspective, no week has gone by, not this week or any other, that I have not seen the [videotape] on TV with my son's body on the sidewalk" as other students raced to safety. "Every single time I see a Columbine story, that footage comes up. There's so much trauma caused by that. It never ends" (O'Driscoll 2000, 3A). Un-like the control a person can exert over looking at a family photo album to revisit one's past, repeated broadcasts of victims' media representation ob-viate the relative control and privacy of the decision of whether or not to look at a photo album or to tell one's story of victimization in conditions defined by the victim-narrator (see Barthes 1981).

These family members of murder victims speak of the reuse of file foot-age as an especially harmful communication practice. They describe the repetition as something they are unable to escape, casting in conscious, attentive form what some media theory presumes is a collective uncon-scious, a compassion fatigue produced by ubiquitous audiovisual media from the perspective of the disinterested or desensitized audience (see, e.g., Gitlin 2001; Moeller 1999). For covictims of murder, their experience of the repetition of media footage of their dead loved one occurs not in the wash of ubiquitous media, but in the directness of reception. In this case, the repetition of representation may be for everyone and seemingly everywhere, but it speaks directly to covictims in their particular location as murder's direct witnesses. As murder victim families, they receive repeated footage of their loved one's murder, not as part of a constant media flow, but as a weapon of depiction targeted directly at them. In these contexts of seemingly incessant repetition that define current mass mediation, the broadcast of images of dead victims to their families — who receive them as members of the media audience — functions as a form of personal com-munication about themselves and the victim, but the representation is not for them; it is of them, but not under conditions most victims perceive as for them. For survivors of murder or other violent assault, primary victims see a moment from their past as it is defined not by themselves but by the news media: a moment about oneself but potentially shared with everyone.

Repetitive video coverage of victims therefore inverts what Paddy Scan-nell (2000) describes as the for-anyone-as-someone structure of mass media texts; that is, their ability to speak as personal forms of communi-cation with audience members. For victims of crime, representations of themselves or their dead family member function more as for-someone-not-anyone media texts, despite being made possible within the very indus-trial structures of mass-mediated address Scannell discusses, particularly around crime and disaster news. According to Scannell, "Broadcast pro-grammes and daily newspapers appear to have a peculiar communicative structure. They are heard, seen or read by millions (by anyone and every-one) and yet, in each case, it seems, they speak to listeners, viewers or readers personally, as individuals. They are, it could be said, *for* me or any-one" (5). Scannell argues that media texts are neither impersonal, mass-produced goods nor customized, personal goods (e.g., a custom-built bike or a family snapshot). They can address viewers of television news sound-ing like custom-made forms of communication because of the intimate quality of their pseudo-personalized address.

The representation of victims, even when not of their own family, speaks to covictims not *as if* they are personally addressed to them: they *are* per-sonally addressed to them. While victims of violent crime are members of the larger news audience, it is not the mode of address of representations of victims that constitute the personal in this case, but covictims' recep-tion of the representation; victims are a different kind of audience mem-ber from all the others precisely because they belong not to an imagined community of crime victims but to an actual one—and one that, like the organization Parents of Murdered Children (POMC), organizes itself to keep an eye on the media's portrayal of murder. The structures of recep-tion of representations of victims by crime victims as I describe them here does not mean that all victims interpret representations of crime's victims in the same way or even as being harmful, as other research on crime vic-tims' interpretation of crime news and entertainment suggests (see Madriz 1997; Schlesinger et. al. 1992; Weis and Fine 1998). Yet, according to a vic-tims' rights perspective, the potential for harm along these lines of recep-tion by crime victims is structured into the very process of making news about crime victims.

While not indicative of all victim activists' approaches to the media, some of the mothers of murdered children I spoke with who head local chapters of POMC engage with media as opportunities to tell the truth about murder. They seek to hold media accountable for what they see as the glamorization of murder and murderers. POMC's national executive di-rector, Nancy Ruhe, cites the organization's Murder Is Not Entertainment (MINE) campaign, through which the parents of murdered children can send MINE Alerts to other activists and parents in their organization when they see or hear media depictions of murder they interpret as harmful to victims and their families. Ruhe detailed how one survivor saw an adver-tisement for a new show on the cable network VH1 about prisoners playing in musical bands (*Music Behind Bars*). A MINE Alert went out across the organization's phone and email tree, and, according to Ruhe, one prison shut down its music program as a result of their flak campaign (author interview, 6 July 2005). Whether the alert had this demonstrably direct effect or not, talk of it is indicative of the kind of power and possibility victims' rights advocates see not only in using the media, but also in organizing themselves to publicly criticize it from the audience position of murder victims' families.

Another chapter leader, Patricia Gioia of Schenectady, talked to me in impassioned tones about her experience watching the HLN show *Nancy Grace* five days a week. In Gioia's opinion, Nancy Grace, who is the survivor of her fiancé's murder ("She's a crime victim and a lawyer," Gioia emphasized), hosts a show that represents one of the few programs on television that is centered on crime victims. Grace covers high-profile court cases from a crusading victim's standpoint, essentially "getting the coverage of crime right," according to Gioia, in the attention she gives to missing persons and the struggles of families of crime's victims (author interview, 31 July 2006). Gioia also spoke of watching coverage of the Laci Peterson murder and Scott Peterson's murder trial, remaining deeply interested in the case because Peterson's body was found very close to the Berkeley marina where Gioia's daughter Mary was murdered.

Ruhe's and Gioia's self-described critical attention to the media's coverage of murder, murder trials, and prisons interprets such representation not from the perspective of its possible pleasures and capacities to entertain, but from the perspective of victims keeping watch on how the cultural talk about murder takes account of the grief parents of murdered children experience. While they seek to hold media corporations accountable for their entertainment depictions of murder, they see the possibility media access holds for extending victims' rights perspectives on murder cases in programming like *Nancy Grace*, a show that, because of its crusading host, powerfully gives voice to a victim perspective on murder that supports state punishment.

Gioia and Ruhe challenge the notion that the for-anyone-as-someone audience dynamic of broadcasting situates nonvictims and victims on an equal footing in the media audience, that is, in a structure of impersonal, industrial mediation and personal address that places nonvictims and victims alike in equal relation as witnesses to crime victim testimonials. Viewed from the position of the news as a structure of media witness-ing, Frosh describes this witnessing as the "social space of uncommitted observation and impersonal witnessing in which people are *sufficiently the same*—sufficiently interchangeable and equivalent—for each person to be able to imagine what it might be like to be in another's shoes" (2006, 281).

The presumed equivalence between audience members in their relation as impersonal witnesses to media coverage of crime and other news sub-jects is precisely the problem at stake in representation for crime victim activists. They challenge the equivalences Frosh draws between the ability of audiences to imagine themselves in others' shoes by asserting that the experience of being a victim of violent crime is not like any other experi-ence and cannot be imagined as it is lived. From the perspective of victims' rights, victims stand out as unique subjects in the production and reception of crime and crime victim news, as witnesses whose bodily and linguistic testimony portrays the emotional, physical, and social aftereffects of crime. They are precisely not witnesses to crime and to the news media in the same way audiences are to the witnessing texts of crime and disaster news. Thus, while victims' rights perspectives on crime have long asserted, as Lois Haight Harrington did in the preface to the *Final Report of the President's Task Force on Victims of Crime*, that "crime makes victims of us all," victims' rights media activism is premised on the view that crime uniquely makes particular victims, and so do the media.

Bruce Shapiro (1995b), a contributing editor at *The Nation*, the execu-tive director of the Dart Center for Journalism and Trauma, and a victim of violent crime himself, writes about the disorienting experience of witness-ing oneself in the news: "On the local evening news, I have unexpectedly encountered video footage, several months old, of myself writhing on an ambulance gurney, bright green shirt open and drenched with blood, skin pale, knee raised, trying desperately and with utter frailty to find relief from pain . . . a picture of my body, contorted and bleeding . . . a propaganda image in the crime war" (23). He describes his lack of control over how the story of his victimization is retold. He has lost the ability to assert posses-sion of his personal experiences, becoming a commodity in the circuits of crime news.

In his interaction with the news media, Shapiro pays witness to his own stabbing and testifies in bodily form to the emotional and physical dimen-sions of the violence he has suffered. The news media then turn that act of witness and its powers of testimony into a news product for others to consume, a process by which audiences and the news industry itself "become the recipients of someone else's testimony" on crime and its victims (see Frosh 2006, 269). News audiences in this construction function as witnesses to crime and crime victims through their interactions with news media insofar as they become the recipients of journalistically packaged testimonies of crime victims like Shapiro. Shapiro's testimony constitutes not his own choice to speak to the press and be imaged by them; he is instead turned into a set of testimonial video images that he does not himself depict. Shapiro's own response to looped video coverage of his knife-wounded body is not about the troubled gap between what he feels and what he can say about it, in terms that other scholars have defined as the key problem in the construction of witnessing as an epistemological divide between experience and representation (see Peters 2001; Caruth 1995; see Leys 2000 for a critique of this tendency in the scholarship). From Shapiro's perspective, the injury of seeing his body writhing in pain in subsequent news broadcasts about his and others' stabbings at a coffee shop in New Haven rests with the disjuncture between his own experience and interpretation of the crime as one of its victims and the ways in which the news recasts his body-as-testimonial object regardless of, and without recourse to, his own relationship to his act of witness. His act of witness is no longer for him in particular, but for others who have no particular or necessary relation to the violence he has suffered.

When Shapiro and other victims describe the experience of seeing themselves on the news or recount their interactions with the news media as forms of secondary victimization, they describe an injurious chasm that forms between themselves as personal, physical, and emotional witnesses to their own suffering and the industrial production of their testimony for others who are unburdened by the ontological, affective, and epistemological dimensions of being witness to suffering firsthand. The problem for crime victims like Shapiro is the status and use of their testimony and its representation in the industrial culture of crime news. Talk of secondary victimization or harm by the news media offers a way to describe the experience of the news media's abstraction of victims' suffering in the form of their own testimony, a form of speech which becomes no longer, if ever, only about them, but a broader news discourse about crime's victims.

Shapiro appears in the NCVC's handbook on the media *Privacy and Dig-*

nity. Another testimonial in the handbook reminds readers that, because news turns crime into a commodity to be sold for profit, "only in the rarest instances are victims portrayed as victims" (10) and not as products to be hawked. It suggests advocates educate the news media in the victims' rights perspective that crime news should serve its victims' (varied) interests in criminal justice. After recovering from his brutal knife attack, Shapiro began speaking out against the punitive politics of victims' rights. His criticisms of victims' rights developed out of the ways he saw his own assault being used in calls for especially harsh punishments against his attacker in the name of victims' rights (Shapiro 1995a, 1997).

Shapiro's critiques of the punitive politics of victims' rights, however, are not discussed in *Privacy and Dignity*, illustrating how the politics of representation asserted within victims' rights media texts enable some political perspectives to be aired while others, like Shapiro's criticism of victims' rights, become less visible. Contextualized within this handbook, Shapiro's quote speaks to his inability as a crime victim and as a journalist to control how the news media commodify the video of his assaulted body, a line of argument completely in line with the critique in *Privacy and Dignity* of the news media's abstraction of crime's impact on its victims who suffer from it. It also illustrates how the concept of secondary wounding committed by the news media is about the wounding capacity of representation — that is, the capacity to be harmed in and through practices of depiction. Shapiro's larger critique of how such commodified images of victimization also function as powerful political evidence in the crime war is absent from this training text, a fact that speaks to the ways in which victims' rights both can and cannot become part of the explicit discourse of its activism.

Victims occupy a unique position in which they are subjects of news media attention, witnesses to their own experience of victimization, and also witnesses of the news production process. They see the news media as only others in their position can see them, as the people and practices responsible for news media coverage of crime victims. As witnesses to its production practices, crime victims can denaturalize the practices of news making because their position as media victims is constituted by it (Couldry 2000).

In the mid-1980s, the crime victim movement began to actively develop media training materials to counter sensationalized media representations of victimization and reports of the insensitive treatment of victims by news and talk shows. The first symposium on crime victims and the media was held in 1986 at Texas Christian University in Fort Worth, also the location of the Sunny von Bulow National Victim Center, which had just opened. The main impetus for media activism and training within the mainstream of the crime victim movement comes from victims, who report being treated insensitively or uncaringly by journalists, news photographers, and talk show hosts. Stories of victims' poor treatment by the media circulate widely in the movement. On two occasions, advocates who work for different organizations told me the story of a man invited to *The Montel Williams Show* to talk about his daughter's murder by a cyber stalker. The producers of the show told the man that his participation would warn others of the dangers of cyber stalking. During the taping of the show, however, Williams never gave the father a chance to talk about his daughter's death as the father had apparently wanted to and instead proceeded to blame the daughter for her murder because she used the Internet. Additionally, just after his daughter's murder, the man's younger, preteen daughter was watching cartoons on Saturday morning when the station broke into the programming with a special news report showing video footage of her older sister's body falling out of the door of her car after she had been stabbed to death. The father contacted the local news affiliates in an effort to get them to stop airing the video, but they refused to do so until the end of the day. At the time, the police had not yet notified anyone in the family of the woman's death (author interview with Diane Alexander, NCVC, 14 June 2000; author interview with Anne Seymour, 1 November 2000). Stories like this foster the moral outrage and ethical justification that fuel the movement's media activism, especially as it is directed at the news industry.[2]

As Frosh suggests, perhaps the abstraction of witnessing from the experience of having suffered violence or crime to that of the representation of that experience of violence might broaden the conception of crime victim testimonial and the significance of crime news. Witnessing conceived in this way sidesteps the crisis of veracity that theorists and commentators on witnessing have analyzed between experience and the inconsistencies or inabilities of its representation and addresses the issue instead as a question of the possibility of communication between media audiences and texts of witnessing—those news testimonials made by crime victims but not for them. As Frosh suggests, news about crime victims is not primarily for victims, but for others. That requires the abstraction of both victims' stories about their experiences of crime and of video displays of their wounded bodies, de-realized portrayals that crime victims repeatedly describe as injurious to them and to their dead family members. Victim harm, in this formulation, is built into the very conditions that structure media witnessing of crime victims. This is a form of harm that cannot be prevented by changing reporters' behaviors toward victims, particularly during news interviews, an approach that much of victims' rights media training prescribes (see chapter 4).

Asserting Rights to Representation in the News

You are in a unique position to put a human face on crime victimization.
NCVC press kit for victim advocates, "Bringing Honor to Victims," National
Crime Victims' Rights Week, April 2002

Where victims directly interact with news media and talk shows, victim advocates see two opportunities. One is to serve victims' needs to be represented vis-à-vis the news media. Advocates then act as media representatives for victims. This work translates into teaching victims about the rights they have in their relationship with reporters and news photographers and their ability to shape the news story by controlling what kind of information on the victim they provide. Some advocates in the field refer to this work as both an opportunity and an obligation for victim advocates (Seymour 1990, 1999a, 1999b). While victims do not have legal rights in this interaction, advocates teach them that they do have social rights: the rights to participate and not participate, the right to answer only the questions they want to, and the right to stop participating in a news interview at any time. They not only become witnesses of the news production process as audiences, but also witness and participate in its production firsthand. Victim advocates talk about this participation in terms of victims' abilities to control parts of the interview process.

While consciousness of the importance of media coverage of victimization has been a staple of the U.S. crime victim movement, its advocates paid little direct attention to media activism until the late 1980s and early 1990s. One limitation has been a lack of resources to produce training materials. With the increased funding of the Crime Victims Fund through the Office for Victims of Crime in 1994, more resources became available to help produce and distribute media training materials to victim advocates. At this time, funding for the annual resource guides for National Crime Victims' Rights Week comes from the Office for Victims of Crime. Programmatic media planning and training have historically been hampered by the movement's decentralization and the relatively conflicted relationships among the central players within the victims' rights movement (particularly around their disagreements over the purpose, inclusions, and exclusions in the various legislative bills that have proposed a federal constitutional amendment for victims' rights) and between them and antiviolence victim advocacy based in public health and prevention (see Rentschler 2003). As a result, media training materials are being produced by different organizations and aimed at diverse political and practical ends, often with little coordination and little direct knowledge of each other's work.

Within this decentralized movement context, however, a number of media training materials offer similar sets of techniques and basic advice to communications staff in advocacy organizations, victim advocates, and survivors of crime and violence. How these techniques are used, however, differs substantially depending upon where they are being used within the field. Some of the material meets what Charlotte Ryan describes as the first goal of media activism: turning news into contested terrain (1991, 4). For some victim advocates, this means telling a different story about victimization by crime, one that speaks from a victim's perspective in order to change how it can be politicized as an issue of violence and how it can be prevented (see Bennett and Edelman 1985). For many organizations within the movement, this translates into establishing long-term relationships with the news media and providing information to reporters. For others it means producing alternative narratives to the ones typically offered in media coverage of crime and victimization. Such narratives focus on violence rather than on crime, where violence "refers to behaviors that are injurious to others" and "crime is best defined as behavior deemed offensive to (and by) the state and therefore subject to punishment" (Stabile 2006, 2–3). As a result, they also attempt to shift the media agenda on crime toward prevention and collective, non–law enforcement responses to violence, a set of alternative strategies I discuss elsewhere (see Rentschler 2010).

Victims' rights advocates perceive news as a site of struggle over the meaning of crime and the representation of crime victims. In such documents as the NCVC's two publications *Privacy and Dignity* and *Crime Victims and the Media*, NOVA's training manual *The Victim Advocate's Guide to the Media*, and the video *Crime Victims and the News Media*, created for the NVAA's yearly victim assistance curriculum, victims' rights organizations articulate their claims about victims' rights to news media representation. Organizations like the NCVC in Washington, D.C., according to one sociologist, want to "control the storytelling prerogatives of the media" (Weed 1995, 90). As national umbrella organizations, NCVC and NOVA provide service and training to other victim advocacy organizations. Their training documents and video demonstrate how crime victim advocates build networks with media institutions and journalism programs in order to represent crime from the position of movement-defined crime victims: the families of murder victims. They put training materials in the hands of advocates and journalists (see chapter 4) in order to to raise the media visibility of their crime victims and to change how the news media treat their subject-victims in the process.[3]

In these documents, victims' rights advocates describe their training as a proprietary battle over who owns the story of a crime. In this line of thinking, "If the victim or their family 'owns' their crime story, then the victim should be able to squelch the retelling of the crime story or at least be able to insist on a dramatization that shows a conflict between villains and victims" (Weed 1995, 90). Through her publication of the victims' advocate training text *Crime Victims and the Media* (1990), Seymour helped carve out the political discursive terrain on which victims' rights activism directed at the news media would be formulated. This booklet, along with *Privacy and Dignity: Crime Victims and the Media* (2000) and *The Victim Advocate's Guide to the Media* (published after 1995; the manual contains no publication date), teaches victim advocates how to put victims' rights into practice with the news media. They teach advocates how to educate their crime victim clients to see themselves as rights-bearing subjects and how to facilitate the movement of media-friendly victims, especially the families of victims who have been killed, into news portrayals of crime.

The foreword to *Privacy and Dignity: Crime Victims and the Media* explicitly portrays the victim whom the handbook addresses, the family: "Like wounded animals surrounded by packs of hyenas or wolves, the family of a murdered child, parent or grandparent is surrounded by reporters who ask in a kind of devil's chorus how they feel and what they want in the way of retribution. . . . We've also seen families in lethal domestic violence cases having to endure first a devastating death, and then the demolition of a victims' character in the newspapers and on TV before a trial even starts" (2000, 3). The handbook characterizes its purpose as the restoration of privacy and dignity to the families of crime victims, who have become, in their view, media victims. Advocates "can recruit the media as an ally" in movement attempts to portray crime through the suffering of its victims by first criticizing the intrusive behaviors of some of the press in their coverage of high-profile violent crime. Quotes printed in large letters at the beginning of the handbook interpret the press's behavior toward victim families as forms of incivility and misconduct and warn readers that the families of crime victims should cultivate a form of risk consciousness in their interactions with the news media. Through the expertise of psychiatrists like Frank Ochberg, handbooks like *Privacy and Dignity* explain how crime victims can assert control over news media behavior in the context of the news interview by first coming to understand how their interactions with the news media always bear risks. As crime victims are instructed how they can exert control over the news interview, they are also told that the conditions in which the news interview and its subsequent news story are bound can never be within the control of crime victims.

In other words, the victims are taught to interpret the news media's behavior as a series of risk-producing, affectively laden, interpersonal encounters defined through their potential to harm news victims. By interpreting the news interview as a form of risk-producing communication between reporter and news victims, these training guides aim to cultivate a form of risk consciousness that translates into more victim control over the communication transaction of the news interview.

The news interview bears the majority of the burden of harm within the idea of the news media as a wounding agent of newsworthy victims of crime, partly because it is also seen as the most trainable of news-making practices. Decisions about news layout, headlines, advertising, language, and news photography do not appear in *Privacy and Dignity* or the other handbooks. They focus instead on how victim advocates should prepare themselves to be interviewed by the news media: "What I would say to victims is: It's important to know that you have choices. Every victim can shape the interview. You can establish a time, a place, have someone with you, even talk over the purpose of the interview. But what you can't do is choose the comments that will be quoted, the pictures that will be selected, or the headlines that will be used. You can't even control whether a lingerie ad will run next to your story about sexual assault" (Ochberg in *Privacy and Dignity*, 4).

Privacy and Dignity never defines victims' rights in its pages, but its information is nonetheless portrayed through a victims' rights perspective on news representation. On page 7, the handbook states that advocates "must empower victims to use the media to bear witness to the impact of crime and violence in our society," urging advocates to see relations with the news media as the means to serve the larger crime victim movement. Statements from well-known victim activists who are also surviving family members of murder victims—including Ellen Levin, the mother of the murder victim Jennifer Levin; Marc Klass, the father of the murder victim Polly Klass; and Brian Rohrbough, whose son was killed in the Columbine High School shootings on 20 April 1999—describe the intrusive behavior of the news media and the need for rights to privacy through which they can grieve their loss. Even more significantly, the political stakes of media attention for crime victims' families come through especially clearly in the words of Dan Levey, the brother of a homicide victim: "I used every opportunity to keep the case in front of the public. I didn't want people to forget my brother's face, the face of a victim of heinous crime. And I wanted to shame the perpetrator who had been charged, by letting people see his face, too. Reporters, who were sympathetic and sensitive and as outraged as I was, remained interested in the case and helped keep my brother's memory alive, and . . . ultimately helped bring the perpetrators to justice" (28). Levey asserts that the cultivation of interest in the victims' life among sympathetic reporters and the willingness to provide family photographs of murder victims catalyzes the criminal justice system to punish offenders for the families of victims. According to Levey, retaining the memory of his brother required that he put his death on display for the news. To assert his own rights to retell the story of his brother's death and his own interest in seeing his brother's killer punished, Levey invests in the forensic power of the news media: to put victims' bodies on display in remembrance of their lives.

Levey's quote, more than any other in *Privacy and Dignity*, lays out the ethical and political possibilities victim advocates see in their engagement with the press. While these training texts warn of the potential injuries victims can suffer through their encounters with the news, Levey speaks to another dimension, that of possibilities of publicity and the ability to transform the politics of victimization through the cultivation of relations with sympathetic reporters — casting the relationship between news and victim as more than one of potential harm, namely, as a site of potential political, social, and personal transformation. In order to do this, Levey asserts that his murdered brother should be represented equally with his perpetrator, that understanding murder requires giving both murderers and victims face. To do so requires the development of, in Levey's words, emotional and political bonds with reporters. The media handbooks illustrate how closely linked the victims' rights movement perceives news media coverage of crime and the workings of criminal justice to be, where each can be cultivated as a platform for the rights of crime victims to have a voice in the formal procedures of punishment.

Most of *Privacy and Dignity* details specific steps that advocates and their victim-clients can take to make interaction with the news media more about what crime victims want and need. On page 19, the text lists sixteen choices available to victims in the news, such as their ability to request that they be allowed to fully present their side of stories about victimization and their right to refuse all interaction with the news media. The political language of victims' rights gets articulated to codes of behavior that advocates and crime victim families can embody. Readers learn that victims' rights emerge in the cultivation and management of social interaction between news subjects and reporters, where the assertion and maintenance of boundaries between the two positions occur (see also *Crime Victims and the Media*, 7–10; *The Victim Advocate's Guide to the Media* sec. 1, 35–36).

The NCVC's earlier publication by Seymour, *Crime Victims and the Media*, explicitly links victims' rights media training to the political struggle for victims' rights: "It is imperative to develop an ongoing, professional relationship with the media in your community. A 'one time only' interaction may serve your intent and purposes, but a continual sharing of resources and information will enhance not only **your** interests, but those of the entire victims' rights movement" (1990, 1). Every media training hand-book that victim advocates publish continually stresses the importance of establishing long-term relationships with individual reporters. They train advocates how to determine whether journalists will be empathic to their cause through examination of their previous coverage of crime victims. The resource guide for National Crime Victims' Rights Week in 2008 reassures advocates that they need not be "news junkies" to get to know reporters, instead urging advocates to search the websites of local news organizations to regularly monitor crime reporters (2008, chap. 4, 1).

At the national level, advocates express admiration for and reward par-ticular news anchors and morning show hosts for their portrayal and treat-ment of victims. One advocate I interviewed, Marcia Kight, whose daugh-ter Frankie Ann Merrell died in the Oklahoma City bombing and who at the time worked for NOVA, displayed an autographed photograph of then-anchor and cohost of NBC's *Today Show* Katie Couric on her desk at work. Kight spoke of the compassion Couric showed victims in her sym-pathetic and sentimental coverage of the Oklahoma City bombing. Like other anchors, Couric had a job to do. She had to produce disaster cover-age that could portray the impact of the event in emotional terms. While one can interpret her encounters with family members of the blast victims as shrewdly strategic, to Kight, the tactical interface with the press through the person of Couric felt like a moment of caring encounter. The vision of victims' rights activism surrounding the press that Kight gestures toward through her autographed photo of Couric holds out the possibility that the media's need for disaster and crime coverage might not preclude an em-pathic personal encounter between the reporter and the victim. Whether this meeting is strategic or instrumental could in fact miss the point, for victims' rights activism presumes the necessity of crime and disaster cover-age, and reporters need to get the story.

Most of the advocacy concerning the media warns of the unsympa-thetic reporters and talk show producers whom victims are presumably more likely to encounter than the Courics of the business who are beloved by advocates. Seymour draws a clear distinction between news media and talk shows in her training seminars. According to her, tabloid talk show hosts disguise their interest in victims as sympathy in order to encourage their participation. And while some national victim advocacy organizations are unwilling to help talk shows get access to high-profile victims through their organizations, talk show producers may be turning more to local victim service providers than national organizations to gain access to victims. According to Seymour, "*Dateline* and *60 Minutes* continually do stories on victims. What we have today are media now going to local service providers as sources. And that's a good thing. We do train people to be careful with their contact to the media in prosecution cases and around victim safety" (phone interview, 1 November 2000). Talk shows continue to call victims directly to request their participation on the show. Advocacy organizations find themselves in a difficult position vis-à-vis talk shows because they continue to cover victim issues. Some victims also express a desire to appear on talk shows (see Livingstone and Lunt 1994; Priest 1995). As service organizations, their job is to serve victims' needs even if that need is defined as participation on a talk show.

While talk shows provide a mass-mediated, yet highly personalized mobilization context for discussing victimization, they also frame the solutions to victimization as primarily those of recovery and redemption. Talk shows dramatize victimization as a series of experiences a person travels through, from suffering and grief to a kind of patched together, tenuous wholeness. They narrate victimization as an experience one eventually triumphs over, if not now, then at some point in the future with the right kind of therapy.

Victim advocates have developed some basic guidelines for victims to follow in their participation on talk shows. The document "Talk Show Guidelines," produced by NCVC attempts to prevent victims from experiencing revictimization by talk shows by training talk show producers and victim advocates how to recognize victims' rights and experiences. With the support of fifteen national victim advocacy organizations, NCVC disseminated these guidelines to talk show producers and staff across the United States. The guidelines suggest which victims should and should not appear on talk shows (adults, not children), when they should appear (long enough after the trauma to be fairly stable and out of crisis), and how they should be treated (with care and with assistance from counselors and advocates if they so desire). The guidelines refer to victims' reports of feeling retraumatized in their interactions with talk show hosts and audiences. They also refer to the common signs of post-traumatic stress disorder in an attempt to educate talk show producers and victim advocates about trauma's long-term manifestations. The guidelines include a "Bill of Rights for Crime Victim Guests on Talk Shows" that outlines victims' rights of participation in order to demystify the news production process.[4]

This demystification work addresses itself to the very meaning of news from the industry's perspective. In its press packet for the National Crime Victims' Rights Week campaign "Bringing Honor to Victims" in 2002, the NCVC defines news for its advocate clients in terms specifically linked to possible crime victim news stories that advocates can propose. Dividing news along the typical industry standards of hard, breaking news and soft feature pieces, the press kit explains how the passage of new victims' rights legislation or a local crime's effect on the community can be constituted as hard news, while stories of individual crime victims who rebuild their lives through victim advocacy can become soft news features. Advocates are told that the media will typically view National Crime Victims' Rights Week as a feature piece and are provided with statistical overviews from which to draw data on victimization for news stories.

More explicitly, the NCVC's *Strategies for Action* series of media training materials, through which the National Crime Victims' Rights Week materials are produced and distributed, builds full media packages for victim service and advocacy organizations. In addition to training advocates in how to understand the news media and its systems of production, it models ideas for media-centered events and language, putting into practice a victims' rights "media grammar" in the form of quotations and speech bites that also speak to the ways in which victims' rights abstracts the politics of civil rights activism and its political language for its own instrumental uses.

Their annual media packet for National Crime Victims' Rights Week in 1998, the theme of which was "Victims' Rights: Right for America," includes four pages of inspirational and motivational thoughts drawn from radically different historical and political traditions to be used as themes in speeches, presentations, and special events. The quotations are grouped into themes, and advocates are told how to use them for specific purposes. The first group includes motivational excerpts from Confucius, such as "Choose a job you love, and you will never have to work a day in your life," to be used "when addressing individuals who provide services to crime victims" (18). Others are suggested for addressing the need for a balanced justice system, such as the following quote from Oscar Wilde: "Discontent is the first step in the progress of a man or nation" (19). Other quotes are

directed at advocacy messages about the need for a victims' rights constitutional amendment, including one from the farmworker and radical labor
activist César Chávez: "We are confident. We have ourselves. We know
how to sacrifice. We know how to work. We know how to combat the forces
that oppose us. But even more than that, we are true believers in the whole
idea of justice. Justice is so much on our side, that that is going to see
us through" (19). Advocates are reminded that "securing a victims' rights
amendment will not be an easy or quick task" and that the use of carefully chosen quotations can "motivate individuals interested in pursuing
the amendment" to the Constitution for victims' rights (20). A quote from
Hannah Arendt closes the media packet's section on the use of motivational thoughts to highlight the significance of advocates' commitment to
their cause: "Action without a name, a 'who' attached to it, is meaningless"
(21).

From political theorists to gay writers, historical figures and civil rights
leaders to radical farmworker activists, the annual media packets for National Crime Victims' Rights Week embody the interesting marriage of different, and often opposed, political traditions in the movement for victims' rights. But the media packets do not serve as meaningful encounters
between these traditions so much as they abstract and then reify a discourse of victims' rights that is possible only through their decontextual-
ization and the political oppositions that exist between civil rights struggles
against racial oppression and profiling by the police and victims' rights calls
for more participation in the work of policing crime. Eschewing the constraints and troubling oppositions of the different movements and political traditions their excerpted authors come from, the annual media packets
stick to the more propagandistic fundamentals of what to do with words.
Rather than produce a sample speech, the *Strategies for Action* guide offers
advocates "speech bites," smaller chunks of text that can be incorporated
into advocates' own speech-making practices. The bites come themed in
concepts produced specifically for that year's campaign, including parallel rights, fundamental rights, fairness, courageous participation, treating
victims' rights seriously, observing justice, justice for all, liberty and justice, and fair treatment. Under parallel rights, the guide offers the following speech material: "There seems to be a misconception about victims'
rights—that somehow it's a zero-sum game—that victims' rights can only
be gained at the expense of offenders' rights. If that were true, it would be

wrong for America. Yes, that just is not the case when it comes to crime victims' rights. Victims and advocates are simply seeking to create parallel rights for victims in order to give victims access to information and a limited role in the process. That's the least our society owes to those it failed to protect" (22). Despite the history of victims' rights assaults on defendants' rights, the text attempts to smooth over the political oppositions in the movement through the language of "rights balance." Other speech bites similarly describe victims' rights as a constitutional issue through the language of fairness and shared justice. In an especially straightforward speech bite, the guide declares, "Our Constitution should protect victims of crime just as it protects those who are accused of committing the crime — justice should be for all" (23), insisting that victims' rights be defined in relation to, if not in opposition to, defendants' rights.

Along with ten pages of sample newspaper editorials, letters to the editor, and public service announcement (PSA) text, the quotes and accompanying imagery for posters, buttons, and other visual media in *Strategies for Action* for 1998 formulate an extensive movement-based grammar in which advocates can talk together about victims' rights through a shared language and set of media strategies. These annual media packets also clearly articulate movement concepts about victims' rights and their understanding of the media from a victims' rights framework. In public service announcement text, sample letters and news articles, and notable quotations, *victims' rights* becomes an organized set of media and movement strategies for communication in ways that link the concept of victims' rights to other civil rights frameworks, but in highly abstracted and decontextualized terms.

Perhaps no one is more cited or referred to in the media packet than Martin Luther King Jr. In a sample forty-five-second PSA announcement, the guide uses King to articulate victims' rights with the civil rights struggle:

> "Injustice anywhere is a threat to justice everywhere." Thirty-five years ago Martin Luther King, Jr. was fighting for civil rights. Now we are fighting for the rights of crime victims. What are the injustices facing crime victims today? Not receiving information about the status of their case; being barred from the courtroom; and learning their offender has been released from custody by turning the corner of Main Street and coming face to face with their rapist, mugger or the murderer of their

loved one. So much has been accomplished in the fight against the injustices suffered by crime victims, but so much more needs to be done to truly guarantee justice for all crime victims. This week as we commemorate National Crime Victims' Rights Week, we are focusing on securing rights, resources, and respect for crime victims. You can help in this effort. Please call (*your organization*) at (*your number*) to join the fight for fairness and justice for all. (36)

While other scholars have noted the links between victims' rights as a strategy of mobilization for rights to participation and those for voting rights in the civil rights movement (see Bumiller 1988), this use of King does not even pause to consider the conflation of victims' rights to participation in the courtroom with the violent racial oppression challenged by leaders like King. What I fear is that King becomes just another American tradition on which victims' rights advocates can draw for their own uses, without having to attend to the substance and context of his discourse within the civil rights movement of the 1960s. Ten years later, in 2008, another American tradition would be drawn upon in the national Office for Victims of Crime and the NCVC campaign packet for National Crime Victims' Rights Week, "Justice for Victims, Justice for All" to stoke the national imagination of victims' rights: the U.S. pledge of allegiance to the flag. In both cases, the nationalist flag ritual and King are reduced to symbols of something for which they never stood — victims' rights.

The media handbooks and press kits contain more than just practical information; they are suffused with a normative critique of how the news media create victims in their reporting practices and an imagination for how the news and other media outlets can amplify the language and images of victims' rights through the appropriation of its discourse as well as that of other movements. What they do not address, however, are the very politics of representation concerning who gets to speak as a victim in and through the movement to the media, and from what traditions these advocacy discourses come. As the examples discussed here indicate, training texts construct the news media–victim relationship as one of necessary harm, where the media create their own victims as an effect of their trained behaviors. News coverage of crime, in this line of thinking, creates the barest of conditions of possibility for victims' rights to be expressed in the news through victim representatives.

Advocates, in response, seek to create what they see as a more hospitable news and talk show environment for those people who seek out the opportunity to appear as victims in these media, because they think doing so might help their legal case, will constitute a therapeutic public testimonial to their dead family member's life, or raise public consciousness of victims' rights legislative and service initiatives. While advocates interpret the problem of news coverage of crime as one of social and institutional conflict between reporters, survivors, and the families of crime victims, the answer these texts offer is for advocates to learn how to better strategize their relations with the media, to foster media-friendly practices, and to speak collectively through a movement language and images of victims' rights built from the archives of other movements. The training texts discussed above evidence how national victim advocacy organizations in the United States consciously think about their representation in the news media and seek to cultivate relations with the press on their own terms. How advocates themselves talk about the press reveals how they imagine the power of media and the possible use of its tactics for victims' rights causes.

four

Undisclosed Sources

Victims' Rights and Journalism Training

As the last chapter illustrated, the media activism of the victims' rights movement does not seek to radically transform the terms of debate on issues of crime and victimization in the U.S. press. Instead its organizations seek to become reliable news sources in order to participate more routinely in news production, encouraging advocates to "think like a reporter" (e.g., "Justice for Victims. Justice for All" Resource guide, 2008, chapter 4, 1). If their focus tends to be on telling the victim's side of a crime story already being told in the press via police and court sources, they do little to challenge the typical story formats and basic assumptions that mainstream news makes about crime and its victims beyond amplifying the voices of victims and their advocates in storytelling on crime.

A body of new curricular materials in some journalism schools in the U.S. extends this approach to the press by training students to adopt a victim orientation to news making. One goal of such training is to nurture among journalism students a victim perspective on the news so that they learn to make news in ways that victim advocates identify as being both less harmful to and less productive of victims *of* the news. It does so by combining a victims' rights approach to their representation in the news with a trauma-oriented perspective on the psychological experience of victimization and news making. In the process, the new journalism training materials link the victims' rights orientation toward the rights of families of murder victims to a trauma orientation to victimization whose focus is on large-scale acts of violence and terrorism. Such a shift in scale, from murder to terrorism and major crimes, relies upon the concept of secondary victimization so central to victims' rights advocacy. Journalism education trains students to utilize the familial orientation of more victim-centric news reporting in their coverage of major crimes and mass victimization. In their training, students are also taught that the procedures of reporting can harm news sources, thereby creating their own production-based injuries secondary to the crime, car accidents, house fires, and other accidents and catastrophes they cover. Journalism training further teaches students that they too can experience psychological distress and harm from reporting, constructing reporters as secondarily injured parties in the news making process as well.

This chapter examines journalism education as a pedagogical site of translation in which victims' rights discourse and trauma talk converge to offer more victim-centric ways of creating and depicting the news of crime and catastrophe. These ways of representing victims are cultivated through empathic modes of comportment and practice by journalism students. In this way, victims' rights discourse, translated into a trauma framework of victimization through what I term trauma training, indexes the victims' rights movement as an undisclosed source for news outlets and, more strategically, for journalism education.

In a recent training film for journalism students called *Covering Columbine*, a male reporter with a look of resignation on his face, says to the camera, "I'd rather cover a war than a school shooting." It is an interesting statement to hear a reporter make in a time of war and military occupation by the United States, when the daily news contains regular reports on reporters and news cameramen who have been shot, assaulted, and killed in war zones around the world. His statement signals a shift in some reportorial representations of danger, victimization, and grief in journalism and in the training involved in becoming a professional journalist. Films like *Covering Columbine* and *The Languages of Emotional Injury* connect discourses of trauma and danger typically associated with the subculture of war correspondence to that of the journalism of school shootings and other domestic acts of mass violence. The dramatic video *Covering Columbine*, for instance, details in the style of a documentary the tragedy of the Columbine High School shootings on 20 April 1999, from the perspective of several distraught local reporters who covered the event. Several of them cry openly in the video as they report from the suburban streets of Littleton, Colorado, the town where Columbine is located. In one scene, a local television reporter stands in the spring rain on the day after the shootings, her face marked with red splotchy streaks from the tears she cannot hold back. She weeps so profusely that she is unable to continue speaking.[1] Another admits, "I don't know how much longer I can do this. I might open a bait shop."

Training texts and films refigure news of crime and disaster as a kind of wounded and wounding practice, for victims and reporters alike. This chapter analyzes how these training films and manuals bring into representation a strategic discourse of trauma that reveals the encounters between victims' rights advocacy and journalism. Journalistic trauma training films and manuals are part of a recent set of curricular initiatives in U.S. journalism education that articulate a discourse of trauma to the particular professional cultures of U.S. news making. This discourse of trauma refers to the representational frameworks that iterate the reality of extraordinary and overwhelming physical and psychic damage (whether from crime, accident, psychological abuse, or histories of oppression and colonial violence) as trauma, including the formal rules and informal guidelines through which it can be represented, the social positions through which different subjects can and do articulate it, and the institutional contexts that create the conditions of its representation (see, e.g., Foucault 1972).

The discourse is strategic because it applies a concept of trauma to the news production process in order to tactically redefine the journalism of crime and disaster as the journalism of collective victimization, even when such traumas must be portrayed through injuries to particular individual victims. For the news business, trauma training reinvests the value of crime news in terms that might enable more victim participation in news making, thereby increasing the value of crime news and at the same time creating less psychologically harmful work environments for news workers and victim sources. Trauma training, then, has several functions, some of which explicitly serve the news industry investment in news as a commodity form and others that simultaneously seek to articulate other social values to news making. While trauma training materials reveal the news media orientation to amplify victims' voices "from a shadowy . . . role in crime narratives to a pivotal position" (Reiner 2002, 392; see also Zedner 2002), they are also attempts by reporters and educators to bring more conscious and socially connective practices of care into the cultural production of news and its workplaces.

Training artifacts provide a unique vantage point from which to analyze how discourses of trauma are being used to create different reportorial techniques for representing victims and giving them new meaning. As E. Ann Kaplan has recently argued, trauma is increasingly an issue of "translation . . . of finding ways to make meaning out of, and to communicate, catastrophes that happen to others as well as to oneself" (2005, 19). Training materials are both the means or mechanism and the site of trauma's translation between victim advocacy, trauma science (where trauma has been codified and studied), and journalism education. Its texts retextualize the discourse of trauma and the political discourse of victims' rights into ready-to-use patterns of journalistic conduct (see, e.g., Gal 2003), revealing what Michel Foucault called the "explicit programmes; . . . calculated, reasoned prescriptions in terms of which institutions are meant to be reorganized, spaces arranged, behaviors regulated" (1990, 80).

Covering Columbine and other DVDs, training manuals, online curricular modules, tip sheets, and textbooks translate trauma from a medical discourse of post-traumatic stress disorder (PTSD) to a more victim-centered news discourse on the traumatic experiential dimensions of crime and violence. From an industry perspective, trauma training seeks to prioritize two things at once: the needs of local television news industries and twenty-four-hour cable news networks for dramatic crime, disaster, and accident news and the calls by victim advocates for more active victim participation within news-based storytelling on crime. In the process, it seeks to develop more reparative and less antagonistic modes of practice within print and television journalism's cultures of representation and their encounters with victimized news sources.

In particular, the propositional content of training documents—their explicit plan for changing how reporters think about and do their jobs (e.g., Foucault 1990; Bourdieu, 1990)—portrays the news interview as a space of intersubjective and sentimental, painful feeling (e.g., Berlant 2000) and organizes this portrayal into therapeutic models of reportorial conduct. According to the training, news interviews are painful for reporters because they may not want to and often do not know how to approach and question victims and their families. Interviews are deemed to be harmful to victims and their families because they exert little control over reporters' lines of questioning and the content of the final news product. Through interpersonal communication techniques, novice journalists learn how to eradicate behaviors deemed intrusive or potentially harmful to victims and to cultivate a more empathic demeanor that will encourage news subjects to participate more fully in the news construction of crime and disaster. Role-playing and videos teach students how to interview news subjects who have survived or witnessed disastrous events and how to write stories about their dead victims from templates complete with language suggestions, interview questions, directions for acquiring family photographs; perhaps most significant, they teach students how to construct commemorative narratives of victims killed in major acts of violence like the Oklahoma City bombings and the 11 September 2001 terrorist attacks through profiles of life, which portray victims via familial remembrances of their life (see chapter 5). The stated goal of this training is to enable journalists to create an interview environment more hospitable to victims and their families, who might otherwise feel secondarily wounded by their interaction with the news media.

The texts examined here include the training film *The Languages of Emotional Injury*, the print manuals *Tragedies and Journalists* and *Crisis Journalism*, the Dart Center for Journalism and Trauma's online curricular modules "Journalism and Trauma" and "Covering Terrorism," and the textbook *Covering Violence*. These educational media create an alternative discursive space through which journalism educators, medical professionals, students, working journalists, victim advocates, and victims are put into communication (Herbst 1994, 1996). They do so within a political imagination of victimization influenced by victims' rights rhetoric in which family members position and experience themselves as victims in order to assert rights to representation in the criminal justice system and the media.

The Emergence of Trauma Training

Journalistic trauma training emerged in part out of interactions between victims' rights organizations and journalism educators, the first formal meeting of which occurred, as noted earlier, in 1986 at a national symposium on crime victims and the media (see Thomason and Babbili 1986). Victims' rights activists criticized reporters for their insensitive treatment of crime victims and their families during news interviews and in news stories that portray victims in an inaccurate and sensational light (Thomason and Babbili 1986; Levin 1995; Roper 1996; Viano 1992). In particular, advocates identified the news interview as a site of revictimization. If the news media can hurt the people they cover while also claiming to give them voice, advocates asserted, then journalists must alter their conduct to create a better platform for victims to claim their rights and their access to representation.

Journalism schools began to turn to trauma curricula in the early 1990s in order to address these criticisms by victim advocates. They initiated professional training protocols in how to cover and manage major catastrophic news events. While victim advocates' media training texts sought to teach advocates how to court news media attention and frame the news interview as a matter of victims' rights to representation, trauma training translates these claims into specific modes of conduct and knowledge about victim experience through the framework of trauma. The latter adopt some aspects of victim advocates' claims that the news production process is harmful to victims while also creating the possibility of articulating in different terms what constitutes victims' perspectives on crime. Trauma training goes a step further and recognizes that the news production process is also potentially traumatizing to news workers in that they bear the emotional and political burden of bearing other's testimonies of suffering. Trauma then becomes a language for talking about the work of journalism.

University journalism programs with trauma training in their curricula represent an emergent set of ideas and practices in the field.[2] Some schools, for example, the Dart Center for Journalism and Trauma associated with the Department of Communication at the University of Washington, have created stand-alone programs. Others, like IUPUI (Indiana University–Purdue University, Indianapolis) and the University of Colorado have no specific programs but incorporate training exercises into their existing curricula. Additionally, some programs establish formal relationships with academic experts in traumatic stress and psychiatry and with individual victim advocates and advocacy organizations; the Victims and the Media Program at Michigan State University and its collaboration with the Michigan Victim Alliance is one such program. Their working relationship explains why trauma training depicts the context of the news interview as a dialogic place of painful feeling: because survivors, their families, and victims' rights advocates have identified the interactions between reporters and news sources as particularly troubling, if not traumatic, while the profession of journalism continues to see the news interview as one of the most significant sites for news production (see Gans 1979; Schudson 1995; Clayman and Hermitage 2002).

Trauma training is an effect both of social movement organizing on behalf of crime victims that sought to publicize victim traumas through the news media and of a professional movement to reorient and remake the work of journalism. The annual conference of the Association for Educators in Journalism and Mass Communication includes panels on trauma and journalism education. It has become a key topic of discussion in trade journals within the profession, including the *American Journalism Review*, the *Columbia Journalism Review*, and *Nieman Reports*. The Society for Professional Journalists publicizes trauma training, its educators (it gave Roger Simpson of the University of Washington a teaching award in 2001), and other resources for reporters seeking information and training opportunities on the topic; the society also covers trauma training in its newsletters, the *SPJ News* and *Quill*. Additionally, the Committee to Protect Journalists, the International Federation of Journalists, and Reporters without Borders have all published their own reporting guides for journalists preparing to cover war, conflict zones, riots, protests, and other contexts deemed to be potentially hostile to news workers. These texts are primarily geared toward teaching risk management strategies and safety tips, but in addition they address the psychological and potentially traumatizing dimensions of reporting from the journalist's perspective (see Rentschler 2007). Beyond the professional organizations of journalists, the most visible evidence of trauma training's ascendancy can be found at the International Society for Traumatic Stress Studies, whose annual conferences are scheduled with several panels on journalism's training initiatives in this area. They too publish reports on trauma and the media that include advice to reporters.

Articulating Trauma and Journalism

Much of the received knowledge on trauma's status as a subjective and corporeal state is articulated and codified through the symptomatology of PTSD and its description of traumatized subjectivity, on which the models of trauma in journalistic training are based. Through its classification schemes, "the medical wound, trauma, became the psychic wound" (Hacking 1996, 85). PTSD is the main source of medical classification for trauma and diagnostic proof of victimized subjectivity. What constitutes trauma within the PTSD diagnostic is an internalized neurobiological reality, a traumatized psyche. According to the feminist rhetorician Jennifer Wood, medical discourses of trauma like PTSD tend to locate the effects and solutions to social violence "'in' individuals rather than the social conditions in which they live" (2003, 298).

In cultural theories of trauma, the divided psyche of PTSD signifies a fractured episteme. Neurobiological theorists such as Bessel van der Kolk, from whom the literary theorist Cathy Caruth borrows her definition of trauma as unclaimed experience, define trauma as a "literal imprint . . . that gets lodged in the brain in a special traumatic memory system that defies all possibility of representation" (Leys 2000, 6; see also Caruth 1996). In this conception, the physiological mechanisms for processing trauma capture traumatic bodily traces in a repeating loop in the brain that prevents its subjects from processing it in narrative form — a "shattering break or cesura in experience that has belated effects" in the form of nightmares, quick startle responses, and overwhelming sensory cues that signal the traumatic event (LaCapra 2001, 186; see also Caruth 1995; Leys 2000, 229). Traumas appear not as "recollected representations — the usual understanding of the term 'memories' — but as literal icons and sensations" that lack narrative frameworks of expression but are deeply embodied realities of traumatic injury (Leys 2000, 250). In this construction of trauma, its sufferers cannot narrate it to others but instead involuntarily and compulsively display its symptoms over and over again in the ways discussed above (Leys 2000, 252). The therapeutic cure to traumas defined in this way, that is, as an inability to narrate, represent, or even directly reference past injury, involves the imposition of narrative frameworks onto the repetitive bodily memories of the trauma victim.

As a medical condition, PTSD accounts for an array of experiences that cause emotional and psychological trauma in ways that normalize social conditions previously viewed as moral or character failures of its victims, such as sexual abuse and military combat (see J. Davis 2005, 118; Turner 2001; Shay 1994; A. Young 1995). The medical diagnosis of PTSD constructs its victims as faultless vis-à-vis their traumas, which in the case of soldiering and combat stress has meant defining the causes of traumatic stress away from soldiers' participation in the violence of war (see, e.g., Turner 2001). PTSD is a construction of political and social subjectivity (W. Scott 1990). While the diagnostic category of PTSD avoids blaming victims for their assaults and their psychological troubles, it can also make it more difficult to analyze the social conditions in which violence occurs, and in some cases erases the participation of those who suffer trauma in violence. It also provides little in the way of distinguishing why and how violence can be traumatizing for some, while not for others. By shifting emphasis away from the violent event that caused trauma and by extension the agent(s) responsible, PTSD focuses almost exclusively on the victims' experience and their bodies' attempts to reintegrate their fragmented and otherwise broken subjectivities. The diagnostic category of PTSD, then, avoids placing blame upon the victim for his or her traumatic experience by placing the trauma inside the body of the one who suffers it, disarticulating the sources of trauma from the agency of its victims and the specificities of its eventfulness (Finkelhor 1988, cited in J. Davis 2005, 117).

The syndrome's model of traumatized subjectivity was formed in part through the activism of social movements and medical institutions, whose own accounts of victimization and victim harm enabled the shift in moral frameworks from victim responsibility and culpability—a cornerstone of victimology studies in the 1940s and child abuse research in the 1950s (e.g., von Hentig 1948)—to one of victim innocence (e.g., J. Davis 2005; Jenkins 1998). What Joseph Davis calls the "trauma model of victim harm" (2005, 109–39) signifies the importation of social movement and medical scripts about the moral innocence of victims and the guilt of offenders into the public sphere, a claim the feminist trauma researcher Judith Herman made earlier in her landmark book *Trauma and Recovery*. According to Herman, traumas come to public consciousness only through the activism of political movements, whether through the activism of Vietnam veterans (e.g., Shay 1994; Turner 2001; A. Young 1995), feminists, or child sexual abuse survivors (see J. Davis 2005; Whittier 2009). "The study of psychological trauma," Herman argues, "must constantly contend with [the] tendency to discredit the victim or render her invisible. . . . To hold traumatic reality in consciousness requires a social context that affirms and protects the victim and that joins victim and witness in a common alliance" (1992, 8–9) — a perfect description of trauma training's attempts to bring reporter and victim into alliance through the production of victim-centered news on crime. Thus trauma as a medical construct of PTSD and trauma as a cultural construct of the emotional, psychological, and physical injuries of systemic violence come into conflict. The former seeks therapeutic fixes to traumatized patients based on an interiorized reality of divided subjectivity separated from social conditions in which that reality occurred, while the latter seeks to politicize the lasting and debilitating harms of state violence and institutionalized oppression by externalizing trauma onto the conditions of its social production.

Journalism education seeks to bring these two constructions of trauma together through trauma training — one as a medical reality requiring treatment, the other as a state of wounded collective identification mobilized through networks of movement activism. Its linkages between the medical and movement models of trauma, however, are themselves unevenly developed and sometimes contradictory, as the training texts themselves demonstrate. The training DVD *The Languages of Emotional Injury* (2003) produced by the Dart Center for Journalism and Trauma illustrates Herman's assertion that public consciousness of trauma emerges from the collective contexts of antiwar and feminist activism. The video presents highlights from a special symposium held by the Dart Center at which the psychiatrist Frank Ochberg, the journalism educator Simpson, and a group of poets and journalists speak to a university audience on the topics of writing about war, racial and sexual oppression, rape, and incest — forms of violence whose very meaning and language have been powerfully defined through social activism. Across the lectures and video interludes, the film asserts that emotional injury can be caused by kinds of structural violence that are different but nonetheless share the same traumatizing effects. At the end of the film, Ochberg tells viewers that psychiatrists, poets, and journalists all learn how to listen to others' unspoken words about traumatic experience. According to Wendy Chun, "a politics and practice of listening is a necessary complement to a politics of testifying. . . . I am suggesting a politics that does not valorize the act of speaking in and of itself: a politics that listens to a person's speech or silence and then grapples with the question of how to respond to it. In other words, I am suggesting a politics that begins, rather than ends with, the speaking subject, that begins with the other who addresses us with her speech or silence" (1999, 138). As a starting point, listening to others' testimonials of harm requires a kind of vigilance that attends to the specificity of individual experiences of injury. Rather than knowing the story in advance, as Stuart Hall (1984) described journalism's narrative construction of reality, the journalism of trauma training must avoid "reducing the personal to the impersonal and the unique drama to a human interest story," the kind of passive listening that enables interviewers, in the words of Bourdieu, to "economize on thought, on emotion, in short on understanding. . . . Even when one mobilizes all the resources of professional vigilance and personal sympathy, it is [still] difficult to shake off the inattentive drowsiness induced by the illusion that we've already seen and heard it all, and to enter into the distinctive personal history to attempt to gain an understanding—at once unique and general—of each life story" (1999, 614). Without such vigilance at the level of listening and a "grasp of the conditions, inseparably psychological and social, associated with a given position or trajectory in social space" (1999, 613), victims, their families, and witnesses become just another news source rather than the starting point for more fully social attempts to tell stories of violence that recognize the people whose lives are cut through with its traumas.

Trauma training seeks to cultivate practices of listening that in effect might upset the typical practices of account production that news making requires, and the referentiality between violent cause and traumatic effect on which its event orientation to crime and disaster is based. In *The Languages of Emotional Injury*, Ochberg instructs viewers to go forth and listen to victims' stories of injury and the signs of their wounded bodies and psyches as a collective practice of account giving. Such listening might serve as a supplement, if not a challenge, to the fact-finding practices of journalism and law and the ways in which they can foreclose possibilities for listening, where "an absorbing interest in the factual details of the account . . . serve[s] to circumvent the human experience" of suffering (Felman and Laub 1992, 73 quoted in Chun 1999, 137).

The Languages of Emotional Injury is perhaps the most explicit of all the training materials in its representation of an epistemic model of journalistic labor figured through trauma. While its explicit message lies in the spoken words of the poets, journalists, and educators it features, its audiovisual strategies for portraying trauma carry a greater burden of meaning in the film. The DVD moves through scenes with a combination of jarring edits and at other times sentimental music and straightforward, lecture-based address. Divided into short interludes linked by transitions that range from spoken pieces of poetry and soothing music to sharp screams and gunshots, the film depicts the conditions and experiential dimensions of psychological and physical injury as unnerving and almost hostile in its disorienting effects. Just seconds after the opening of the video, loud, crackling gunshots aurally interrupt pans of still photographic shots of nature scenes, coupled with glitchy video cuts to black-and-white photographs of physically injured victims. The significations of the video's verbal, visual, and aural components are confirmed not only through the hosts' and performers' narration, but also through the disorienting position in which the film places its viewers. The video upsets the typical talking head and teacher-centered training format, creating a filmic viewing experience that is more experimental in approach.

While the film's title suggests that it offers a language of emotional injury, the combination of sonic cues and the stark visual contrasts between colorful photos of nature and grim, high-contrast black-and-white photos of physically traumatized people carries the film's primary message: the representation of trauma may lie less in the construction of a new language to describe social harms and individual traumas than in the aural and visual depiction of the victim's injured body. Through various strategies the video portrays the injured and affect-laden body as the most trusted medium through which traumas of victimization can be expressed and then turned into news. Through its stills of news photographs of disaster victims and the performing bodies of journalists and poets who bear the burden of others' testimonials to histories of incest and civil war, the video posits trauma as a reality grounded in the bodies of post-traumatic subjects and their witnesses. In this way, the film "anchor[s] in the conviction that special truths can manifest themselves in traumatized bodies" (Douglass and Vogler 2003, 12). All through the film, video of performers is interrupted by more pans across still photographs of victims' bodies and families' stunned expressions of incomprehension and grief. Many are news photographs of witnesses and family members that have been republished in other training documents, such as the Dart Center's pocket-sized training manual *Tragedies and Journalists: A Guide for More Effective Coverage.*

One of the photographs displays a police officer and a paramedic who are helping a stunned woman leave a site that has been leveled by either a bomb, perhaps from the Oklahoma City federal building in 1995, or a weather disaster. Her face is streaked with blood (Hight and Smyth 2004, 5). Joe Hight, the coauthor of *Tragedies and Journalists*, is an editor at the *Oklahoman*, a daily paper in Oklahoma City that first codified many of the strategies local reporters are now being trained to use to commemorate the lives of local victims of mass violence. While it is impossible to tell exactly what has happened to the bloodied woman in the photograph, her body offers forensic visual evidence of the violence of some event. In the absence of any referent to its source, however, it is the trauma on the woman's body that becomes visible — "the speaking and crying wound" as Dominick LaCapra puts it (2001, 182) — not the violence that created it, mirroring the thesis that trauma is by nature nonreferential.

Unlike forensic television programming such as the *CSI* television franchise, in which the "spectacle of crime digitized" disappears the subject by creating a surgical point of view that travels through exterior wounds into the body's interiors, *The Languages of Emotional Injury* relies on a forensic framework that pictures the whole human body inscribed — scarred, cut, bloodied — with violence (Gever 2005, 447; see also Grosz 1995, 33–36, Tait 2006). In portraying the wounded body, it places the burdens for understanding the social dimensions of victimization as trauma onto a set of reading practices in how to interpret the social causes of the physical markings of violence inscribed into bodies. Yet because it lacks a clear sense of referentiality to the event that caused the woman's bleeding, the photograph serves as material evidence of journalism's own troubled relation to trauma discourse and the challenge of its nonreferentiality. If journalism requires referentiality between what sources look like, say, and do and the events being reported on, then trauma training's own use of photographs of traumatized victims without clear reference to a violent event indicates the very possibility that another kind of news that references not violent events but the traumatized subject may be part of what is on offer in trauma training. This form of news making on victims may mark a move away from the eventfulness of crime and disaster, as victims' rights discourse did in the shift from crime to criminal justice, toward the portrayal of traumatized subjectivity unmoored from the social structures and agents that create and do violence.

Perhaps journalism starts to play more explicitly with the distinction between writing trauma and writing about trauma that LaCapra asserts within the context of historiography. The distinction between writing about trauma and writing trauma rests in the difference between recounting the past and reliving it. Writing trauma, for LaCapra, is metaphorical. He posits the impossibility of representing trauma as something "related to particular events." Traumas "cannot be localized in terms of a discrete, dated experience. Trauma indicates a shattering break of cesura in experience *which has belated effects*" (2001, 186, emphasis added), a delayed temporality without clear progression or end point, an extended model of temporality that conflicts with the news value of immediacy and timeliness. LaCapra criticizes the film *Shoah*, for instance, for its exclusion of testimonials from figures who, according to the trauma theorist Shoshana Felman, could recount past traumas without having to relive them (2001, 187). The trauma of the Holocaust codified in *Shoah* portrayed traumatized subjectivity through its inability to represent the past, caught in the cycles of posttraumatic reality. The point is that journalism figured through trauma training could also overly codify traumatized subjectivity and write trauma in ways that appear only through the symptomatology of PTSD. Journalism, like history, inevitably relies upon the "aboutness" of particular events and their timeliness. Through trauma training, journalism replaces one form of referentiality, that of the event, with another, the traumatized subject and her or his body. Trauma training begins to articulate the limits to journalism's investment in the referentiality of wounded bodies to violent events when cast in terms of nonlinear and aproximal temporalities.

Perhaps "this inevitable 'aboutness' or referentiality . . . is a principal limit in the field when compared with art and literature (especially fiction) or even philosophy—fields in which the imagination or speculation may have freer reign." Again, journalism, like history, "is always about something specific, and it necessarily and constitutively involves referential truth claims" (LaCapra 2001, 203). Trauma upsets the very system of referentiality on which journalism works. This is why *The Languages of Emotional Injury* portrays journalism as but one kind of writing practice among others, such as poetry and fiction, that write trauma by serving as translation machines and carriers of traumatic experience, gaining access to the hidden depths and sometimes "pathological secrets" of trauma's victims (e.g., Leys 2000, 2–3).

Yet unlike novels and fictional films, "journalism remains constrained by its somewhat reified but nonetheless instrumental respect for facts, truth and reality." "Were it to loosen its adherence to these foundational tenets," according to Barbie Zelizer, "journalism would lose its distinctiveness from other modes of cultural expression, argumentation, representation, and production" (2004, 102–4). Even as journalism functions as another mode of representation, like novels and popular films, it is still invested in the veracity of facts and the referentiality of reality that make reporting on traumas particularly troubling. Based on reports by victims and their families, the harms of journalistic practice result from failures of factual accuracy: spelling victims' names incorrectly, publishing incorrect information about their jobs, printing the wrong birth date, and so on. The problem of trauma understood in this light might suggest that journalism must be read "against its own grain while giving that grain extended attention" (Zelizer 2004, 101), just as a historical document, according to LaCapra, "requires that one begin by not treating it simply as a source for facts or as an ink blot one protectively reprocesses but as a complex artifact that may indeed have a grain or variety of grains with their own dynamic and force of resistance" (2001, 204). In other words, trauma training does not argue against the belief in facts, truth, and reality on which journalism relies, but it redefines their value in terms of their significance to families looking to the news for accurate reports on their dead family members' lives.

The manual *Tragedies and Journalists*, unlike the film *The Languages of Emotional Injury*, explicitly tells its readers how to translate seeing the bodies of injured victims into writing stories of social or collective trauma. In the caption that accompanies the photograph of the bleeding woman, readers are told to "focus on describing the victim's life" (2003, 6). That is, the encounter with the wounded body and the faces of victims ought to be approached as "a kind of *hinge* or threshold" between the exteriority and interiority of traumatized subjectivity: "it is placed between a psychic or lived interiority and a more sociopolitical exterior that produces interiority through the *inscription* of the body's outer surface" (Grosz 1995, 33). In inscriptive models of reading the body, the interpreter is "more concerned with the processes by which the subject is marked, scarred, transformed, and written upon or constructed by the various regimes of institutional, discursive and non-discursive power as a particular kind of body" (Grosz 1995, 33).

The call to "describe the victim's life" through the interpretive encounter with the bloodied body is a call to see the injured body as an expression of an externalized trauma internalized to create a traumatized subjectivity. The further admonition to make the injured body speak life rather than death means that reporters should interpret the traces of injury as signs of life. Much like Walter Benjamin's description of the detective in the stories of Edgar Allan Poe as a "physiognomist of the interior," in trauma training, journalists learn to see the signs of trauma as the traces of life, not of death. In this view, "to live means to leave traces" (see Werner 2001, 7, quoting Benjamin's "Paris, Capital of the 19th Century," 155). If the detective "must consider this flexible relation between interiority and exteriority when reading the physiognomy of a room's interior to solve a crime" (Werner, 13), the journalist in trauma training must consider the flexible relation between wounded bodies, the struggle to survive, and the position of witnesses — as observers and translators — within this struggle. Trauma training texts like *Tragedies and Journalists* teach students to use the external signs of the body to articulate a discourse of life after victimization.

In similar terms, *The Languages of Emotional Injury* teaches the viewer to construct news of trauma, not through the dead bodies of victims, but through the injured bodies and minds of its living victims — where trauma signifies survival and the struggles of survivors living in grief. When dead victims are reported on, in the case of news coverage of catastrophic events such as 9/11, reporters are advised to focus on the significance of their lives, rather than on the details of their deaths, a discursive injunction against talking about death as anything but the absence of a once-lived life, what the feminist literary critic Nancy Miller refers to as "the happiness that was" the victim's life before he or she was killed (2003, 126). Documentation of the lives of the dead functions less as a record of events than an "archive of feeling," where the news serves as "repositories of feeling and emotion." These repositories of feeling are not only "encoded . . . in the content of the texts themselves but in the practices that surround their production and reception" in the work of journalism and news audiences (Cvetkovich 2003, 7). Trauma "puts pressure on conventional forms of documentation, representation and commemoration, giving rise to new genres of expres-

sion, such as testimony, and new forms of monuments, rituals and performances that . . . call into being collective witnesses and publics" (2003, 7).
Through trauma training, news is being refigured as a testimonial performance that calls upon reporters to serve as witnesses to others' victimization and be the bearers of secondary victims' storytelling prerogatives on
crime and criminal justice.

News as a Space of Recovery

As these examples suggest, training journalists to speak in the language of
traumatic stress signifies that crime and disaster journalism should play
a role in secondary victims' search for psychological recovery from their
grief and loss. Journalists are asked to become not just scribes but active
enablers of victims' recovery. William Coté's and Roger Simpson's textbook *Covering Violence* instructs its readers that "humane reporting . . . requires a new set of assumptions about the person who suffers trauma and
new thinking about how to apply those ideas to the basic work of journalism. . . . If news practices take trauma into account, reporting their stories
can help victims" (2000, 8). Coté's and Simpson's argument for "a new set
of assumptions within journalism" defines victim-oriented news practice
as a means to victims' recovery from trauma. Their textbook and the Dart
Center online module cited above suggest that journalism should become
more identified with the victim by adopting a trauma framework, through
which victims are constructed as a particular expression of traumatized
subjectivity. When news is modeled as an emotional contact zone between
reporter and victim, crime and violence are no longer spoken of as effects
of social injustice best remedied through social services and more equi-
table distributions of wealth and resources. They are instead discussed as
problems of victim pain and reporter empathy — a "place of painful feeling"
in which the news interview can function as a form of therapy.

Training manuals suggest that the news can create spaces of recovery for
news audiences, victims, and journalists through the display of and collective interaction with the wounded subjects of major disasters and violent
events. According to *Crisis Journalism*, newspapers should provide a forum
in which "Americans want to talk about the crisis; they need to talk about
it. Provide the forum, even if it means stealing space from other sections.
Run e-mail and letters and phone-call transcripts in the news columns;

get as much diversity of opinion as possible. Let readers vent, but make it constructive. Keep a firm handle on hatred" (Hazlett 2001, 4). *Crisis Journalism* portrays 9/11 as an extraordinarily catastrophic event that defies conventional practices of news representation, a claim cultural theorists of trauma echo in relation to other practices for representing the traumas of sexual abuse and the Holocaust (e.g., Caruth 1996; LaCapra 2001; Cvetkovich 2003). While I do not disagree with this descriptive assessment, the claim that events like 9/11 and the shootings at Columbine High School require different forms of news representation signals a particular moral prescription for journalism: that the news media bear responsibility for the depiction of news subjects and news readers' potential traumas and their practices of recovery, marked in particular by the scale and intensified affective register of catastrophic, multiple-victim events. The news is asked not simply to cover its community but to enable the community to define the experience of catastrophe and seek solace through the news portrayal of its struggles for meaning and its desire to commemorate the dead. To fulfill this obligation, reporters must learn to navigate the "available cultural and national scripts and truth-telling conventions" (Hesford 2004, 108) for representing various forms and causes of human suffering, scripts and conventions that are deeply indebted to the language of trauma science and the construct of post-traumatic stress disorder as a pathology of wounded subjectivity not normally accessible through conventional means of documentation. Trauma "demands an unusual archive" (Cvetkovich 2003, 7) against what one journalist calls the "white noise" and "banality of trauma" in the "crowded marketplace of human suffering" (Nina Bernstein in *The Languages of Emotional Injury*).

Covering Violence also articulates the burden to represent trauma as a social obligation to which reporters are bound. It describes news as frontline preparation for audiences to think about and respond to traumatic events. To fulfill this pedagogic role, photojournalists must photograph the scenes of violent events and their victims while reporters must learn how to interact with victims and survivors in the context of the interview in order to write more victim-serving news: "The journalist's obligation to represent the public means, above all, going where human beings are most at-risk. For better or worse violence is an important part of the report we want journalists to bring back to us. . . . Citizens in a democracy *must* know about violence if they are to make responsible decisions about how to protect themselves, their families and their communities. The job of the media is to tell them, accurately, fairly, and comprehensively" (2000, 223). In this vision of the profession, journalists are agents of public protection who bear moral responsibility to educate the public about hazards they may face and the means they have to respond to them. This point is echoed by Bonnie Bucqueroux, coordinator of the Victims and the Media Program at Michigan State University, who argues for the significance of disaster news from a public service perspective, in which news audiences need to see images of tragedies like nightclub fires and the Oklahoma City bombing in order to commence community-based processes of recovery (Schwanbeck 2004). Victim advocates argue that the news fails in this particular pedagogical and protectionist mission, mistaking the display of local and distant victims for knowledge of their experiences, or, as Susan Sontag (2003) argues, knowledge about how one could and should respond to such suffering (see also Moeller 1999).

From trainers' perspectives, the journalism of crime, disaster, and terrorism is morally and socially obligated to become more centered on victims. The way to cultivate more victim-centered reporting is to focus the news interview and news story on an interpretive framework that approaches victims and their accounts through the window of their possible traumas. "Better reporting about trauma," say Coté and Simpson, "can help readers and viewers gain empathy for the suffering of victims and enrich our awareness of the powerful role trauma plays in our collective lives" (2000, 8). Their approach to covering victims in the news echoes the position of Anne Seymour, the author of the book *Crime Victims in the Media*: "to give a face and voice to victims" that is attuned to the traumatic experiences of victims (from author interview, 1 November 2000).

Journalism educators and victims' rights advocates alike believe that journalists' careful management of communication will elicit more victim-centered news stories. By simply altering their behavior, according to these training materials, journalists can elicit newsworthy displays of emotion from victims and their families. From this vantage point, trauma training appears to instrumentalize empathic reportorial conduct to encourage victims to participate in news stories. Simpson describes trauma training as a process of learning to treat interviews "as sequences of actions by reporters and responses of trauma victims": "A good journalist takes some time to get a sense of how the interview subject is doing. Give him or her a sense of control. Tell them who you are, and what you're going to write. The sensitive reporter will talk to a person first, before walking into the home with a camera. . . . I'm optimistic that we can help newsrooms become more humane working environments and that reporters can be more creative in their approach to trauma" (Simpson, quoted in Zalin 2001). Simpson teaches students to set up interviews by foregrounding an ethic of care. While journalism training asserts that care is a feeling reporters can communicate to their interview subjects, its texts present formal techniques of communication that represent the careful management of interpersonal communication in the news interview as care itself. That is, care is a managed orientation to news subjects; it does not require proof of feeling on the part of reporters, yet journalists' own feelings of emotional injury can serve as a kind of affective evidence for this performance of care.

Interviewing techniques become the practical craft for demonstrating care and emotional exchange in reporters' relation to news subjects, suggesting more broadly that care can be viewed as an externalized performance that creates the appearance of shared feeling without necessarily requiring it. The technical delivery of an ethic of care includes interactions in which reporters appear to cede some decision-making power over the form of the interview and its content to the victim or survivor. Training in empathic interpersonal communication techniques provides students with an interview program they can use to construct victim-oriented news — a set of behavioral and linguistic conventions for organizing the speech acts of interviewers and interviewees. They learn which words to use, how to position their bodies, how to conduct their expressions, and how proximate they should be to their subjects. Students learn to use physical and verbal conventions to communicate that their news story will be co-constructed with the victim.

Students learn to open the conversation with formal and rather clichéd statements that express sympathy, such as "I'm sorry this happened to you" or "I'm glad you weren't killed" or "It's not your fault" (e.g., Carter and Bucqueroux n.d.; Hight and Smyth 2004; *Reporting on Victims of Violence and Catastrophe* 1999). Such statements avoid casting blame on the news subject while acknowledging the survivor's experience (Coté and Bucqueroux 1996). They fulfill basic expectations of support, reassurance, and sympathy without personalizing the tragedy. Students are also encouraged to give victims a business card, telling them they can contact the reporter later to talk or to correct mistakes that may have been made in the news story. Business cards are a formal means of expressing friendliness and openness to the victim, while also establishing authority. They communicate that the reporter is willing to continue the interaction, which also has an instrumental use, such as continued access to a potentially good source. Furthermore, students learn to explain the purpose of the story and why an interview is desired, which lets the news subject know the journalist's intentions for how the story will be told, giving them an out if they do not wish to participate.

Many of these techniques aim to communicate to interviewees that they can exert control over the interview process or even choose not to participate. In the Michigan State University video *Reporting on Victims of Violence and Catastrophe*, Sue Carter, a professor of journalism, admonishes students to demystify the tools they use during the interview, to lay bare the apparatus of the interview context. Cameras, lights, microphones, and other recording technologies should be demystified, she argues, to increase victims' sense of security and increase their willingness to participate in the interview. Giving interviewees a reasonable estimate of the length of the interview shows respect for their time. Asking victims if they want to be interviewed rather than starting an interview without their permission offers them a choice. If they agree to the interview, asking them where they would like to talk and telling them they can signal for a break, request that lights be turned on or off, use tissues, and alter the physical environment also gives victims a sense that they have some control over the interaction. Asking how victims would like to be referred to, whether they want to be called a victim or a survivor or neither, lets them decide how they will be publicly represented. These strategies encourage victims to participate in news making by shifting the perception of the interview away from the news media's interest in the story and toward families' interests in telling a story of the victims' life before they were injured or killed. In *Reporting on Victims of Violence and Catastrophe*, Carter warns viewers, "It is difficult, it is appropriate, to ask for a picture, perhaps of someone who has been killed by a drunk driver. It's a hard thing to do. It has to be done gently." She advises students to explain to families how important it is to celebrate the life, rather than the death, of the person who has died through the news display of family photographs.

Familial depictions of victims within the family unit become powerful ideological visual terrain on which victims come to matter and count as

moral agents. Family photographs and video footage of victims and survivors are used to transform crime victim stories into commemorative
news features that have recently been codified into a genre I call the profile of life (Chermak 1995, 85–108; see also Jermyn 2003; A. Williams 1993).
Trauma training educates reporters in how to construct news stories that
shape the meanings of crime, disaster, and terrorism through the familial
remembrances of dead victims. Reporters learn to see victims through
what Marianne Hirsch calls the familial gaze, that is, "the conventions and
ideologies of family through which they seem themselves" (1999, xi) and
which are currently being institutionalized throughout the news industry
(see chapter 5).

None of the techniques taught in journalistic trauma training guarantees victims' control over the final form of the interview. Rather, the
training emphasizes how reporters can change the feeling and tone of
their exchange. Training can make the process of the news interview more
transparent to news subjects and journalists, but it still prioritizes the news
media's need for dramatic coverage over the victim's possible need to tell
her story. If the primary goal is to get the victim's story, then getting the
victim to participate will always be more important than figuring out what
participation, if any, is most helpful to the victim. Trauma training pre-
serves the structural relationship between journalist and victim or survivor
because empathy is a performance, not an intersubjective orientation. As
Wendy Hesford warns of those who witness human rights testimonials,
the real danger lies in the belief that witnesses can not only stand in for the
narrator-victim, but also incorporate the victimized other into their professional selves (2004, 107). To do so is to misrecognize and misrepresent the
differences between the subjectivities of victims and their families and the
professional roles of journalists as bearers of their testimonies.

Through the educational media of training manuals and videos, the concept of trauma is being translated from a medico-scientific and therapeutic
discourse into a distinctly news-oriented one grounded in the reportorial
cultivation of its language and a unique articulation of storytelling about
injured and dead victims' lives, told from the perspective of their families. Training films such as *The Languages of Emotional Injury* and curricular manuals like *Tragedies and Journalists* illustrate how politically targeted
and therapeutic practices of representation are actively being cultivated
among journalism students and educators via their interactions with vic-

tim advocates. Their moral construction of the depiction of victims' deaths and familial grief is directly linked to the victims' rights movement and its investments in telling the stories of crime and criminal justice from a victim perspective.

Journalistic trauma training defines the process of news making as a space of painful feeling for reporters and news subjects, a space in which the news interview is imagined as both a therapeutic and a potentially hurtful interaction, an extension of the harms committed through the event that created the victim in the first place. Current training practices treat journalism as a set of highly intimate, interpersonal relations between journalists and their subjects in ways that can mask the news media's economic investment in the coverage of crime and twenty-four-hour news cycles on major crimes and terrorist attacks, and the political investments the victims' rights movement has in amplifying the voices of victims. In fact, their focus on the news interview as a space of emotional encounter may instead camouflage the political economy of crime and disaster news and the moral and economic value of victims within the news industry in ways that may bind the news profession more closely to the movement for victims' rights. The work of such a binding process is visible in the ways training encourages reporters to interpret the news-making process as a recuperative encounter between the reporter as a representative for victims and a repository for victim testimonials and the victim as familial representatives of the injured and dead.

What is more likely to make the news interview a place of painful feeling is the industrial imperative for news coverage that pushes reporters and photographers to cover victims and grieving families in situations in which they might best be served by being left alone. Even though its roots are in the victims' rights movement, trauma training does not shift this power balance toward individual victims, even though it claims to. Instead it raises the visibility of victims' rights perspectives on crime and criminal justice by training news personnel in how to recognize and professionally identify with victims' traumas and familial grief in order to transform them into news. The life stories of the injured or dead family member amplify powerful moral codes of innocence and guilt in reporting on crime and criminal justice. Trauma training helps turn these representational codes into lasting institutional realities within the news industry—at precisely the same historical moment as the obituary pages have risen in cultural and professional significance within journalism. Victim commemoration now plays an increasingly visible role both on and off those pages. As a result, the sentiments of loss and grief for victims expressed in these training texts may make it increasingly difficult to hear the "punishing power" of politically dominant victims' rights claims to representation (Wood 2003) against the powerful calls to commemorate and never forget victims' lives.

The social history of death is a precious source
of information about the social history of life.

ERNEST MANDEL, *Delightful Murder*

five

Profiles of Life
News Memorials to the Dead

"Tell me the secret of a good life!" Marilyn
Johnson exclaims in her book on the trade
of obituary writing—the modern "dead beat"
to which she belongs (2007, 5). Johnson's book
is an ode to obituary writers and the imagina-
tive literary styles they employ to cover the lives
of everyday people in the pages of the press in
what she terms the "egalitarian obituary" (67).
The egalitarian obituary "captures . . . the essential Americanness of this kind of obit," gesturing
toward the national fantasy of universal white,
middle-class ordinariness and the historical recuperation of the largely invisible lives of unknown women and African Americans (citing
Gay Talese, 117). As Christine Kay, the metropolitan editor of the *New York Times*, describes
the egalitarian obituary format in regard to the
paper's award-winning "Portraits of Grief" feature on the lives of 9/11 victims, obituaries are
a genre that can "encompass dishwashers from

Windows on the World, firefighters, stockbrokers, and successful executives" (quoted in Johnson 2007, 65). What resonated with readers of the *Times*, Kay surmised, was that an obituary for a trader could read exactly like one for a janitor.

The obituary page and obituary writers were rising in social status at the same time national victims of mass violence in the United States were becoming more visible, thanks to the victims' rights movement and twenty-four-hour news channels. Through trauma training initiatives in the nation's journalism schools, journalism students are also being prepared to write obituaries commemorative of victims in a style similar to the egalitarian obituary and with a similar "democratic ethos." The obituaries of crime and terrorism victims embrace a form of affective or sentimental politics of remembrance for crime's and mass disaster's effects. Rather than being expressly political in character, they resemble the "juxtapolitical" forms of sentimental cultural production that Lauren Berlant analyzes in *The Female Complaint*. The juxtapolitical constitutes those forms of collective life that happen "to the side or under the radar of politics" (2008, 27). In obituaries for victims, the "register of importance is *not* in the idiom of politics" but in that of familial grief and remembrance. They portray "ordinary scenes of survival" in extraordinary circumstances (2008, 24). Following Berlant, this chapter does not critique victim memorialization for its failures to be more political. Instead, it seeks to understand how the genre of the victim obituary emerged out of families' desires to publicly remember their killed loved ones in a news environment that may be becoming somewhat more hospitable to victims, thanks to journalism and trauma programs and victims' rights media activism. The resulting obituary-like practices for commemorating the lives of the killed occur to the side of the political rather than being explicit political strategies in and of themselves. They may occasionally cross over into the political realm; their proximity to political agency and practice modifies, amplifies, and mobilizes political action through their affective register. They are affective practices and texts, witnessing texts to familial grief for national victims.

Perhaps the best exemplar of this style of obituary, or profile of life, is the "Portraits of Grief" feature in the *New York Times*. Yet six years before this award-winning reporting on 9/11 victims ran, the editors and reporters at the *Oklahoman* in Oklahoma City crafted the first multiple-victim newspaper memorial: that to the 168 adults and children killed in the bombing of the federal building on the morning of 19 April 1995. Joe Hight, the managing editor of the *Oklahoman*, brought the lessons he and his reporters learned from his paper's victim commemorations to journalism educators at the Dart Center for Journalism and Trauma. He also helped found the Center for People and the Media Program in the Department of Mass Communication at the University of Central Oklahoma just outside of Oklahoma City. In 2003 he wrote the training text *Tragedies and Journalists: A Guide for More Effective Coverage*, published by the Dart Center (see chapter 4). Journalistic trauma training codified the features of the *Oklahoman*'s commemorative format and has systematically been training students how to write commemorative news features on killed victims. The profile of life is the principal genre of victim-oriented news writing to emerge from trauma training.

The profile of life obituary format conceptualizes human life in terms of those deemed worthy of being grieved by the national circumstances of their deaths. Against the nineteenth-century fantasies of democracy in death that Johnson and Kay revive, profiles of life constitute a "hierarchy of grief . . . where lives are quickly tidied up and summarized, humanized, usually married, or on the way to be, heterosexual, happy, monogamous," while others are cast out of the category meriting grief (Butler 2003, 20–21). As Judith Butler suggests, if we were to commemorate the lives of victims who are not "our own," "if there were to be an obituary, there would have had to have been a life, a life worth noting, a life worth valuing and preserving, a life that qualifies for recognition" in national terms (2004, 23).

Mass commemorations of the dead victims of terrorism and major crimes share some of the stylistic features of the profiles of local individuals that run in such special features as "A Local Life" in the *Washington Post* and "Lives Lived" in the *Globe and Mail* of Toronto. But unlike these profiles, in which the lives of largely unknown citizens are narrated as being singular and unique, either by an obituary writer, as is done at the *Post*, or by a family member, friend, or former colleague, as at the *Globe and Mail*, the profiles of life examined here speak simultaneously as individual and mass. Reading through the 2,310 "Portraits of Grief" published in the heavy tome that Time Publishing released in 2002, I was struck by how much life circumstances and social difference matter in them. African American heritage, immigration status, class immobility, white privilege, and the sexual divisions of family and work, for example, strongly and profoundly define the differences between the lives of those individuals who share having been killed together, differences whose meaning comes to matter as further evidence of how violence democratizes all life, despite its differences, in death. While the memorials mark out difference, they also depict the magnitude of the losses caused by the terrorist attacks. Singular obituaries commemorate the lives of local citizens. A profile of life commemorates the life of a person who has been killed at the same time as many others and is a victim. The simultaneity and magnitude of their shared deaths make victims' lives all the more worthy of being recognized. Profiles of life are not just familial remembrances of individuals' lives. They represent an industrial imperative to both commemorate dead victims of major criminal acts and portray the magnitude and significance of their killing in national and international terms.

This chapter draws on several sources in which profiles of life have been published: the special commemorative features section in the *Oklahoman* called "Together in the Heartland," devoted to the 168 victims of the bombing of the Alfred P. Murrah Federal Building on April 19, 1995; and various commemorations of the victims of 9/11, including the "Portraits of Grief" in the *New York Times*, republished in a six-hundred-page book titled *Portraits 9/11: The Collected 'Portraits of Grief' from the New York Times*, now in its second edition; the commemoration in *Newsday*, also republished in book form in 2002 under the title *American Lives: The Stories of the Men and Women Lost on September 11*; memorials to New Jersey residents killed in the attacks in the *Star-Ledger*; and *Rolling Stone* magazine's short commemorative feature on a group of victims whose rock fandom and subscriber status became the basis for the magazine's commemorations.

These examples in no way constitute the entirety of newspaper and other online and print culture profiles of life on dead victims, but they are representative of the style, flexible form, and content of the genre as employed to describe an act of domestic terrorism and an act of international terrorism. While the feature on the bombing victims in the *Oklahoman* became the template for subsequent news commemoration of multiple victims killed in acts of major crime and terrorism, the commemorations of the victims of 9/11 in the New York and New Jersey newspapers further codified the form and the practice of its production through the journalistic routines of the reporters who worked on the project. Yet the "Portraits of Grief" feature has achieved most of the professional and scholarly recognition for these practices of commemoration.

What can be said of the lives of the dead in victim profiles is defined primarily by familial desire to cast the lives of the dead as meaningful, successful, good. And, as news obituaries of the dead from these major acts of crime illustrate, the remembrances of the lives of the dead was a central part of the argument for launching military strikes against Afghanistan in October 2001, invading Iraq in March 2003, and prosecuting and executing Timothy McVeigh for his role in the Oklahoma City bombing. I want to examine the decisions and practices around which the inclusions of the dead in the victim obituary are made as an extension of a victims' rights framework coded into the trauma training practices discussed in chapter 4. Whereas Johnson argues that the egalitarian obituary marks the democratization of death through its presumption that all lives are equally memorable, when viewed from the perspective of victims' rights, the victim obituary presumes precisely the opposite: that while death may be the ultimate democratizer (for we all die), death by major acts of criminal violence, terrorism, or criminal negligence marks some lives as more worthy of recognition in death than others. In commemorating the lives of the dead, these obituaries also prohibit talk about the circumstances of victims' deaths. They also presume that victims' lives must have been morally innocent. Following Butler, I ask, "how the obituary functions as the instrument by which grievability is publicly distributed" (2003, 23). If the obituary is "an icon for national self-recognition" and "the means by which a life becomes noteworthy," it represents the combination of familial needs to commemorate the loss of individuals and the creation of memorials to a nation's dead (23). As Butler and Ernest Mandel both suggest, the very possibility of representing human life and enabling its social recognition is predicated on how nations and communities socialize death and organize their mourning practices in forms like the profile of life (see also Noys 2007).

The Profile of Life Format and Its Language of Victims' Rights

The profile of life draws from the familial, intimate, and anecdotal spaces of grief and their story-based practices of remembrance. Rather than focus on the profile of life as a generic format of obituary that applies to potentially all lives, this chapter attends to the specific format of the collectivized profiles of life that depict the lives of victims of major criminal or terrorist acts. Such collective obituaries to mass victims give conventionalized form to the representation of everyday life. They do so through commemorative formats that place the lives of victims killed in acts of terrorism and mass murder on an equal scale of significance. Not only are they a special version of the profile of life genre, but in addition their practices of collective portrayal and archiving set them apart from day-to-day news obituaries. These profiles of life in the context of mass death point to a powerful set of fantasies about the meaning and constitution of life in the context of having been made victims of major mass crimes. Their perspective on victimization and their recognition of the family as victim resonate with the orientation of the victims' rights movement toward secondary victims and its media grammars of representation.

Profiles of life attempt to describe what one reporter at the *New York Times*, Janny Scott, called, in the wake of 9/11, the "tiny but telling details" that define a life as being both good and unique (*Portraits 9/11/01*, ix). They often include material gathered from interviews with surviving family members, who serve as the main sources of anecdotes, descriptions of personal idiosyncrasies, and family and school photographs that, when packaged as a profile of life, come to define life and its losses in primarily familial terms. As a result, profiles of life employ the movement's media language of victims' rights and its amplification of the covictim voice.

Like other daily papers in the 1980s that began the practice of profiling the lives of deceased city residents according to the interest they might provoke rather than to the status or station of the deceased (Johnson 2007), profiles of life recognize the small accomplishments of a victim's life, the significance of local and neighborhood figures, and the emotional work of familial and interpersonal relationships. In this obituary format, newspaper readers read about the meaningfulness of the dead victim's life as members of the family wish to have that life remembered: it is their memories of rites of passage, personality traits, hobbies, or favorite pastimes of the dead. In Nancy Miller's words, victim profiles of life "anecdotalize familial grief" on a national scale, detailing the "happiness that was" the victim's life before victimization (2003, 126). The quotidian detail, as Miller argues, is "the index of poignant loss" (122): "In the face of collective disaster . . . the anecdote was seized upon as a form suited to rendering the familiar acts of ordinary life. Like the snapshot, the anecdote . . . catches life in everyday dimensions. Often the details are not harnessed to a narrative; rather they provide points of entry into character: personality traits, habits, quirks, hobbies, mottoes, which are cumulative in effect but not shaped into a story" (115). The goal of a profile of life is to speak well of the dead by narrating the good in their life in the form of its everyday details.

Most death notices represent the dead through their familial relationships, yet profiles of life give the form unique political valence in their extension of victims' rights claims to media representation and political recognition. Profiles of life promise a form of social recognition through the news that speaks to the significance of a loved one's death in ways the typical death notice simply cannot. To the families of people who have been killed in murders, bombings, and other acts of terrorism, the profile of life offers a way to publicly remember the lives of the dead. In some cases, it also links the remembrances of their lives to calls for harsher sentencing, antiterrorism legislation, and increased border security. In other cases families use it to express their investments in violence prevention and antiviolence initiatives aimed at bringing about social justice, such as the group September 11 Families for Peaceful Tomorrows. This group challenged the ways in which newspapers and the administration of George W. Bush used the grief and anger of survivors to make the case for U.S. military aggression against Afghanistan. The grief families experience at the murders of their family members calls out to be recognized, but what that recognition comes to mean politically and ethically and whether it achieves recognition and of what kind are specific to context, person, and organization.

The profile of life recalls the lives of the dead primarily through victim photographs and familial remembrances. Photography, the anthropologist Susan Hirsch argues, ensures that the "dead victim is present" (2000, 2), whether in a court of law or on the newspaper page. Hirsch's husband was killed by a bomb that exploded at the U.S. embassy in Tanzania in 1998. In describing her experience dealing with the prosecution at the murder trial of the al-Qaeda operative who was held responsible for her husband's death, she notes the significance to the prosecutors of the display of photographs of the victims. Over the course of the trial, the testimony of each family's witness was accompanied by photographs of the dead, first in portraits that showed the victims alive and smiling and then in photographs of their dead bodies. During the testimony of Hirsch's nephew on behalf of the family, the prosecutor first displayed a photograph of Hirsch's husband cropped from their wedding photo followed by a photograph of his badly burned, nearly unidentifiable body. After the prosecutors had promised Hirsch that they would not show the photo of her husband's charred remains during the trial, an experience she describes as especially harmful to her, they "explain that photos of victims before the bombing would show the impact of my loss, while the photos of dead bodies would attest to the horror of the crime scene. Legally, they need to make both points" (2000, n.p.). The profiling of victims' lives and deaths in the courtroom is not done for the benefit of families, above all when plaintiffs like Hirsch specifically desire to be protected from images of their loved one's dead body in the course of the trial.

Although profiles of life are not evidentiary documents in the context of the courtroom, as the photographs of victims in the al-Qaeda operative's trial were, they seek to recognize the subjectivity of the dead by treating their life stories as claims-making instruments and as commemorations. Photographs portray the dead as social subjects whose deaths by acts of terrorism or mass murder refigure the significance of their lives. The call to remember the dead in profiles of life has less to do with dead victims' own agency while alive than with the status of their vicarious agency in the political, social, and familial contexts of their death. As Elizabeth Klaver argues, "Agency resides in a much higher register than the subject, an order of performativity located somewhere between subjectivation and self-determination. . . . The dead most definitely can be considered 'subjects,' or at least 'being-as-subjects.' . . . The dead also 'do' something in the world. . . . They just do not have agency, though in Western culture we have a tendency to project agency onto them" (2004, 108). The photographic representations within the profile of life give face to the dead in life through their families, as the victims' rights movement does. They "contextualize tragedy by placing the victim within the context of bereaved *families*," creating a "presence absence . . . of the murder victim" (Jermyn 2004, 85, 87). When victims are not portrayed in relation to a family unit, the implication is that they might be in some part blameworthy for the victimization they suffered. Their position in a loving, conventional family signifies their moral worth as victims: "To not be in a family would be to not be a proper victim" (Jermyn 2004, 185). Placing victims within familial formations "perpetuates the notion that it is primarily through their roles within the conventional family unit that individuals can be positioned, identified and legitimized, thus endorsing the hegemonic institution of the family" (Jermyn 2004, 176).

My particular interest lies in the politics of recognition that form around and through these victim obituaries in their conventionalization of the discourse of victims' rights. The news imperative to memorialize some dead victims is part of a larger political battle being waged to raise the profile of crime victims through their families' rights to legal and media representation as victims, who in the process come to stand in as national victim representatives. The promise that profiles of life will bring recognition to the lives of dead victims through their family's public remembrances exposes the tenuous links between media representations of victims and their social recognition. In commodity form, the profiles create industry-specific conditions for representing families' needs for recognition of dead victims' unique individuality in life; they are both memorials and commodities.

The Dart Center training booklet *Tragedies and Journalists* distills the profile of life genre into five tips reporters can follow to produce a victim memorial. *Tragedies and Journalists*, among other training texts, teaches students how to streamline the process of writing profiles of life by providing them with a set of writing guidelines. In its "Tips for Writing about Victims," reporters learn to ask questions about the lives of victims who have been killed to elicit the kinds of anecdotes Miller describes above: questions such as "Can you tell me about Jerry's life?," and "What did Jerry like to do? What were his favorite hobbies?," define the content of the profile of life through the mundane aspects of everyday life (see figs. 1.1 and 1.2). Students should, according to Hight and Smyth, the authors of the booklet, "try to clarify [when interviewing survivors] that you seek to profile their lives before they disappeared and not to write their obituaries" (2004, 3).

Gaining access to family photos reinforces the idea that the profile will offer an intimate, familial remembrance of a once-living individual. Profiles of life are generally published with one or more photos of the victim. In an interview in the Michigan State University training video *Reporting on Victims of Violence and Catastrophe*, Sue Carter advises her student viewers to explain to families how important it is to celebrate the life, rather than the death, of the person who has died through the news display of private family photographs. Family photos not only identify the victim but also place him or her firmly within the family unit. As Allan Sekula writes, "Pho-

Tips for writing about victims:
1. Focus on the person's life. Find out what made the person special: personality, beliefs, environment (surroundings, hobbies, family and friends), and likes and dislikes. Treat the person's life as carefully as a photographer does in framing a portrait.

2. Always be accurate. Check back with the victim or victim's representative to verify spellings of names, facts and even quotes. The reason: When you first talk to a victim, he or she may be confused or distracted. Double-checking can ensure accuracy. It also may provide you with additional information and quotes that you can use.

3. Use pertinent details that help describe victims as they lived or provide images of their lives. Example: "Johnny loved to play the guitar in the evening to entertain his family, but it also helped him escape the stress of his job as a sheriff's deputy."

4. Avoid unneeded gory details about the victims' deaths. After the Oklahoma City bombing, certain reporters chose not to reveal that body parts were dangling from the trees near the federal building. Ask yourself whether the images are pertinent or will do unnecessary harm to certain members of your readership or broadcast audience.

   Also, avoid words and terms such as "closure," "will rest in peace" or "a shocked community mourns the death." Use simple and clear words as good writers do for any story.

5. Use quotes and anecdotes from the victim's relatives and friends to describe the person's life. Especially those that tell how the person had overcome obstacles. Seek current photos of the victim (but always return them as soon as possible). This way, you know what the person looked like in life.

I.I and I.2. *Tragedies and Journalists*, "Tips for Writing about Victims."

tography welded the honorific [function of bourgeois portraiture] and repressive functions [of police photography] together" (1986, 10).

Profiling Life, Marginalizing Death

As a genre, the victim profile of life uniquely collectivizes individual obituaries into archival newspaper features, functioning as a way to catalogue the bodily evidence of recent terrorist attacks and major acts of murder-

2. The grim reaper, from *Newsday*, 16 September 2001.
Newsday Illustration/Gary Viskupic

ous violence in which their victims were produced, but in a way that replaces the forensic portrayal of dead bodies with distinct textual features
and photographic markers of the dead as once-living subjects. Outside of
the profiles of life in the pages of the newspaper, however, images of death
contextualized the once-living lives of the victims, sometimes in overly dramatic graphic art. On 13 September 2001, in *Newsday*, a graphic of the grim
reaper ran on the op-ed page right in the middle of the fold. His hooded
figure stands between the two towers of the World Trade Center while his
scythe cuts a diagonal path through the buildings as an airplane approaches
the north tower from the right (see fig. 2). As this image suggests, there
was no news taboo against portraying death as a character in the context of
the immediate aftermath of the 9/11 attacks, yet avoidance of talk of death
became an editorial mandate at those newspapers running special commemorative features on the dead within the obituaries themselves. Most
death notices include mention of the individual's death. Profiles of life do
not. Rather than a taboo against death talk, images such as this one of the

grim reaper, while possibly in bad taste, function as "spaces for exposure to death." Arguing against the "cliché of the death taboo," Benjamin Noys suggests instead that modern cultures of death are better thought of as social experiences in which people are exposed to death and its representation (2007, 4). Understanding the precise nature of that encounter through profiles of life can reveal the cultural politics of talk about death that the political discourse of victims' rights enables.

Profiles of life expose newsreaders to the dead, but they do so through a discourse of life that relegates talk of death and its representation to other forms, like the news graphic on the editorial page of *Newsday*. Gathered in feature formats, profiles of life display a unique, text-based architecture of life-in-death, sometimes in diagram form, as in the graphic depiction (although devoid of bodies) of the bombing of the federal building in the *Oklahoman* and in the textual and photographic interface *Rolling Stone* magazine and newspapers like the *Star-Ledger* used in building textual museums to the lives of the dead, including lists of their names, and in the physical memorial monuments built to victims, like that of the Oklahoma City bombing memorial museum, with its room dedicated to the 168 victims and a field of chairs that greets visitors on the grounds surrounding the museum building. Inside the museum, victims' lives are memorialized in Lucite boxes that contain a photographic headshot of the victim and one physical artifact from his or her life: a small bottle of hairspray for a former hairdresser, a teddy bear for a toddler boy.

As an example of a profile of life, Steven D. Jacoby, chief operations officer of the second-largest wireless pager company in the United States when he died on American Airlines Flight 77, which crashed into the Pentagon on 11 September 2001, appears in several online and print commemoration sites for 9/11 victims. His is the first profile published in the wake of the attacks, appearing on 13 September 2001, in *Newsday*'s series "The Lost." The profile notes the time of Jacoby's death as the moment his pager sent its last signal, at 9:30 A.M. More than once the profile comments on the irony of Jacoby's death in the kind of catastrophic conditions the wireless pager network he helped to build were meant to address. His business associates and friends describe him as a thoughtful, caring man who had a good mind for business. Included in the profile is mention of the fact that his wife, Kim, chose not to comment on his death immediately after it occurred.

On the website 9-11heroes.us, former business acquaintances of Jacoby and people seeking information about his family origins (some were trying to find out whether they were related to him or his family) posted messages under a simple textual identification stating his name, age at time of death, city of residence, and the flight on which he was traveling when he was killed.[1] In an odd juxtaposition, the memorial page includes a series of full-color video clips of the members of Rockabilly US, the show band from central Florida that sponsors the site. Included also is a YouTube video clip of the band singing an original song, "The Day America Cried," a tribute song to the victims of 9/11 that blends the ballad style of the 1960s with lyrics from "America the Beautiful." The band is fronted by a middle-aged male singer wearing a blond toupee and backed by six young females in kitschy costumes, backup singers and dancers, and a full band. The website is a blend of Branson-style show—the Missouri tourist destination for live country music performance, comedy, Middle American variety shows, and theme parks—with victim memorial. Despite or perhaps because of its odd combination of band publicity and victim memorial, 9-11heroes .us is the perfect example of how unusual and sometimes blatantly self-propagandistic the formats of popular commemorative sites can be.

The site is also, however, very much like other forms of victim commemoration, telling visitors who might wish to post messages exactly how and what kind of material is most appropriate for memorialization:

> Post your memorial thoughts: Share your feelings and memories of grief and sadness concerning the 9-11-2001 attack, or of positive memories. If you knew this person, help us to build a small 'bio' of the person and share with us something about his/her life:
>
> · what kind of person he/she was,
> · what nice points you remember about him/her,
> · what kind of relationship you had with him/her,
> · what you two perhaps did together,
> · what he/she meant to you,
> · or other things about him/her that might be especially encouraging for other people.
>
> This website is intended solely as a means of allowing all of us to express our grief and sympathy on behalf of the people who lost their lives, and also our love and compassion towards those who lost loved ones and

friends in the 9/11/01 tragedy. The site is strictly for memorial mentions of those who passed away in the tragedy, not of other people who have passed away.

The site is not meant to be a general memorial to the dead but an exclusive space for 9/11 remembrances, a feature the website's manager had to make explicit. Following this prescription, the site warns visitors that mention of who might be responsible for the terrorist attacks or any negative comments about the victim or "passing judgment upon any person or group will not be published on this site. We do NOT want this site to be a base for expressions of hatred, but only for expressions of LOVE!" The memorial page for Ann Judge from Great Falls, Va., who also died on Flight 77 includes heartfelt expressions of grief ranging from those of family friends, like ten-year-old Amanda Kerr's — "Ann was our family's best friend. She loved me and I loved her. Ann is and always will be in our hearts and thoughts forever. I love you Ann, and miss you like crazy!" — to simple statements like the one by Ben Donahue, who classified her death as undeserved.[2]

According to the editorial note at the beginning of *Rolling Stone* magazine's memorial feature on 9/11 victims, the people profiled there include a "firefighter who fronted a punk band. Another was a financial executive who . . . planned to take his wife to a Black Crowes concert at the end of September in 2001" (*Rolling Stone* 2001/2, 45). To highlight *Rolling Stone's* commemoration of rock fans and musicians, many of their profiles are accompanied by photographs of victims playing guitar at rock shows, being photographed with their favorite rock stars, and disc jockeying at clubs in addition to wedding and employment photographs. John Heffernan's profile describes him as a loving father and a dedicated punk rocker who one of the Ramone brothers helped get a recording gig. The photograph that accompanies his profile shows him performing at a rock concert (see fig. 3). With electric guitar in hand, he strikes an impromptu rock pose, his face turned toward the camera, eyes closed, and his mouth agape as he sings.

In another profile in *Rolling Stone*, Josh Birnbaum appears in a photograph spinning records at a party in May 2001. According to his profile, Birnbaum was a twenty-four-year-old assistant bond trader at Cantor Fitzgerald and had graduated from Columbia University in May 2001. By night, Birnbaum worked as a disc jockey under the name Samsson, after his father,

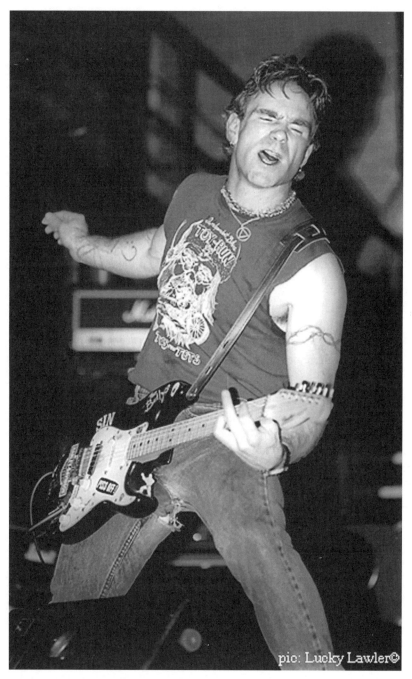

pic: Lucky Lawler©

3. John Heffernan, *Rolling Stone* magazine. "A Firefighter who kept his rock dreams alive."
By permission of Walter Stachnik.

Sam, who had given him ten thousand dollars as a college graduation gift. Birnbaum used the money to purchase DJ equipment and a number of records so he could follow his true passion in life, his music. In his spare time he burned compact discs of electronic music he mixed and shared them with friends. According to his friends, Birnbaum's goal was to leave the bond trading business and become a full-time musician. His profile, like so many that follow the conventions of the profile of life, is listed under his name and a personalized caption that reads, "A Last Phone Call to Mom" in reference to a call he made to his mother, Marcel, shortly after a plane hit the tower of the World Trade Center building in which he worked. That phone call, according to his mother, consisted of the following plea from a son to his mother: "Mommy, something hit the building and I need to tell you that I love you. I love all of you."

Such intimate moments of communication between mother and son capture the rich affective burden of the profile of life for surviving family members. They also mark the final connection between the once-living dead and the survivors. They serve as a means for those surviving families linked together through their family members' deaths in the airplane attacks of 11 September 2001, to commemorate their losses through specific mementos of their communication — their final phone conversations, photographs of them engaging in activities they enjoy, playing records and performing live on guitar. Final phone calls are specifically noted in several profiles, calls whose timeliness in the moments before death marks the last vestiges of life across wireless networks.

As Elaine Scarry has argued, the use of cellphones by air passengers and their family members on the ground on two of the flights hijacked on 11 September 2001, signifies a form of intimate timeliness and an American ethos of self-defense: "The conversations enabled extraordinary events to be tested against the norms of everyday life. They were both intimate and an act of record-making: how else to explain Mark Bingham's self-identification to his mother, 'This is Mark Bingham.' He both gave his mother the statement that the plane had been seized by hijackers ('You believe me, don't you?') and in effect notarized the statement by giving a verbal signature" (2002, n.p.). Scarry uses the example of cellphone telephony on United Flight 93 before some passengers on board caused it to crash in a field near Shanksville, Pennsylvania, as a sign of decentralized democracy at work — where the communication between passengers and family members on the ground was used to confirm information about the other hijackings, to develop a plan to respond to the hijackers of their plane, and to communicate familial and personal intimacies. The quotes she cites from those conversations are marked by their highly familiar and familial dimensions of intimacy and its conditions of communication in the high-stress, disastrous context of a hijacked airplane. People on board called their wives, husbands, stepmothers, close friends, and mothers not only to confirm information about the other hijackings but also to pray and express their love to each other. "Each of the passengers who was in conversation with a family member," Scarry explains, "stated aloud his or her love for the listener; Todd Beamer asked Lisa Jefferson to convey his love to his family. The family members reciprocated: 'I've got my arms around you,' Elizabeth Wainio's stepmother told her" (2002, n.p.).

Profiles of life, these examples suggest, put into text and image the familial dimensions of intimate communication so central to victims' rights discourse, particularly in the last communication before death in its connection to the familiar intimacies of communication in the everyday. In constructing profiles of life, family members or other intimates tell parts of the life stories of the dead to reporters, who then turn them into obituaries defined through a rhetoric of life that rests on the everyday dimensions of communication. Profiles of life at their core are about the relationship of the dead to the living. The dead's last act of communication plays a central role in reconstructing their subjectivity in life, not only as a speaking subject but also as a member of a family unit.

Most profiles, such as those described above, come bundled in packages with others in special feature sections of newspapers, segregated from the rest of the daily news. The majority of profiles of life contain a single photograph of the dead, usually a family snapshot, a work identification photograph, a formal portrait, a school photo, or sometimes a photocopied candid shot distributed on missing persons flyers, for example, around the scene of the World Trade Center bombing. The special section titled "Together in the Heartland" that appeared in the *Oklahoman* followed the police investigation of Timothy McVeigh's and Terry Nichols's truck bombing of the federal building in addition to presenting victim profiles called "Those who Died," which ran in April and May 1995. The paper's news memorials became material for the national memorial museum to the bombing now located at the former site of the Murrah federal building. The feature section "A Nation Challenged" in the *New York Times* combined "Portraits of Grief" with news stories on U.S. military strategy in Afghanistan, war reporting, and the federal investigations into the attack sites in New York City, the Pentagon, and Shanksville. Across all of these news features, the profiles of life attempt to give body to the lives of the dead in order to socially recognize them by expressly not portraying their dead bodies or describing the circumstances of their deaths, as their families had done via cellphones on the morning of 11 September. This is an aspect of the profile of life made all the more apparent in the architectural depictions of mass disaster in the case of the Oklahoma bombing and their profiles of killed children.

Memorials to the Dead: The Oklahoma City Bombing

To dismember is to fragment a body and its memory; to remember
is to make a body complete.
MARITA STURKEN, *Tangled Memories*

On 7 May 1995, the *Oklahoman* ran a full-page listing of every person killed in the bombing of the Alfred P. Murrah Federal Building in downtown Oklahoma City on 19 April 1995. Printed as part of a special feature in the paper's A-section called "Together in the Heartland," the listing of the casualties marks the end of the *Oklahoman's* commemoration of the bombing dead in victims' life profiles (see fig. 4). Along the left-hand margin of the page and covering the whole bottom half under the fold, the bombing dead are listed by name, followed by their age at the time of death, and, where applicable, their occupation and employer. Many of the dead were infants and babies, some as young as three months old, who were at a child care center in the eight-story building. As of the issue dated 7 May 1995, three victims' bodies as yet unaccounted for are listed on the page as "Presumed Dead." Another sixteen people are listed as hospitalized.

The page is particularly striking for the ways in which it gives body to the dead in architectural form. The list of the dead, missing, and injured stands like eight erect pillars holding up the four architectural diagrams of the federal building's bombing sequence at the top of the page. At the top of the right half of the page, four black-and-white diagrams reconstruct the building's structural collapse over the two-minute interval of the bombing.

THE SUNDAY OKLAHOMAN Section A May 7, 1995 **19**

Together in the Heartland

Bombing Casualties

Following is an alphabetical list of people confirmed dead, missing or still hospitalized as a result of the April 19 bombing at the Alfred P. Murrah Federal Building. Included is Rebecca Anderson, who died during the rescue effort.

Dead

Lucio Aleman Jr., 33, safety engineer, Federal Highway Administration.

Richard Arthur Allen, 46, Yukon, claims representative, Social Security Administration.

Ted Leon Allen, 48, Norman, community planning, Housing and Urban Development.

Baylee Almon, 1, Midwest City.

Diane E. (Hollingsworth) Althouse, 45, loan management, Housing and Urban Development.

Rebecca Anderson, 37, nurse.

Pamela Cleveland Argo, 36, Oklahoma City.

Saundra "Sandy" Avery, 34, Midwest City, development clerk, Social Security Administration.

Peter Avillanoza, 56, fair housing and equal opportunity director, Housing and Urban Development.

Calvin Battle, 62.

Peola Battle, 56.

Danielle Nicole Bell, 15 months.

Oleta Christine Biddy, 54, Oklahoma City, Social Security service representative.

Shelly Turner Bland, 25, asset forfeiture specialist, Drug Enforcement Administration.

Andrea Y. Blanton, 33, Oklahoma City, secretary, Housing and Urban Development.

Olen Burl Bloomer, 61, budget assistant, U.S. Department of Agriculture.

Lola Renee Bolden, 40, Army Sgt. 1st Class, Birmingham, Ala., assigned to the Oklahoma City Recruiting Battalion.

James E. Boles, 51, administrative officer, U.S. Department of Agriculture.

Mark A. Bolte, 27, highway engineer, Federal Highway Administration.

Cassandra Kay Booker, 25, Oklahoma City.

Carol Louise Bowers, 53, Yukon, operations supervisor, Social Security Administration.

Peachlyn Bradley, 3, Oklahoma City.

Woodrow "Woody" Clifford Brady, 41, Oklahoma City.

Cynthia Lynn (Campbell) Brown, 26, special agent, Secret Service.

Paul G. Broxterman, 43, Housing and Urban Development.

Kimberly Ruth Burgess, 29, Tinker Air Force Base, Federal Employees Credit Union.

David Neil Burkett, 47, Housing and Urban Development.

Donald Earl Burns Sr., 63, construction analyst, Housing and Urban Development.

Karen Gist Carr, 32, U.S. Army Recruiting Office.

Michael J. Carrillo, 44, Federal Highway Administration.

Rona Linn Chafey, 35, Oklahoma City, Cleveland County sheriff's secretary assigned to the Drug Enforcement Administration.

Zackary T. Chavez, 3, Oklahoma City.

Robert Neal Chipman, 51, Edmond, financial analyst, Oklahoma Water Resources Board.

Kimberly Kay Clark, 39, Oklahoma City, legal division, Housing and Urban Development.

Dr. Margaret Louise "Peggy" Clark, 42, veterinary medical officer, U.S. Department of Agriculture.

Anthony Christopher Cooper II, 2, Moore.

Dana Brown Cooper, 24, Moore, director, America's Kids day-care center.

Harley Cottingham, 46, special agent, Department of Defense.

A Split Second Of Destruction

A moment-by-moment diagram of the April 19 bomb blast that destroyed the Alfred P. Murrah Federal Building.

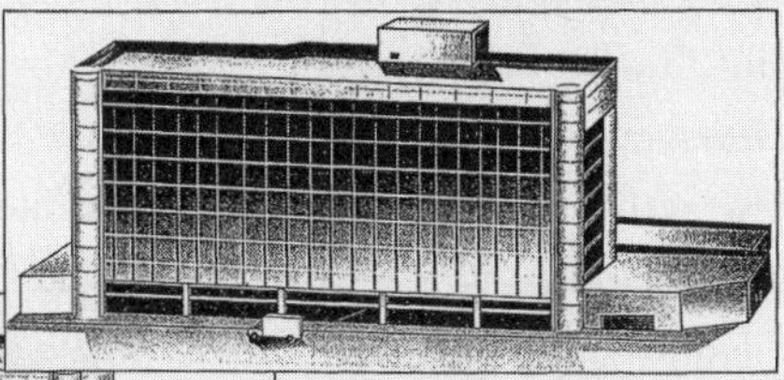

At 9:02 a.m., Wednesday, April 19, a yellow Ryder rental truck parked at a meter on 5 Street explodes into a spray of steel, chrome and glass. Gases from the two-ton bomb roar out at 6,500 feet per second, erupting into a cone-shaped wall of scorched air.

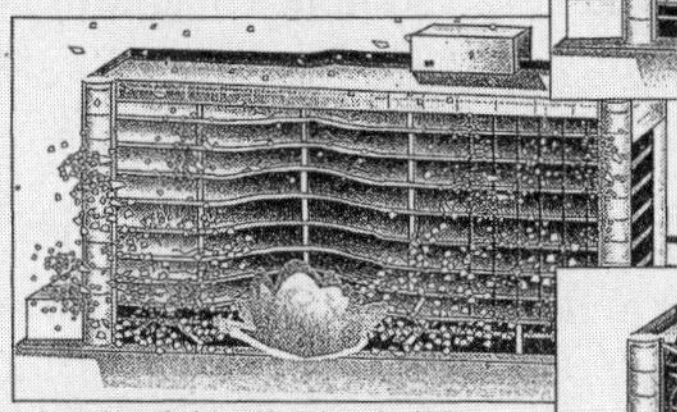

In seven-thousandths of a second the shock wave slams into the building, putting nearly a half-ton of pressure on every square inch of the building's surface. The wave lifts all nine floors, snapping the two-inch steel rebars in the concrete support columns, causing them to crumble.

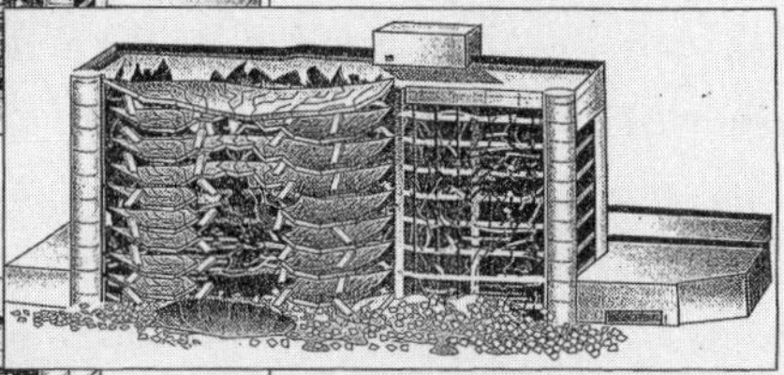

The rapid rise and fall of the floors crushes everything below. Desks, chairs and file cabinets become dangerous projectiles. As the blast wave dissipates, the floors collapse. Three of the building's main support columns are destroyed, so the entire north face funnels into a tremendous pile of rubble on the street. In a tenth of a second it is done.

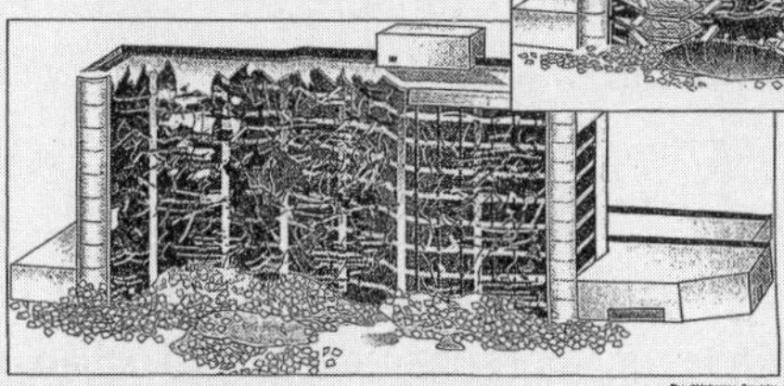

The Oklahoman Graphics

Kim Robin Cousins, 33, Midwest City, Housing and Urban Development.

Aaron Coverdale, 5.

Elijah Coverdale, 2.

Jaci Rae Coyne, 14 months, Moore.

Kathy L. Cregan, 60, Oklahoma City, claims representative, Social Security Administration.

Richard Leroy Cummins, 55, senior investigator, U.S. Department of Agriculture.

Steven D. Curry, 44, Norman, General Services Administration inspector.

Brenda Daniels, 42, Oklahoma City, America's Kids day-care center.

Sgt. Benjamin L. Davis, 29, U.S. Marine Corps Recruiting Station, operations clerk, Oklahoma City.

Diana Lynn Day, 38, Housing and Urban Development.

Peter DeMaster, 44, special agent, Department of Defense.

Castine "Brooks" Deveroux, 49, Oklahoma City, closing clerk, Housing and Urban Development.

Sheila R. Gigger Driver, 28, Oklahoma City.

Tylor Eaves, 8 months, America's Kids day-care center.

Ashley Eckles, 4, Guthrie.

Susan Ferrell, 37, attorney, Housing and Urban Development.

Carroll June "Chip" Fields, 48, Guthrie, Drug Enforcement Agency.

Katherine Ann Finley, 44, Federal Employees Credit Union.

Judy J. Fisher, 45, Housing and Urban Development.

Linda L. Florence, 43, Oklahoma City, properties disposition, Housing and Urban Development.

Donald Lee Fritzler, 64, Oklahoma City.

Mary Anne Fritzler, 57, Oklahoma City.

Tevin Garrett, 18 months, Oklahoma City.

Laura Jane (Washington) Garrison, 61, Oklahoma City.

Jamie Genzer, 32, Wellston, loan officer, Federal Employees Credit Union.

Margaret Betterton Goodson, 54, Social Security claims representative.

Kevin Lee Gottshall, 6 months, Norman, America's Kids day-care center.

Ethel Louise Griffin, 55, Edmond, Social Security claims representative.

Colleen Guiles, 59, Oklahoma City, senior underwriter, Housing and Urban Development.

Capt. Randolph A. Guzman, 28, Castro Valley, Calif., executive officer, U.S. Marine Corps Recruiting Station.

Cheryl Bradley Hammons, 44, Oklahoma City.

Ronald Vernon Harding, 55, Oklahoma City, claims division, Social Security Administration.

Thomas Lynn Hawthorne Sr., 52, Choctaw, Social Security customer.

Doris A. Higginbottom, 44, purchasing agent, U.S. Department of Agriculture.

Anita C. Hightower, 27.

Gene Hodges Jr., 54, Norman, evaluation supervisor, Housing and Urban Development.

Peggy Louise Holland, 37, Oklahoma City, civilian computer specialist, U.S. Army Recruiting Office.

Linda Coleen Housley, 53, Oklahoma City, Federal Employees Credit Union.

George M. Howard, 45, Housing and Urban Development.

Wanda Lee Howell, 34, Spencer, teacher, America's Kids day-care center.

Robbin A. Huff, 37, Bethany, loan officer, Federal Employees Credit Union.

Dr. Charles E. Hurlburt, dentist, Oklahoma City.

Jean Hurlburt, Oklahoma City.

Paul Douglas Ice, 42, Midwest City, senior special agent, Customs Service.

Christi Y. Jenkins, 32, teller, Federal Employees Credit Union.

Norma Jean Johnson, 62, executive secretary, Department of Defense, Defense and Investigative Service.

Raymond Lee Johnson, 59, Oklahoma City, senior volunteer, Social Security Administration.

Larry J. Jones, 46, Yukon, computer specialist, Federal Highway Administration.

Blake Ryan Kennedy, 18 months, Amber.

Carole Khalil, 50, Oklahoma City, U.S. Department of Agriculture.

Valerie Koelsch, 33, Oklahoma City, marketing director, Federal Employees Credit Union.

Carolyn Ann Kreymborg, 57, Oklahoma City, loan management, Housing and Urban Development.

Teresa Lea Lauderdale, 41, Shawnee, realty specialist, Housing and Urban Development.

Kathy Leinen, 47, Federal Employees Credit Union.

Carrie Ann Lenz, 26, Choctaw, contract employee, Drug Enforcement Administration.

Donald Ray Leonard, 50, Edmond, special agent, Secret Service.

Airman 1st Class Lakesha R. Levy, 21, U.S. Air Force.

Dominique London, 2, Oklahoma City.

Rheta Ione (Bender) Long, 60, Oklahoma City, secretary, U.S. Department of Agriculture.

Michael L. Loudenslager, 48, Harrah, planner/estimator, General Services Administration.

Aurelia "Donna" Luster, 43, Guthrie.

Robert Lee Luster Jr., 45, Guthrie.

Mickey Bryant Maroney, 50, Oklahoma City, special agent, Secret Service.

James K. Martin, 34, highway engineer, Federal Highway Administration.

Gilberto X. Martinez, 35, Oklahoma City.

James A. McCarthy, 53, Housing and Urban Development.

Kenneth Glenn McCullough, 36, Edmond, special agent, Drug Enforcement Administration.

Betsy Janice McGonnell, 47, Housing and Urban Development.

Linda McKinney, 47, office manager, Secret Service.

Airman 1st Class Cartney J. McRaven, U.S. Air Force.

Claude Medearis, 41, senior special agent, Customs Service.

Claudette Meek, 43, Oklahoma City, Federal Employees Credit Union.

Frankie Ann Merrell, 23, teller, Federal Employees Credit Union.

Derwin Miller, 27.

Eula Leigh Mitchell, 64.

John C. Moss III, 51, Warren, Ark., chief of public affairs, U.S. Army Recruiting Office.

Patricia Nix, 47, Edmond, Housing and Urban Development.

Jerry Lee Parker, 45, Norman, area engineer, Federal Highway Administration.

Jill Diane Randolph, 27, Oklahoma City, Federal Employees Credit Union.

Michelle Ann Reeder, 33, Oklahoma City, administrative staff, Federal Highway Administration.

Terry Smith Rees, 41, Midwest City, acting director of public housing, Housing and Urban Development.

Mary Leasure Rentie, 39, Bethany, organization management personnel specialist, Housing and Urban Development.

Antonio Reyes, 55, fair housing, Housing and Urban Development.

Kathryn E. Ridley, 24.

Trudy Rigney, 31, Midwest City, draftswoman, Oklahoma Water Resources Board.

Claudine Ritter, 48, Moore, collection officer, Federal Employees Credit Union.

Sonja Sanders, 27, Federal Employees Credit Union.

Lanny L. Scroggins, 46, Oklahoma City, accounting, Housing and Urban Development.

Kathy Lynn Seidl, 39, Shawnee, investigative assistant, Secret Service.

Leora L. Sells, 57, Housing and Urban Development.

Karan Denise Shepherd, 27, Moore, loan officer, Federal Employees Credit Union.

Chase Smith, 3, Oklahoma City.

Colton Smith, 2, Oklahoma City.

Master Sgt. Victoria L. Sohn, 36, Moore, U.S. Army.

John T. Stewart, 51, Oklahoma City, Housing and Urban Development.

Dolores Marie Stratton, 51, Moore, civilian personnel clerk, U.S. Army recruiting office.

Emilio Rangel Tapia, 50, Oklahoma City.

Victoria J. Texter, 37, Oklahoma City, Federal Employees Credit Union.

Charlotte A. Thomas, 43, Social Security appointment clerk.

Michael G. Thompson, 46, Social Security Administration.

Kayla Marie Titsworth, 3, Oklahoma City.

Ricky L. Tomlin, 46, division program specialist, U.S. Department of Transportation.

LaRue Treanor, 56, Guthrie.

Luther Treanor, 61, Guthrie.

Larry L. Turner, 43, special agent, Defense and Investigative Service, Department of Defense.

Jules A. Valdez, 50, Housing and Urban Development.

John Karl VanEss, 67, Chickasha, Housing and Urban Development.

Johnny Allen Wade, 42, Oklahoma City, planning and research engineer, Federal Highway Administration.

David J. Walker, 54, environmental specialist, Housing and Urban Development.

Robert Nolan Walker Jr., 52.

Wanda Lee Watkins, 49, Midwest City, clerk, U.S. Army.

Michael Don Weaver, 45, Edmond, attorney.

Julie Marie Welch, 23, Oklahoma City, claims representative and interpreter, Social Security Administration.

Robert Glen Westberry, 57, Daytona Beach, Fla., special agent in charge, Department of Defense, Defense and Investigative Service.

Alan Gerald Whicher, 40, Oklahoma City, assistant special agent in charge, Secret Service.

Jo Ann Whittenberg, 35, Oklahoma City, program assistant, Housing and Urban Development.

Frances A. Williams, 48, community planning, Housing and Urban Development.

Scott Dwain Williams, 24, Tuttle.

William Stephen Williams, 42, Cashion, operations supervisor, Social Security Administration.

Clarence Eugene Wilson, 49, chief counsel and acting manager, Housing and Urban Development.

Ronota A. Woodbridge, 31, engineer, Federal Highway Administration.

Sharon Louise Wood-Chesnut, 47, Oklahoma City, claims representative, Social Security Administration.

Tresia Worton, 28, Federal Employees Credit Union.

Victims Not Recovered

Christy Rosas, 22, Moore, Federal Employees Credit Union.

Virginia M. Thompson, 56, El Reno, Federal Employees Credit Union.

Presumed Dead

Teresa Alexander, 33, Oklahoma City.

Antonio Ansara Cooper Jr., 6 months, America's Kids day-care center.

Gabreon DeShawn Lee Bruce, 3 months, Oklahoma City.

Hospitalized

CHILDREN'S HOSPITAL

Critical:
P.J. Allen, 20 months.

Serious:
Nekia McCloud, 4.

Fair:
Brandy Ligons, 15.
Christopher Nguyen, 5.

PRESBYTERIAN HOSPITAL

Critical:
Brandon Denny, 3.

Serious:
Susan Walton, 44.

ST. ANTHONY HOSPITAL

Critical:
John Youngblood, 52.

Serious:
Sharon Littlejohn, 28.

Fair:
Pam Briggs, 29.
Enetrice Smiley, 36.

Good:
Nancy Ingram, 64.
Stan Rombaum, 63.
Roya Sims, 28.

SOUTHWEST MEDICAL CENTER

Critical:
Patti Hall, 57, Oklahoma City.

UNIVERSITY HOSPITAL

Fair:
Dana Bradley, 20.

VETERANS HOSPITAL

Critical:
William G. "Gene" Martin, 40, Oklahoma City.

4. *The Oklahoman*, 7 May 1995, A19.

In the upper-right diagram the building is pictured intact, at the time the truck McVeigh was driving is parked on the sidewalk in front of the building. The next three diagrams depict the process of the building's structural destruction. There are no dead bodies or living people depicted in any of the architectural drawings, nor are there any photographs of the bombing's victims. In fact, nothing living is depicted in the diagram: no trees or plants, no humans, no animals; only a cement, steel, and glass office building with a truck parked alongside its basement. Even the truck disappears as the bomb is depicted in the process of exploding, replaced in the second diagram by a gray cloud of smoke and debris. The building's windows are shown shattering and flying outward into the street. Inside the building, all that appears in the simple architectural drawing are the floors and the vertical beams that hold the building's structure in place. While the diagrams offer still portrayals of the building's structural disassembly from the blast of the bomb, the progressive representation of the bomb's effects maps its movement over time. The third and fourth diagrams from the top, show the continuing collapse of the building: the roof caves in, vertical support beams break and buckle, while the floors disintegrate and collapse. Increasingly large piles of rubble are shown in the area where the truck was located just prior to the ignition of the bomb. The building's physical destruction stands in for the traumatized body.

These diagrams construct for readers a forensic model of the bomb's physical damage to the building itself, yet they offer no evidence or portraiture of the human deaths it caused. The evidence of the bombing's human victims instead lies in the list of names of the dead, missing, and injured. There are no bodies to be memorialized in this section of the paper, only "a chronology of names" that "represents bodies destroyed and inscribed . . . with the identity" of the dead. Names and building diagrams, as Marita Sturken has described in reference to the Vietnam Veterans' Memorial in Arlington, "act as surrogates for the bodies" (Sturken 1997, 72). Unlike the physical monument and memorial grounds that now stand in Oklahoma City at the site of the federal building, the building diagrams and the inscription of names on the newspaper page nonetheless represent the commemoration, "in a collective mode," of the individuality of the dead in a single site. As Daniel Sherman has noted about the plans for the World Trade Center memorial to the victims of the 9/11 terrorist attacks in Manhattan, "As an organized gesture, the very act of naming the dead confers a collective value on names that once, indeed not long ago, lacked any such quality" (2006, 138).

The layout and design of this page in the *Oklahoman* illustrate how the profiles of the dead that precede it function as memorials to their lives. They also illustrate the disembodied ways in which death can be accounted for in relation to major crimes and terrorism committed against U.S. victims cast as national. To speak in terms of death appears to require a distantiation through representations of the magnitude of lives lost — in the list of names and in the diagrams of the building. The *Star-Ledger* followed a similar pattern six years later in the wake of the attacks of 11 September, building a columned list of the 701 victims from New Jersey which gives names, hometowns, and ages ("New Jersey's Terror Victims," 1 January 2002, 30). This compilation signifies both the magnitude of loss and the victims' specific individual identities (identified with the barest of population information). *Newsday* also listed the names of the dead in "9/11/01: The Lost," in their final issue of 2001 on 31 December. In "Places of Grief" on 21 October 2001, *Newsday* located the dead by their place of residence in Metro New York through cartographic representation; rather than list the dead by name at this time, the paper placed them in quantified groups (e.g., 1–5, 6–20, 21–60, and 61–205) that mapped them in the New York City boroughs and the New York, New Jersey, and Connecticut counties of their residence. Like the diagram of the bombed federal building in the *Oklahoman*, the graphic in *Newsday* used an image of twisted metal remains, this one of a World Trade Center tower, a graphic that seemingly rises out of the waters of the Hudson River. On the left side of the map, an image of a broadcasting or cellphone tower appears to rise out of Warren County in New Jersey. The map of the dead is framed on one side by the physical remnants of one of New York City's iconic skyscrapers while on the other the communications tower points to the capacity to communicate beyond New York City. The places of grief appear to be concentrated around clusters of death's magnitude while also residing in the physical, artifactual remnants of the bombing's destroyed architecture. The fact that the communications tower appears undamaged in the image might suggest that grief is located not only in New York, but also, as the article below it states, in a "broad band of death." In spite of the editorial mandates not to speak of death in the life profiles, these diagrams and graphic representations attempt to portray not death but the broad reach of grief's wake across the local population and nation. They are the social constructions of nationalized grief into which the lives of commemorated victims became grieve-able.

The memorial page in the *Oklahoman*, unlike monuments to the dead that celebrate individual sacrifice (as in war) or commemorate defeat, instead "officially recognize[s] the sorrow and validate[s] the grief (of victims' families and friends)" (Sturken 1997, 75). It is not a monument to heroism and heroic sacrifice, but to the murder of innocents who neither chose nor volunteered for service on the front lines of national battle. It names the dead and collects them in one place; it does not do the work of commemorating their lives—the profiles of life printed in the pages before the diagram do that work. Like the Vietnam Veterans' Memorial Sturken describes, one has to look to the letters, familial remembrances, artifacts, and other materials that attempt to reconstruct the lives of the dead in order to understand the commemorative and political work they do. "In the commemorative realm," Sherman notes, "both names and places . . . appropriate the personal on behalf of the political" (2006, 123). Naming, "in the form of the inscription or recitation of the names of those being honored, has over the past two decades become perhaps the most easily identifiable element in American commemoration" (122).

Appearing just over two weeks after the bombing and nine days after the first victim profile ran in its pages, the *Oklahoman's* victim memorial page tells readers to never forget the dead. This command attempts to return subjectivity in death to those whose lives after death came to signify the magnitude and national significance of acts of terrorism, among other forms of criminal violence. The tenuous promise of the memorial practices to "never forget" is especially revealed in the commemoration of the young infants killed in the Oklahoma City bombing. It is in their profiles where the rhetoric of life in victim commemoration is most unequivocally asserted.

The Pro-Life Framework of Children's Profiles

The feature section on the bombing victims, "Those Who Died," in the *Oklahoman* was the first news articulation of the profile of life around a high-profile act of terrorism in the United States to be directly linked with the movement in journalism education toward victim-oriented curricula.

The published profiles describing the lives that the bombing victims led before their deaths enabled the 168 dead to appear as unique individuals and reminded newspaper readers of their material, bodily existence.

I am interested in the rhetoric of life used to describe the children profiled in "Those who Died" in terms of the links that might be drawn to antiabortion politics and their rhetoric of life and the framing of the killing of fetuses through abortion as murder. Both profiles of life and antiabortion discourses are pro-life. Like abortion rhetoric, the profiles of life produce a "discourse obsessed with untimely, unwarranted death." And while "antiabortion discourse is equally obsessed with life to the extent that images such as [Lennart] Nilsson's [biology film on human reproduction called *The Miracle of Life*] offer proof that abortion is murder," the profile of life also codes death through images of the now-dead though once-living subject. That is, they are both discourses of murder—different as they are in their conceptions of what murder is—wrapped up in the meaning of what constitutes biological and familial life. Additionally, antiabortion rhetoric, like that of the profile of life, defines life as "the ability and imperative to procreate" (Stormer 1997, 182), signifying in explicitly biological terms what the profile of life also communicates about the family as a site of social reproduction and value. In the profiles, to have had a life signifies, above all, that one belonged to a (primarily) reproductive family unit.

Profiles of life specifically highlight the reproductive relations of family in the remembrances of killed children. Unlike pro-life discourse in the abortion debates, however, profiles of life draw upon a discourse of life about the already born. The meaning of this life particularly comes to matter after the person has been killed, in ways that are not all that different from how the "lives" of fetuses on antiabortion posters and videos represent life within a broader political discourse of abortion as murder. They are not the same discourses of life but similar ways of talking about life in terms of the life potentials cut short in the deaths of living children and in the abortions of yet-to-be-born babies. "Pro-life," according to the rhetorician Nathan Stormer, refers to an "outlook that deems the creation of human life a value that supersedes cultural and individual considerations and that centralizes life's worth in reproductive structures and practices" (1997, 173).

The particular pro-life portrayal of the dead after the bombing comes through most clearly in the profiles of young children and infants who were killed in the child care center at the federal building. On the first day profiles appeared in the paper, 24 April 1995, reporters created an extended obituary for four-year-old Ashley Megan Eckles and her grandparents Luther and Larue Treanor, who were killed while waiting in the Social Security office in the federal building just moments before their scheduled appointment at 9:15 A.M. Ashley would be profiled again, in shorter form, on 25 April. Unlike an individual profile, the first one of Ashley describes the Treanor family and Luther's plans for starting a cattle farm after twenty-nine years of delivering milk to stores and schools in Oklahoma City. The Social Security check Luther hoped to pick up that day in the office would have been one of the first payment installments for buying the farm after his years of delivery work. The photograph that accompanies the profile, with the headline "That was Dad's Dream, To Retire and Raise Cattle," is a snapshot of Ashley in summer shirt and shorts sitting outside on a warm day on what appears to be a picnic table. While the profile is really about the family, not Ashley or her grandparents specifically, her photograph stands in as visual evidence of the familial loss of the Treanors and the Eckleses from the perspective of her parents (A13).

Ashley's newspaper profile on 25 April 1995 tells a bit more about the girl's life from the perspective of her surviving family. Her aunt Lois describes her as "a happy child who knew no strangers. She had a big heart" (A11). The photograph that accompanies her profile is a cropped version of the full-body one that appeared on 24 April. The paper from 25 April also profiles four other children who were killed in the bombing. The profile of three-year-old Zackary Chavez includes a photograph of the grinning boy, and the text describes his love of quarters. His great-grandfather Cereaco Hernandez is quoted: "He was a cute little guy. You would try to give him a dollar and he would say, 'No no — give me a quarter'" (A11). In a framed inset on the same page, Christopher Cooper is profiled along with his mother, Dana, the director of America's Kids daycare center in the federal building, both of whom were killed in the blast. The father of Christopher and husband of Dana described the boy as "Mr. Personality" (A11). Next to the Coopers' profile, the brothers Colton Wade and Chase Dalton Smith are depicted in a photograph that shows the two boys embracing and mugging for the camera. The text of the profile tells readers that their favorite television show was *Barney* and that, according to their mother, Edye, "They were happy. They were free-spirited. They were sweet" (A11).

Baylee Almon, the infant girl whose limp body was photographed in the arms of an Oklahoma City fireman just after the bombing, is profiled without an accompanying picture and without any additional information from the family, both unusual omissions in the profiles of the children killed that day. The commentary on the news photograph of her dead body in her obituary distinguishes hers from the others, for she was first portrayed, forensically, as a corpse and only later as an infant girl worthy of having her life commemorated. Readers learn that she had celebrated her first birthday just one day before the bombing. Yet Baylee is not so much profiled as pictured in a traditional obituary. In addition to noting when and where she was buried, the obituary states, "Of all the thousands of photos taken at the site, the photo of Baylee captured the horror of the bombing and took it straight to the heart of a sorrowful nation" (A11).

Far more attention is paid to her death and to the site of her burial than in any other child's profile. Less commemoration than an obituary, the profile talks about her death, its image, and its rituals of remembrance. She represents what Berlant (1997) calls the infantile citizen, that contemporary model citizen imagined as the innocent female infant who neither participates nor fully represents the nation, but needs its protection. Baylee's obituary goes one step further to suggest that the nation failed her: she became a victim of an assault on the nation through McVeigh's and Nichols's bombing of the federal building, but in addition she was victimized again by the apparatus of national publicity that made her dead body a symbol of national assault. She is both the quintessential victim of the victims' rights movement — the child murder victim — and the symbol that the movement uses to draw attention to the harmful uses to which representations of victims are put in the name of depicting national loss. In that Baylee had already been used in this way, perhaps the absence of a portrait, the lack of an attempt to replace a photograph in life for a photograph in death, was the family's way of refusing to let Baylee be used anymore as a national symbol of the bombing.

Many of the profiles draw on the formal features of obituaries. They often include a photographic portrait of the dead individual in life and general details about his or her family relations and survivors and basic descriptive characteristics of the kind of person the dead embodied. Most have no byline, although the longer feature versions of the profile of life do. The longest of these was written for an infant girl named Danielle Nicole Bell on 28 April 1995. Danielle's profile details the remembrances of her mother, Deniece, and grandmother Sherita of their fifteen-month-old "blue-eyed, light-brown-haired beauty's" time at daycare in the federal building. The reader learns that her grandmother liked to call her Pooter. Unlike the shorter profiles, which have no bylines, that of Danielle is published under the byline of Bobby Ross Jr., a staff writer, whose profile is headlined "Child's Ready Smile, Affection Remembered." Her young friends Colton and Chase Smith comforted her when she became uncertain about the new people who began running the daycare when it was taken over by new management. But what comes through most devastatingly in Danielle's profile is her mother's anguish at not knowing her daughter was dead for four days. Over that time, as readers learn, Deniece received prank phone calls from people who falsely claimed they had seen her daughter and only later discovered that the police had pulled her daughter from the wreckage just minutes after the explosion. The mother's anger at her daughter's death is directed at the national media for invading her privacy, at the police for failing to inform her in a timely fashion that her daughter was dead, and at federal officials who, she is reported as saying, withheld crucial information—all central claims made by the victims' rights movement about victims' lack of rights to information and participation in the investigation of criminal cases. The profile ends with a statement by the grandmother: "Everybody out there that has a child, be sure to love them and hug them and tell them that you love them because they can be taken away—in a blink of an eye" (*Oklahoman*, 28 April 1995, A20).

On 29 April 1995, a second, shorter profile of Danielle Bell was published, this time without citing her mother's and grandmother's words of anger and grief. Readers learn that the young girl liked the outdoors and birds and that she liked to smile. Her mother refers to her as being "like an angel from God" (A19). Other children's personalities and likes and accomplishments are described by family members: Jaci Rae Coyne loved the "Itsy Bitsy Spider" song (29 April 1995, A19); Dominique London was a two-year-old practical joker (29 April 1995, A19); Tevin Garrett loved to ride his yellow Lion King bike and eat chicken (6 May 1995, A17); eight-month-old Tylor Eaves was just learning how to pull himself upright (7 May 1995, A18); three-month-old Gabreaon DeShawn Lee Bruce was a "loveable baby"; six-month-old Antonio Ansara Cooper Jr. liked to be thrown up in the air; six-and-a-half-month-old Kevin Gottshall II was proud of his six teeth (9 May 1994, A8); three-year-old Peachlen Bradley loved to laugh (May 8, 1995, A9); three-year-old Kayla Titsworth accompanied her mother to do paperwork at the federal building after her father was restationed in Oklahoma City (26 April 1995, A11). In lieu of personal details, the brothers Aaron and Elijah Coverdale, five and two years old, respectively, are pictured in suit jackets smiling for the camera, and the text describes how their father wandered the streets after the bombing "holding photos of his smiling children" (27 April 1995, A15).

The great loss of these children's lives suffered by their families is palpable across each and every profile. In the children's profiles one hears the profound grief of parents who have lost a child to an intentional act of violence. Their unique personalities, their individual likes and dislikes, their accomplishments (like learning to pull oneself upright), their love for their siblings and parents are all recalled. Because they are so young, their profiles are cast in terms that highlight the very potential of their lives cut short and the significance of that potential in national terms. They represent the possibilities of citizenship, interrupted before they had the chance to develop into fully participating citizens.

In her examination of the federal ventriloquism of victims' voices in the passage of crime bills named after them, Jennifer K. Wood suggests that the broader "consequence of this idealized image of the victim as a little, white, middle-class girl is that it facilitates the simplification of crime into a contest between good victims and evil villains" (2005, 10). As young people killed before they had a chance to develop into adulthood, the racially diverse children killed in the Oklahoma City bombing signify the politics of life itself in cases of terrorism in the United States even more than killed adults do. The African American and mixed-race heritage of many of them signifies a different articulation of national victimhood that is explicitly raced as nonwhite, suggesting that they might signify a model of democratic citizenship and its possibilities premised exactly on the implicit politics articulated through children of color.

Profiles of children's lives become especially potent indictments of the terrorist bombing through the discourse of childhood innocence and its articulation to racial hybridity and difference. There is no doubt that these children were innocent; neither they nor anyone who died in the bombing deserved to be killed. If one starts from this premise, that no one deserved to die or should have died, it becomes clearer how the discourse of childhood innocence works both to represent the familial grief over these children's deaths and to morally amplify the desire to punish those who killed them. In identifying the dead one by one, the profiles of life depict the traumas of their loss for the families in terms that help articulate — perhaps inadvertently and sometimes without the knowing participation of families — the need for McVeigh to be subjected to capital punishment. Identifying the dead and speaking to their lives enable the state to punish the perpetrators, if not on their behalf, at least in their names.

Unlike many obituaries, which speak briefly of the cause of death, profiles of life, like those of the killed children above, for the most part tend to avoid talk of death as an explicit editorial strategy in the news production of their life profiles. Editors instructed the reporters that their job was not to write about the deaths of victims but about their lives before death, to keep the representation of death itself — its dead bodies and body parts, overwhelming smells, and bloody scenes — out of victims' memorials. According to Christine Kay of the *New York Times*, who was in charge of the "Portraits of Grief" on 9/11 victims, the profiles "should be about life. . . . they should be snapshots, not obituaries." She directed her reporters to find "the one story people like to remember about their missing loved one, or the single characteristic that most stands out in their memories" (*Portraits 9/11/01*, 683). In a note in the *Oklahoman* for 11 May 1995, the editors take a similar editorial position: "Everyone who died in the Alfred P. Murrah Federal Building was someone. Maybe they were a wife, a husband, a son, a daughter, a co-worker, a friend. They all have a story" (A10).

While profiles of life memorialize dead victims, they also memorialize the family unit. The lives that are memorialized in the profiles discussed here represent not only the individual who was killed, but also the family unit that is now victimized by the loss of their family member, a key tenet of the concept of secondary victimization enunciated by the victims' rights movement. Life matters as an aspect of family relations. The memorial representation of the dead victim is predicated on first seeing the family itself as the victim of the deadly event that killed their individual family member.

Profiles of life specifically memorialize the victimized family unit through a grammar of victims' rights, in which the family and other close intimates represent the main victims in victims' rights. Like other forms of victim agency around which the victims' rights movement organizes (e.g., the right to provide testimony on victim impact in trials), profiles of life give families what Susan Hirsch (2000) calls an "experience of agency" within the representational politics of crime and terrorism news in the face of overwhelming grief. This experience of agency can be seen perhaps most directly in the victim memorials produced by Justice for All at murdervictims.com (see chapter 2) and in the organization Parents of Murdered Children and their online murder wall (see chapter 6). For these organizations, however, victim profiles function as memorial texts that are also used to aid the prosecution of their killers, sometimes for the death penalty. The newspaper profiles of life discussed here make no such claims, at least not explicitly, about the political uses for which victims' obituaries can be mobilized. They nonetheless bear the features of victims' rights' amplification of secondary victims and their claims to represent dead victims. The profile of life is a kinship-based format for making visible the lives of the dead grounded in the familial politics of victims' rights.

In addition to their displays of family-oriented commemorations of victims' lives, the profiles in the *Oklahoman* reveal points of political encounter between two opposing interpretations of the bombing from a victims' rights perspective. The first is contained in the profile of Julie Welch, a young, religious woman killed in the bombing. The reader learns from her profile that Welch was committed to humanitarian missionary work in Latin America and had hoped to devote her life to this calling. She was soon to be married (see fig. 5). Her father, Bud Welch, provided the information for her profile and became an outspoken opponent of the death penalty, on religious and moral grounds, in the wake of his daughter's death. In cities throughout the country he gives speeches against capital punishment; he was outspoken in his opposition to the execution of McVeigh and even visited McVeigh's father in upstate New York. Welch is also a member of the organization Murder Victims' Families for Reconciliation and a founding member of the organization Murder Victims' Families for Human Rights. Welch does not speak about his political activism in his daughter's profile, and no indication of it is included, but Julie's profile nonetheless evidences how her activist father is empowered to speak about his daughter's life after she was killed. Like other parents in these profiles of life, he speaks of his daughter, not for her.

Frankie Ann Merrell, another young woman killed in the bombing, worked as a clerk in the Oklahoma City federal building and was the

Julie Marie Welch

Julie Marie Welch, 23, of Oklahoma City had been working as a Spanish interpreter for the Social Security Administration.

Her goal was to be a Spanish teacher to help improve global understanding.

Welch graduated with a degree in Spanish from Marquette University in Milwaukee, Wis., where she was on the dean's honor list.

She spent a year as a foreign exchange student in Pontevedra, Spain, during high school, and studied for one year at the Marquette en Madrid during college.

Born Sept. 12, 1971, in Oklahoma City, she attended Windsor Hills Elementary and Wiley Post Elementary, Hefner Junior High and graduated from Bishop McGuinness High School.

Welch was planning to marry an Air Force lieutenant.

5. Julie Welch's profile.

mother of a five-year-old girl, Morgan, who now lives under the care of her grandmother Marcia Kight (see fig. 6). Kight became a victims' rights activist after her daughter was killed, forming a bombing survivors' group in Oklahoma City called Families and Survivors United. Later she worked in the offices of the National Organization for Victim Assistance in Washington, D.C. Kight is pro–death penalty and actively campaigned for family members' rights to attend McVeigh's trial in Denver. She was also instrumental in the fight to overturn a court judge's ruling stipulating that family members of the bombing dead could either be present at McVeigh's trial or provide victim impact testimony, but not both. An act of Congress, the Victims' Rights Clarification Act, passed less than two weeks before McVeigh went on trial in 1997, overturned the judge's ruling. While the law applies to all victims of federal crimes, it was passed specifically to enable family members of the victims of the bombing to attend and speak at the trial in 1997. Arguments made in favor of the act accentuated the potential therapeutic benefits for victims whose grief and suffering might be eliminated

Frankie Ann Merrell

Frankie Ann Merrell, 23, was a loving mother to her only child, a person who loved life and always gave of herself.

If any of her friends or their families needed help, Merrell was there.

"She would go out of her way to help them," a friend said.

She was described as of the most caring individuals a person would ever meet and an outstanding mother of her 2 ½ -year-old daughter, Morgan Taylor Merrell.

Merrell, 23, was a teller at the Federal Employees Credit Union for three years.

Born Oct. 25, 1971, in Fort Smith, Ark., she graduated from Putnam City High School. Her husband, Charles Wayne Merrell, said she was a devoted wife, and was pulling her life back together after the death of her father a year ago.

An educational trust fund has been set up for her daughter. Memorials may be sent to the Morgan Taylor Merrell Trust Fund, Bancfirst, Attention: Bud Ham, P.O. Box 26788, Oklahoma City 73126-0788.

6. Frankie Ann Merrell's profile.

by being present at McVeigh's and Nichol's trials and by testifying about the impact of the bombing on their lives (Wood 2003, 296). In this way, victims' rights claims combine therapeutics with prosecution in a "taken-for-granted normative expectation that attending the trial will be healing for . . . victims of crime" and not potentially harmful, a point on which other victims, including Bud Welch, have testified. Victims' rights claims shift the emphasis in the courtroom "from defendants' innocence or guilt to providing therapy for the victim" (Wood 2003, 308), but capital punishment and participation in it by victims' families do not necessarily constitute the most therapeutic response, as relatives like Welch have argued.

The profiles of these two victims in the *Oklahoman*, both reveal and conceal, through an activist father and mother who are identified with victims' rights, the links between the desire to publicly commemorate victims and the political struggle over the meaning of their memorialization within a shared victims' rights framework. The two texts share in the familial commemoration of the dead, the foundation of victims' rights claims making and representation. Yet the specific claims of victims' rights advocacy are concealed in them, as are these parents' opposing ethical investments in victims' rights as a political ideology. The profile of life constitutes a unique, victims' rights–inspired, U.S. news representation of the victims of terrorism and major crime. The language and the photographic portrayals of victims before their death in profiles of life symbolically reference the movement-based argument that victims and their families deserve and require social recognition both for their grief and loss and as rights-bearing citizens (Ochberg 1996). No direct political claims are made through these news commemorations of dead victims. In some cases, for example, in the case of the feature "Portraits of Grief" in the *New York Times*, families used the newspaper profiles of their dead family members as part of the documentation of their loss in their applications for federal victims' compensation (Miller 2003, 129).

The Democracy of Death, Kinship of the Nation

We have to think of the obituary as an act of nation building.
JUDITH BUTLER, *Precarious Life*

Howell Raines, the former executive editor of the *New York Times*, wrote in the foreword to the *Times* book *Portraits 9/11/01,*

> "Portraits of Grief" remind us of the democracy of death. . . . When I read them, I am filled with an awareness of the subtle nobility of everyday existence, or the ordered beauty of quotidian life for millions of Americans, of the unforced dedication with which our fellow citizens go about their duties as parents, life partners, employers or employees, as planters of community gardens, coaches of the young, joyful explorers of this great land and the world beyond its shores. These lives, bundled together so randomly into a union of loving memory by those

terrible cataclysms of September 11, remind us of what Walt Whitman knew: "The United States themselves are essentially the greatest poem." (2002, vii)

On 13 September 2001, the first day *Newsday* ran profiles of 9/11 victims in its commemorative feature "The Lost," B. Donovan opened with a similar description: "When friends and loved ones spoke" of the lost, "they spoke more of personal qualities than of titles or accomplishments." Before the very first profile, Ted English, the president and chief executive officer of TJX Companies Inc., which lost seven company employees in one of the planes that crashed into the World Trade Center, presented the dead as members of a national family, stating, "Our family is forever changed."

The profiles I discuss below appeared first in the *Times* and were then republished in the book *Portraits 9/11/01*. I analyze a number of profiles that in their collected form reiterate similar kinds of life stories about very different people who are linked in death—many worked in the same companies and in the same physical space, but death is what relates them to each other here. The interpretations of the profiles are overdetermined by the caption under each victim's name and beside their photograph. As the captions suggest, the meaning of life in death can be thematized, a point made all the more convincing when different victims' life profiles share the same captions.

One profile, that of Neil Shastri, even references how the commemorative narratives of detailing the lives of the dead often sound like and draw upon clichés, becoming part of the very language of the life profile in ways reminiscent of the talk in journalistic trauma training of the comfort that clichéd statements can provide those who are grieving. Jay Shastri, Neil's twin brother, in describing how Neil immediately befriended people, prefaces this information by saying, "It might sound like cliché right now." I interpret this remark more broadly, not as a limitation of the profile format and its conventions of representation, but as a condition of their articulation. The recognition that victims' life memorials might sound clichéd suggests that everyone's life can be thematized and accounted for in conventionalized form. Perhaps the clichéd, democratizing details of a daily life are also what provide comfort to the families whose remembrances are enshrined in the form. Perhaps they also help organize the details of human life and its remembrance into something manageable.

As one reads through the *Times* book of 2,310 profiles, the description of lives, while filled with specific details and characterizations of individuality, feels weighted by a burden of originality. In my reading of every profile in alphabetical order, by the time I reached the *Bs* it had become clear that the profiles tread rather narrow commemorative scripts into which individuals' lives can be thematized. Some themes repeat across different profiles. Many wives describe their dead husbands as their cheerleaders. Friends and siblings describe dead New Yorkers as having the city or the borough of their residence "in their blood." Lovers describe the first inklings of romance as instances of "love at first sight." Amateur and professional cooks' lives are described as "full of spice." As someone who loves to talk about food and enjoys the pleasures of cooking with others, I found these food-oriented profiles resonant with my own life, as did others: the diabetics whose life profiles talk about their struggles with the disease, and the women whose friends describe their love of cats. These familiar ways of talking about other people's lives and the things they loved suggest that life remembrances are both unique documents of an individual life and accounts of shared tastes and life resemblances others collectively recognize and share in.

That is, lives can be thematized and portrayed in ways some find clichéd, but talk of love and life, taste and pleasure, struggles and successes mark many lives in similar ways. These similarities, these "tiny but telling details," are the things that mark out lives as shared forms of social existence (J. Scott 2002, ix; Miller 2003). Profiles of life are representations of personal and familial life individualized and packaged in like form, in the familial descriptions of their lost members that can be socially recognized precisely in terms of their likeness to others' lives.

Convention provides the format for profiling the unique qualities of a life and also for the ways in which those qualities are necessarily socially structured. For example, in their depiction of gender codes, many of the profiles speak to conventional notions of gender roles, while others broaden the portrayal of gendered lives. Several men's profiles home in on their performances of manliness. The profile of Stephen Adams captions his life as that of "an 18th century man." His wife, Jessica Murrow, describes him as a man whose values and tastes were of another, more noble time. In addition to his enjoyment of Irish dance rituals and drumming, Stephen had just acquired a job as beverage manager at the Windows on the World restaurant on the top floor of the World Trade Center and was working on his craft as a sommelier. While his profile is presented through the framework of manliness, the description of the details of his activities modifies the category of manhood to include highly stylized Irish dance rituals. Another victim profile, that of Andrew Brunn, a tall, heavy-set man, describes him as "the man in flannel" for his informal way of dressing. Sigalit Cohen, Andrew's wife, who admits in her husband's profile to "having a thing for men in flannel," remembers seeing Andrew dancing wildly at a Queens, New York, bar and asking him for his phone number. The profile makes only brief mention of his job in the New York Fire Department, instead highlighting the particular qualities of his awkwardly expressive and simultaneously private sense of his manhood. Manliness in these profiles is a diversified category, one that recognizes different kinds of masculinity and masculine performance. The lives of Brunn and Adams, however, are nonetheless linked through the ways in which they could be thematized around their performance of manhood.

Several other profiles invoke codes of manhood in order to describe the dead as unusual kinds of men, like that of Michael Cahill, who is described, as is John P. Williamson, as a Renaissance man. Williamson was a golf fanatic who built his family home and its furniture and served as battalion captain in the New York Fire Department; Cahill was an accomplished long-distance runner, a dedicated community volunteer, and a senior vice president and claims attorney for Marsh & McClennan, a firm located on the ninety-ninth floor of Tower 1 of the World Trade Center. Their wives remember them as both community men and family men. Although both are described as Renaissance men, their lives differed considerably (*Newsday* also used this characterization to thematize the life of at least one other man, Richard Y. C. Lee, in an article of 8 October 2001 entitled "Renaissance Man Never Forgot About People"). Their likeness as Renaissance men stems from the enjoyment that their wives recognized in their husbands' active and varied lives.

Two women, Janice Ashley and Maile Rachel Hale, are depicted as Renaissance women by their mothers, friends, and college roommates. Hale's mother details her love of dance and chocolate and her ability to overcome her intense shyness in order to hold the position of vice president at Boston Investor Services, while her roommate remembered her skill at throwing parties all by herself. Ashley's friends recount her commitment to having new experiences, like eating ostrich burgers rather than chicken when she ventured out to eat, and say she was a woman "as comfortable on Rollerblades as ordering a meal at a fancy restaurant." Unlike the behavior that signals Renaissance men, however, that of a Renaissance woman appears to be her ability to venture out in the world on her own, to not form a traditional family. Neither Hale's nor Ashley's marital status is mentioned, presumably because neither was married.

The gendered portrayals in "Portraits of Grief" are one of the many ways in which the family unit and other intimate relations of kinship and friendship are imagined in these press snapshots of extinguished lives, but in ways that constitute differently gendered kinship relations. The act of commemoration became part of some survivors' talk about the meaning of kinship within the context of the attacks and the U.S. military response. The members of the organization September 11 Families for Peaceful Tomorrows described the vision of family and community they saw in the wake of the attacks: "We came to realize that human beings pass their days in endless combinations. . . . It was a day that demolished the belief that we could ever be truly independent of each other" (2003, 8).

While "Portraits of Grief" sought to portray the democracy of death through individuated profiles of the 2,310 dead, they still largely relied on a sense that this collective archive profiled the lives of national victims imagined in primarily familial terms, a point that comes through perhaps most powerfully in the profile of Sue Kim Hanson, her husband Peter Burton Hanson, and their young infant, who died on United Airlines Flight 175 from Boston to Los Angeles, where they were headed to visit Sue's family. The caption reads "going yuppie for love," referring to the fact that Peter had cut off his dreadlocks and put away his tie-dyed T-shirts to become a businessman when he married Sue. This mixed-race family is described in terms that highlight the barriers between their families' expectations of their daughter's and son's marriage, the difficult upbringing Sue experienced living with her grandmother in Korea, and the death of her mother when Sue was sixteen.

Despite the preponderance of heterosexual unions and family forms presented in the profiles, differences in family make-up matter greatly in them. The lives of lesbian couples are commemorated in profiles like the one for Pamela J. Boyce, whose partner, Catherine Anello, describes her blunt demeanor, her love of disco dancing, and her pride in serving as the

Lamaze coach for her sister Desiree. In this profile, the fact of their lesbian union is simply a given. In another family profile, Daniel Brandhorst and Ronald Gamboa are commemorated along with their adopted son, David Gamboa-Brandhorst. They were on the same flight to Los Angeles as the Hanson family, returning home from Boston. According to his brother, Daniel, an accountant for Pricewaterhouse Coopers, led two lives, his work life and his family life, suggesting that in some ways Daniel may have lived a closeted life among most of his work colleagues. One colleague quoted in the profile, however, suggests that at least some of his colleagues knew of his and Ron's adoption of David. Another colleague, Scott Pisani, a senior consultant at the firm, describes how Daniel focused more of his intense workplace energy on Ronald and David after the adoption. The profile ends by revealing that Ronald and Daniel had intended to adopt another child.

While some profiles highlight the lesbian and gay familial lives of some of the dead, the focus on family (or, if the profiled victims were not married or in committed relationships, the characterization of them, for instance, as Renaissance women unburdened by the conventional gender roles of more traditional family arrangements) makes their victimization matter in familial terms. The familial definition of their loss ties them together into a national family of victims, victims who have lived, however, in differently gendered, sexed, raced, and classed ways. Some were removed from their families through immigration and cast into narratives of often unrewarded and unfinished citizenship renewal. Others receive recognition via the intimate unions they created, tying their constructions of family to the nation in homonationalist memoriam. Written from the perspective of his Nigerian friend, who was also working in the United States to build a better life, the profile of the former Nigerian lawyer Godwin Ajala describes his struggles working early shifts as a security guard and studying nights for the New York bar exam. Living without his wife and children in New York City, Ajala, in the words of his friend, had a lonely, difficult, and frustrating life. Once he had passed the bar, Ajala planned to bring his wife and three children to the United States. His profile is captioned, without irony or sense of melancholy, "An American family dream."

Other profiles detail ways of life, shared tastes, and practices of the everyday that link the lives of the dead, for example, the women who loved cats and cared for them in their homes, like the former Montréaler Chantal Vincelli, whose friends had to find homes for the seventeen cats she kept in her Harlem apartment (see also Jennifer Smith, "A Loving Woman, A Savior of Cats," *Newsday*, 4 November 2001, A38). Several profiles recount the struggles many of the dead had with chronic illnesses, diabetes in the cases of Michael Collins and Michael Lowe. Lowe was an African American man who had recently been diagnosed as a diabetic; his wife describes how he left his crummy job and the bad apartments they had been living in to find a better place in which to raise their kids and build healthier lives. Lowe's profile, like those of so many of the African Americans and African immigrants included in "Portraits of Grief," tells a moving tale of race and class struggle in the United States.

In these ways, the profiles make visible the different life circumstances of the people killed in the attacks of 11 September. Ajala, for instance, is photographed in a robe and wig from his days as a lawyer in Nigeria. Set against his tale of exile and education in the United States, the stoic image of him dressed in his professional attire points to the great distance he traveled from his life in Nigeria to his struggles as an immigrant worker in New York City. Photographs and life profiles like Ajala's are presented in language, as Butler says, "that communicates the precariousness of life" and its circumstances; a precariousness that, as she further suggests, "establishes the ongoing tension of a non-violent ethics" (2004, 139). In her reflection on the political state of the United States in the wake of the attacks of 11 September, Butler considers the relationship between representation and humanization, "a relation that is not as straightforward as one might think" (140). She writes, "If critical thinking has something to say about the present situation, it may well be in the domain of representation where humanization and dehumanization occur ceaselessly" (140).

The collected profiles of life and the photographs of many of the profiled faces express the precariousness of life against other media portraits, like those of Osama bin Laden's and Saddam Hussein's faces, whose portraits signify danger and terror in the U.S. press, or, as Butler suggests, the U.S. press photos of young Afghan girls removing their *burkas* (an all-enveloping outer garment) as a sign of female liberation (142). Burkas deface the face, "a representational and philosophical consequence of war" (143).

How do the "Portraits of Grief" give face to the bereavement and loss of life experienced by the family members and communities of the people killed in the attacks of 11 September? Do these faces also shroud the forces of war making and militarism that were mobilized in the wake of the at-tacks? Butler warns, "Something altogether different happens . . . when the face operates in the service of personification that claims to 'capture' the human being in question" (144–45), as Raines implies the "Portraits of Grief" do in the quotation cited above. The task of the portraits is not to increase understanding of the attacks, to offer a reason why they happened; rather, they seek to represent a vision of national lives lost, giving meaning to the very question of what constitutes the lives of so many whose deaths occurred at roughly the same time in the same act of terrorism committed against the United States. As Luc Boltanski writes, "The sufferings made manifest and touching through the accumulation of details must also be able to merge into a unified representation," that of national victims (1999, 12). How might these portraits represent the dead "in ways that effect their capture by the war effort," a matter of "effacement through representation itself"? (Butler, 147). And what elements of the profiles are not fully cap-tured by the call to war?

The profiles of life are compelling, affective documents. In the months that "Portraits of Grief" was published, New Yorkers were described in the city's newspapers as being moved to tears when they read them. The mean-ing of the profiles, the narrow constraints in which they could be portrayed, and their abilities to give face to the once living also portrays their power as collectivized, localized, and national documents of loss.

six

Faces of Murder

In his book *The Victims*, the right-wing anticrime advocate Frank Carrington put the politics of the death penalty into stark relief alongside that of victims' rights: "Anyone who has ever seen, in the flesh or in photographs, the body of a murder victim knows that the victim's loss of human dignity is complete and final. To engage in judicial hand-wringing about the human dignity of murderers is to mock the meaning of the lives of their victims" (1975, 186). Twenty-five years later, the stakes of activism by murder victims' families around the death penalty were still being defined in similar terms: the memories of murder victims hinged, in part, on the call to execute their killers.

Carrington was one of the more outspoken victims' rights advocates in the United States, and he saw the death penalty as a direct extension of victims' rights activism. Many victims' rights organizations today carry on this political tradition in groups such as Justice for All, the pro–death penalty victims' rights organization founded by Ellen Levin, the mother of a murder victim, and Parents of Murdered Children (POMC), a nonprofit support organization for the parents of murder victims. While POMC is not pro- or anti–death penalty in its mission, many of its campaigns support the death penalty in the name of murder victims' families.

This chapter examines one particular encounter between POMC and a high-profile, though short-lived, anti–death penalty campaign launched by the Italian clothing label Benetton in February 2000. The campaign centered on a portrait-based magazine entitled "We, On Death Row," an anti–death penalty publication presented in the style of an exposé. This encounter occurred primarily through the medium of portraiture and the political discourse of life, but, unlike the profiles of life discussed in chapter 5, the portraits of murder victims that POMC used to counter Benetton's portraits in "We, On Death Row" did not seek to profile the lives of those who have been murdered. Instead, in their commemorative contexts, they profile the particular circumstances of murder, emphasizing the contexts in which their sons and daughters were killed. In this sense, they might be more accurately called portraits of murder. Benetton's portraits of death row inmates, on the other hand, constituted a form of profile of life in which inmates describe their lives in text printed alongside pictures of their faces.

The portrait-based encounter between Benetton and POMC is both commemorative and political. The forms of portraiture I examine here are not commemorative in the ways profiles of life are; they have a much more fundamental task, which is to portray the humanity of death row inmates and murder victims, respectively. In Benetton's and POMC's memorial portraits, the profile of life takes expressly political form. Benetton's is also expressly commodified as a branded campaign. Benetton's impetus to profile death row inmates in the United States was driven both by marketing and a statement against the death penalty on moral and religious grounds. It sought to recognize the humanity of death row inmates, the worthiness of their lives, and in turn branded the anti–death penalty claims made on their behalf. POMC's murder victim memorial practices have been part of their organization's work since its founding, providing a space for parents to talk together about their sons and daughters who have been murdered. Their memorial work has taken material form in memorial plaques and in an

online "murder wall" where families can post individual memorials commemorating murder victims. While the profile of life news genre developed
from community newspapers' attempts to carve out a space of memoriam
for local victims of major acts of mass violence against the overwhelming tide of twenty-four-hour news channel pressure and was then codified
by editors and journalism educators, the profiles produced by POMC and
Benetton scale the commemorative form of memorial portraiture to the
politics of murder: to the interpersonal violence of murderer against victim for POMC, and to the state's capacity to kill those sentenced to capital
punishment for Benetton.

Returning here to those durable links between law-and-order perspectives on crime and criminal justice and victims' rights activism discussed
in chapter 1, I reinterpret them through the politicized portraits of murder
victims and inmates' lives. As Carrington suggests above, there has long
been a political intimacy between advocates of capital punishment and
advocates of victims' rights. This chapter further exposes and troubles this
intimacy by homing in on the ways the portraiture practices of POMC and
Benetton each claim for their subjects a need to have their humanity restored. POMC took this one step further, arguing that death row inmates
do not deserve any representation, for to represent inmates is to grant
them a form of human recognition that comes, in their perspective, at the
cost of murder victims' own humanity. In their politics of murder, victims
and murderers cannot both be seen as subjects worthy of representation.
The encounter between Benetton's anti–death penalty campaign "We, On
Death Row" and POMC illustrates the often unspoken refusal among some
victims' rights advocates to recognize the humanity of those who do violence, and the insistence that they remain unrepresented in public discourse.

To this end, in 2000 POMC launched a quiet, behind-the-scenes, city-
based counterpublicity campaign against "We, On Death Row." "We, On
Death Row" symbolically linked the brand image of Benetton to vivid depictions of inmates who were awaiting what anti–death penalty advocates
call their state killing (see, e.g., Sarat 1996). Through photographs and
interviews with inmates, "We, On Death Row" attempted to give human
voice and face to the largely invisible social realities of the men and women
on death row, intervening in a media environment relatively devoid of real-
life representations of prison, inmates, and the human experience of death

row. While television is populated with crime news and fiction, the representation of crime, as Elayne Rapping has said, "stops short of the prison gates" (2003, 73). Against the relative cultural invisibility of prison life from the perspective of its inmates, "We, On Death Row" sought to make visible the experience of prisoners' lives, though not their crimes, through portraiture. Part of this process of humanization involved printing interviews of the inmates in which they talked about their relationships with their families and the experience of living on death row. A large part of the humanizing aspect also rested on the large color photographs of the faces of several men and one woman convicted of murder and living on death row in states such as Kentucky, North Carolina, and Missouri.

POMC interpreted Benetton's campaign and its photographic display of convicted murderers as a direct affront to families' memories of the victims of the inmates. One couple in Kentucky reportedly saw a Benetton billboard of the man convicted of torturing and killing their teenage son while they were out driving on the highway. In response, local chapters of POMC sought to create their own billboard victim memorial campaign that would draw on the slogan "Behind Every Murderer Lies an Innocent Victim" and use large photographic portraits of murder victims to counter Benetton's depiction of death row inmates. The organization had little money to buy billboard space, however, and the campaign never got off the ground.[1] This did not stop POMC from organizing a successful campaign against Benetton that had major financial and legal repercussions for the company. Despite the financial constraints that prevented POMC from launching its countercampaign of billboard portraits, the organization could draw on its long-standing practice of using murder victims' portraiture to memorialize their lives in other media while making the case against inmates' representation through letter writing and news coverage.

My interest lies in the physiognomy of murder that crystallized around the Benetton campaign and POMC's portrait-based memorials to murder victims. The space of portrait-based encounter between the two campaigns offers up the ethical and political possibility of the face-to-face encounter in both victims' rights and abolitionist efforts around the death penalty. Their conditions of representation rest on the different needs murder victims' families and anti–death penalty advocates have for picturing victims and killers in portraiture. The two campaigns also draw upon different aesthetics of portraiture: Benetton's draws upon the redemptive imagery of other death row portraiture, while POMC's rests upon the familial conventions of snapshots and the institutional production of formal school photographs. Both, however, draw upon the physiognomic ideal that the primary grounds for human identity and ethico-political subjectivity rest in the depiction and recognition of the face as the primary site of individuals' humanness. In this sense, the face becomes the exterior surface where "the soul finds its clearest expression" (Simmel 1959/2004, 5).

Yet, despite physiognomy's promise that the study of the face, its features and expressions, can reveal the truth of a person's inner character, faciality is also "a very special mechanism" by which the face can conceal as much as it reveals of the nature of humanness (Taussig 1998, 231). Michael Taussig refers to this as the "co-existence of the face as mask and the face as window to the soul" (231). Pictures of faces work on a double logic of both visibility and invisibility. In their physiognomies of murder, "the close-up on the face screens the visibility and invisibility of death" (Gibson 2001, 318); that is, the visibility of murder victims' deaths and the invisibility of life on death row. The face in POMC's and Benetton's campaigns is both a screen through which to interpret signs of human subjectivity and character inscribed on the skeleton and skin of the face, and a mask that also costumes the faces of advocates and families.

For the families of murder victims, the faces of murder victims become a mask they wear to mobilize their claims against death row inmates and their representation. In the Benetton campaign, the faces of death row inmates become screens upon which corporate branding blends with Catholic anti–death penalty argumentation. Neither campaign portrays the faces of murder victims and inmates free of the political claims making through which they are mobilized. At the same time, they bring into visibility the former lives of the murdered, and the lives-in-waiting of those living on death row.

Crucial differences exist between the two campaigns. Benetton's campaign was a highly capitalized but ideologically abolitionist one, achieving visibility for its claims less through its advertising initiatives than through news coverage of the controversy that developed around "We, On Death Row" in February 2000. The campaign could easily travel into news spots partly because it did not look or act like advertising. One journalist called it "a contrived fusion of advertising and journalism" (O'Leary 2000), but it was precisely this fusion that enabled the campaign to receive more coverage in the news than in advertising spaces. POMC is an underfunded, volunteer-run support group organization for murder victims' families. Because their activism is fueled by the grief of familial loss manifested in law-and-order ideologies, POMC's organizing is more in line with reformist victims' rights perspectives on crime and punishment, while Benetton challenges capital punishment as an inhumane practice. Unlike Benetton, however, POMC lacks the resources to launch capital-intensive campaigns. Its organizational infrastructure depends upon the free labor of activist mothers (and, to a lesser extent, fathers) whose advocacy work is based in their homes around their experiences of losing a son or daughter to murder. Theirs is a form of maternal "kitchen table politics" conducted in the domestic spaces of grief and daily life and in the cramped office of its national headquarters in Cincinnati (see, e.g., Eliasoph 1998; Kintz 1997). Unfortunately, because POMC's record-keeping is done by chapter leaders who work out of the cramped spaces of their homes, most of the documentation for their planned billboard campaign in 2000 had been disposed of to create space for newer campaign materials by the time I contacted them.[2]

In light of their disparate ideological investments and unequal access to financial and organizational capital, the Benetton campaign and POMC's countercampaign lay bare the ways in which victims' rights activism that is oriented toward law and order constitutes a politics of representation that seeks to deny representation to inmates. In their politics of representation, the very definitions of what it means to be human and have the right to speak as citizens are at stake. POMC suggests not only that murder is the work of dangerous, predatory, and dehumanized (primarily male) killers, but also that imprisoned men and women forfeit their social rights to representation in the public sphere. Those who are empowered to speak through the politics of murder, according to the organization, are the families, the covictims, who, within the victims' rights imaginary, constitute the victim of violent crime.

While families themselves are not given face in these campaigns, it is through their ability to stand in as activist proxies for the murdered that the primary murder victim is given face at all. Death row inmates are given face in the campaign, not through their family members, but through the work of abolitionist activists, the photographer Oliviero Toscani, and the Benetton marketing team. POMC's campaign suggests that the humanity and political subjectivity of individual murder victims are built on their membership in a loving family, while the purported inhumanity of death row inmates relies on maintaining the invisibility of all parts of their lives, including their location within family units. While Benetton's campaign did not visually represent the families of death row inmates, nearly every inmate talked about his or her family in the interviews contained within the print magazine version of "We, On Death Row." And while the inmates spoke of their families, their families did not (and could not) speak for them. In several cases, the men on death row spoke of how they had been abandoned by their families. Their interviews articulate how belonging to and having the support of one's family would constitute a basic sense of social being they do not have.

Profiling Life on Death Row: The Material
Artifacts of Benetton's Campaign

At the dawn of the new millennium, Benetton reveals the real faces of the
prisoners on death row: the present of those without a future.
Benetton press release, 7 January 2000

When we see the offender as "other," it becomes far easier to sentence
that offender to death.
SUSAN SHARP, *Hidden Victims*

According to a press release issued in 2000, Benetton's "We, On Death Row" campaign aimed at "giving back a human face to prisoners on death row, to remind those *'respectable people (who) are always so sure they're right'* that the debate concerns men and women in flesh and blood, not virtual characters eliminated or spared with a simple click as with a videogame" (Benetton 2000).[3] Benetton framed its campaign about the death penalty in terms of the humanity of death row inmates. In order to do so, debate about the death penalty would have to challenge the desire "among respectable people" to punish those who are deemed to be a danger to the social order and to make the carrying out of capital punishment itself invisible (see Connolly 1995; Sarat 1996).

"We, On Death Row" is an artifact of anti–death penalty strategic print culture and corporate branding.[4] In its pages there are no photographic layouts of the company's recent spring and summer clothing collection, no page numbers, and no description of Benetton's product lines or brand identity, even though its brand logo appears throughout. Building on over ten years of shock advertising associated with its brand, Benetton's death row campaign coupled arresting photographs of inmates with bright red and white logos alongside essays by anti–death penalty advocates and scholars. "We, On Death Row" bore the look of a professional marketing text targeted at a cause more than of an advertising campaign, one that combined the message "buy Benetton" with "abolish the death penalty."

As a corporate clothing label that has tended to market itself around causes often without making any direct political claims, Benetton has shown a lack of sustained commitment to any particular causes. This fact distinguishes it from most cause-related marketing campaigns, which, out of concern for corporate image and the bottom line, tend to establish long-term relationships with relatively normative and family-friendly cause-related activism (see S. King 2006 on breast cancer culture and the politics of philanthropy). Benetton's marketing instead tends to emphasize shock value and the starkness of imagery rather than understanding, a feature Susan Sontag notes of the use of atrocity photographs in newspapers (2003, 89). As a Benetton spokesperson put it during protests against the campaign, "We appreciate any protesters, anybody's opinions or demonstrations. That's a legitimate form of communication. The idea of this campaign was to promote discussion and communication and that's what's happening" (Mark Major quoted in Chen, 16 February 2000). In other words, it was the publicity buzz around the campaign, not the building of a robust, lasting debate on the death penalty and the politics of its representation, that spoke to its success. Furthermore, despite the abolitionist claims made in "We, On Death Row," Benetton used the bodies, faces, and voices of men and women on death row to extend its brand, United Colors of Benetton, and its iconic color-block logo.

The campaign nonetheless deserves some critical attention for the ways in which it made visible the faces, bodies, and admittedly ventriloquized voices of death row residents and for the mere fact of their visibility in a media environment nearly devoid of representations of people living in prison and condemned to death. There is also something striking in the aesthetics of their representation, a way in which the photographs humanize the lives of death row inmates while giving face to their identities as

7. "We, On Death Row" cover image.

convicted killers. As Barbara Ehrenreich has commented, "No amount of cynicism about corporate motives can protect [you] from" the ethical pull of Benetton's photos (2000). Despite the textual constraints that kept the inmates from talking about their crimes and their cases, the portraits gave fleshly form to the often-abstracted debates about innocence, guilt, and responsibility that define whose rights as a human being are protected in the politics of criminal justice—victims and their families—and whose humanity is often denied—that of death row inmates.

As a form of portraiture practice, the Benetton campaign drew on both idealized and realistic modes for depicting the likeness of its subjects. While the figures are not beautiful in and of themselves, the practices of photographic depiction are nonetheless beatific, a feature Karen Beckman (2004) notes is particular to much death row photography. Perhaps most significant, they represent a basic set of conditions through which others can recognize the imprisoned as human beings, even if they are guilty of great violence. They make the otherwise absent figures of those who live behind bars present to the public.

To conduct its campaign, the clothing company hired Oliviero Toscani, the Milanese photographer who photographed several of the company's United Colors campaigns. Toscani's other work for Benetton had used visually shocking photographs of a burning car in an empty street, a sinking ship, a young man dying of AIDS photographed moments before his death, a black woman nursing a white baby, a black stallion mounting a white mare, and the image of a newborn baby with its umbilical cord still attached—all of which appeared in Benetton advertisements. The company's ad campaigns present highly contentious images of social difference and power along the lines of agitprop, presenting provocative images of racial discord and disaster with little or no political background or thematic information on what is being illustrated.

The "We, On Death Row" campaign was equally provocative but grounded in explicit anti–death penalty argumentation. In order to gain access to prisoners, Toscani posed as an Italian reporter in Missouri. In a letter to Missouri state officials, he wrote that Benetton underwrote his journalistic project for the National Association of Criminal Defense Lawyers. After the publication of "We, On Death Row" and its distribution in *Talk* magazine on 9 February 2000, the attorney general of Missouri sued Toscani and the freelance writer Ken Shulman, who had posed as a reporter for *Newsweek*, for trespass and fraudulent representation upon learning that they had falsely represented themselves to gain access to the prison.[5] According to one report, Thomas "Speedy" Rice, a law professor at Gonzaga University, sent letters to several prisons requesting access for Shulman and Toscani starting in 1999 (C. Davis 2001).[6] Rice's letter was reported to have stated that "no profits are generated" from the project, though he did note in the letter that Benetton was their sponsor. In a press release of June 2001 Benetton and the state of Missouri reported the settlement of the suit: Benetton was required to apologize to the families of the inmates' victims and pay fifty thousand dollars to the Missouri Crime Victim Compensation Fund.[7]

The Benetton campaign turned the stories of death row inmates into a related crime commodity while circumventing any discussion of the crimes they committed. The company avoided so-called Son of Sam legal prohibitions that prevent convicted killers from profiting from their crimes through publication contracts and media appearances by not directly commoditizing the crimes; instead, they commoditized their brand through representation of the inmates' discussion of their prison experiences. In their interviews with inmates, Benetton explicitly scripted the interactions to avoid discussion of their possible remorse or any details of their crimes (Chen, 10 January 2000). The crimes they had committed remained an unstated backdrop against the larger discussion of the daily experience of death row and the inmates' recollections of life outside of the prison. The only indication of the crimes for which they were convicted appears in a brief description of each inmate that accompanies the large head shot photographs of them, a description that identifies the crime for which they have been sentenced and the length of their prison term. The campaign's content attempted to humanize the lives of the inmates by describing the smells, sights, sounds, foods, activities, and routines of inmate life and the prisoners' musings on life, mass media, and the violence of popular culture.

In "We, On Death Row" readers and viewers see and read about the men and women of death row whose very life and death are made difficult to represent because of state restrictions on public access to prisons. Despite the textual censures prisoners face, the inmates' portraits and interviews situate them as people whose hard lives before and after their convictions for murder are worthy of reflection and social recognition. As Ehrenreich has commented, "Stare long enough [at the faces in "We, On Death Row"] and you see that each of them is saying: Look, violence is not a singular event, it is always a chain. It begins, in these cases, with a childhood of neglect and abuse; moves on to legally recognized crimes; then feeds itself further on the cruelty of imprisonment and capital punishment" (2000). As Ehrenreich suggests, the Benetton campaign grants death row inmates their humanity by drawing out the commonalities of life experiences that the inmates share — the difficult and often abusive childhoods, the poverty, and the decisions they made that brought them to death row. As such, the portraits function as a kind of composite image of death row from the perspective of those who live and die there, a shared set of experiences linking the lives of those convicted of capital murder. Profiled in a series of portraits, the differences and variances in their lives signify perhaps not their unique individuality so much as the variety of features that define the lives of men and women on death row as a class.

A similar process is at work in a statistical composite portrait of death row inmates in California that produced a life narrative of the typical lifer. The authors of this article from 1969, Robert Carter and A. Lamont Smith, craft a life narrative of a fictional prisoner they call Johnny Cain. According to them, the portrait enables a more humanizing perspective from which to examine their comprehensive review of the state's record on its death row inmates. His life narrative is "fact in that he represents the statistical average; fiction in that there is no Johnny Cain" (1969, 62). Over six pages they narrate the life of this statistical figure: his birth to poor white tenant farmers, his father's alcoholism and physical abuse, his removal from school at the age of eleven when his family left to seek work elsewhere during the Depression and his permanent removal when he was fourteen, his homelessness, his abandonment by his father, his leaving home to ride the rails, his sexual hustling of older men to survive, and his inability to find gainful employment after marrying a young woman who then became pregnant. After describing the arrest and imprisonment of Johnny Cain for several robberies, the composite portrait offers a picture of institutional negligence in which Johnny is assigned to an overworked case officer who has more serious cases to address than his. Shut out of good employment and estranged from his wife and children, Cain turns in desperation to armed robbery, in which he ends up killing a gas station attendant. After a four-hour court appearance, he is convicted of murder and sentenced to death. At the end of the composite narrative, Johnny is put to death by cyanide gas, alone, without personal estate, and with "no relatives, no friends, to share it" (76).

Carter's and Smith's composite, like "We, On Death Row," has the look and feel of a documentary exposé. Both are grounded in lay and professional expert opinion. While Carter and Smith draw on the writing conventions of narrative sociology, "We, On Death Row" uses the investigative writing style of the crusading journalist. For their composite, Carter and Smith begin with a statistical review and summary of the demographics of inmates on death row, followed by the composite narrative of one possible death row inmate's life circumstances.[8] The introduction to "We, On Death Row" includes the voices of moral and legal experts on the death penalty, including the Dalai Lama and Pope John Paul II, an article by Professor Speedy Rice of Gonzaga University School of Law and William Moffitt, president of the National Association of Criminal Defense Lawyers, and an article by the freelance journalist Ken Shulman, who often writes for *Newsweek*. Each quotation and essay in "We, On Death Row" presents a case against the death penalty through the well-worn rhetoric of anti-death penalty activism. It also references the visibility of the Dalai Lama and the Pope in recent news coverage on the death penalty, creating an intertextual dialogue between "We, On Death Row" and more authoritative media coverage of anti–death penalty positions, helping to ensure that the campaign could easily be picked up by news media outlets for additional coverage on the issue and additional media visibility for Benetton.[9]

Pope John Paul II is quoted as describing the death penalty as cruel and unnecessary, while Rice and Moffitt make the case that state killing is a human rights violation (n.p.). In the context of the refusal by the U.S. Supreme Court to hear death penalty cases based on inmates' claims to innocence and a statement by U.S. Congressman Bill McCullom of Florida that it is acceptable to execute innocent people because the risk of killing them is worth the trade-off in the security the death penalty provides, Rice and Moffitt also describe the importance of the Benetton publicity: "It is in the context of this domestic sickness that bringing a human face to the individuals on death row is so important. Our policy of death also keeps the victim of terrible tragedy on puppet strings operated by prosecutors, politicians and victims' rights groups. They are paraded out and danced before the media in order to maintain a climate of rage and support for executions. . . . To death penalty supporters, no evil is too wrong when compared to the need to exterminate these creatures from our society" (n.p.).

Shulman's essay describes the experience of photographing and interviewing the inmates. Admitting that he could recognize both their humanity and some similarities between their lives and his, Shulman also responds to them with pity and a desire for vengeance when he reads details of their crimes. Halfway through his essay, after describing his fantasy of wanting to do the inmates violence, Shulman states,

> I am now more against the death penalty than ever. And not because I have sympathy for the killers. Many of them are likeable. Many of them are changed, especially after having found in prison . . . the time and wherewithal to step out of their knotted lives and reflect on every step that has brought them here. . . . Several of them are most likely innocent. . . . Many of them are mentally ill, or deficient. But my sympathy

goes to their victims, to their families and friends. . . . I am against the death penalty because I believe it gives vent to something very uncivilized within us. Because it makes us . . . a little more like the men I met on death row, more abstract, more cynical, less human. (n.p.)

Shulman questions what William Connolly describes as the desire to punish, to vent rage outward at subjects who can be held accountable for society's ills; the impulse that states, "save the categories; waste those whose conduct or subject positions disturb them" (1995, 64). The front matter of "We, On Death Row" draws attention to the calls for revenge that "animate the desire to punish" (42) in the pro–death penalty activism of some victims' rights groups. In the pages of the print campaign, inmates themselves voice the desire to punish: perhaps in recognition of their own desire, but also perhaps of that which is directed against them and their lives.

One of the ways in which Benetton makes its case against the death penalty is by asserting the innocence of death row inmates who, as Shulman suggests, have been wrongly accused or poorly defended. While the problem of the wrongly accused and poorly defended is a significant and deeply structural one, the focus on inmates' innocence also participates in and reproduces the moral economies of criminal justice. In these moral economies, those who are wrongly accused or innocent of their crimes are deemed worthy of release and, more important, of respect and human dignity, while those who are "actually" guilty deserve punishment. In comparison, the composite portrait of Johnny Cain includes no talk of his potential innocence. The recognition of his humanity is not predicated on depicting his life and crimes through the moral economy of innocence and a good, clean life. Clearly his life is not meant to appear innocent, but it does appear as one lacking in opportunities and access to marketable skills and other institutional forms of support. What is more difficult in today's moral political economy of crime is the recognition that the guilty life on death row is a life worth saving. Smith's and Carter's composite presents a differently humanized portrait of a life on death row that is both undeserved and guilty, worthy of life but also responsible for having killed. Cain's life profile and "We, On Death Row" represent, in this way, different paradigms of anti–death penalty argumentation. By 2000 Benetton's campaign marked an earlier shift that occurred in anti–death penalty discourse from a critique of violent crime as an effect of missing social opportunities and lack of institutional supports to one invested in a religious economy of guilt and innocence.

The remaining content of the magazine includes photographs and interviews with death row inmates, interspersed with two-page graphic displays of publicity slogans printed on solid colored backgrounds (red or black) with large white lettering. Some of the text has been appropriated from statements inmates made in the interviews. A small, green United Colors of Benetton flag appears at the bottom right corner of most pages. These printed slogans are the closest approximation to an advertising convention in the entire publication, and they carry out most of the explicit branding work of "We, On Death Row." The slogans are simultaneously touching and clichéd, not unlike the text of the profiles of life discussed in chapter 5. They combine what might sound like the canned sentiment of television talk shows and the therapeutic language of self-help books, but within a context that situates the statements outside of the normal flow of prepackaged media language. These are the words of death row inmates, not of psychotherapists and talk show hosts, functioning in that way as truth-telling testimonies of people who have been subjects of the criminal justice system and its machinery of punishment.

Since the inmates speak these particular clichés and because they describe their experiences of death row, readers of "We, On Death Row" are positioned to attend more carefully to these words, as forms of speech they are rarely able to hear and read. They are the statements of people who pay direct witness to the border between life and death on death row and whose photographs "eerily double . . . the death row prisoners' uncertain condition of waiting, of being suspended between life and death" (Beckman 2004, 11). Occasionally their statements are grammatically incorrect, reminding readers that some of the convicted murderers on death row in the United States are undereducated and illiterate. The inmates are quoted as saying, "Parents aren't spending enough time with their kids"; "TV is a very big influence. In here we call it Big Monster"; "I think people like seeing other people suffer and killed"; "Every day we have one day"; "Each day in my cell I paint butterflies"; "I want to run nude through Africa before there ain't no Africa left"; and "Myself is my home."

From their quotes to their facial portraits, Benetton's campaign offers a series of episodic snapshots, "telling details" about death row from the perspective of the incarcerated offender (e.g., Kay in *Portraits 9/11/01*, ix).

From front to back cover, the reader moves from quote to two-page photo of an inmate to interview text to another photo of an inmate, then another inmate, and so on. The inmates' photographs appear alongside their name, date of birth, prison sentence, and execution date. They are asked what their life is like, what they would be doing if they were free, how they were treated as children, and what death row smells and sounds like. No particular narrative is being told about each inmate, but their interviews read like autobiographical litanies of despair. Through the inmates' terse descriptions, readers glean something of what life is like on death row. In ways that do not hinge on questions of the offenders' guilt or innocence, the interviews tell the story of the personal and psychic costs of being on death row. A quote by Edgar Ace Hope that appears at the end of the publication sums up the meaning of the inmates' stories: "We are still human. We still have feelings."

In most of Toscani's photographs, only the inmates' faces are in focus. The rest of the surroundings frame the inmate's face against a fluorescent-lighted green background, the effect of poor lighting in the prison and the drab olive green paint on the walls. Each photograph feels private, as if the viewer is peering into a world that is otherwise out of sight, which is true in the case of prisons in the United States. Some of the inmates pose and smile with the warm but stiff affect of a posed photograph. Others stare blankly into the camera. Some appear defiant, standing with their arms crossed as they lean against the hallway walls of death row. Asked about the justness of the death penalty, Samuel Steven Fields, an inmate serving a death sentence for first-degree murder, states, "I would say it's unjust. Because that is the easy way out. I mean, you kill the person, and it's over. But the worst punishment would be to serve life in prison, you know, day after day, you do thirty, forty, fifty years, I mean it gets to be a drag" (n.p.) (see fig. 8). His photograph, lit from below, gives his face a beatific quality, one of the gendered aesthetic features of death row photography Beckman analyzes in the photographic portrayals of the female killer Karla Faye Tucker (see Beckman 2004). According to Beckman, when the nation is "invited to pay attention to the 'beautiful' female body" on death row it is for "the ultimate purpose of its eradication" (2004, 2).

The photograph of Fields, however, suggests that the aesthetics of beatification may not be limited to depictions of female criminality, but can extend to portrayals of criminalized white masculinity. While Fields is not the

8. Samuel Steven Fields.

only inmate in "We, On Death Row" who appears to be white, in one mode of interpretation his whiteness and stoic masculinity intertwine with what Beckman describes as the mainstream fantasies of death penalty activism. "By analyzing how individual images are constructed and circulated," she argues, "we begin to intervene in the often imperceptible work they do to support states in their right to brutally eradicate the bodies they no longer want" (2004, 3). Such eradication, Beckman argues, is legitimated through the photographic depiction of inmates in the aesthetic of seemingly religiously inspired states of redemptive sacrifice, as in the image of Fields with glowing face and in the photo of Harvey Lee Green, whose face is surrounded by a yellow halo and whose hands hold an open Bible. "Rather than provoking justice," Beckman warns, "the 'beauty' of these photographs . . . works by infusing [their] image[s] with a heavenly aura that transforms execution into some kind of perverse blessing" (2004, 25). This is a particularly prescient point in light of Green's portrait, which went to print just months after he was executed for two counts of first-degree murder (see fig. 9).

These portraits may also function, however, to challenge capital punishment rather than legitimate it as the fated (or martyred) conclusion to a murderer's actions. "We, On Death Row" functions as an archive of more

9. Harvey Lee Green, executed on 24 September 1999.

humanized portraiture of the inmate. The photographic conventions of these portraits both draw from the history of police photography, with its emphases on the features of the head and face, and challenge it on the basis of its own contextualized use of the same conventions for bringing "the camera to bear upon the body of the criminal" (Sekula 1986, 15).

I want to consider the centrality of the face in these examples of death row photography to the construction of death row inmates' subjectivity. For portraiture, as Joanna Woodall (1997) suggests, is itself a kind of physiognomic practice: an anatomized practice of identification combined with an aestheticized practice of depictive likeness. As Tom Gunning further suggests, eighteenth-century physiognomic thought anticipated photography's indexical process of production, "directly tracing the shadow of its subject" (1997, 5). An "exemplar of magical thinking," physiognomy proposed to reveal the secrets of human character in the common features of the human face. Physiognomic thought rested on a principle shared later with cinematic and other visual technologies that "the expressive human face" serves as "a pivot between individuality and typicality, expression and destiny, body and soul" (Gunning 1997, 2). It could reveal, as Foucault suggested, "visual marks of invisible analogies" (quoted in Gunning 1997, 2). "With the advent of photography, the human face became less a realm described in generalities . . . than a zone of intense scrutiny on an individual basis" (Gunning 1997, 6).

"We, On Death Row" stresses the unique qualities of each inmate as a condition of their being grouped together in the pages of Benetton's magazine, qualities expressed in the features of their faces. Joseph Amrine, who is shown in extreme close up, is introduced in Ehrenreich's article on the campaign simply: "There is Joseph Amrine, 44 years old and 14 years on death row." By her own admission that one cannot help but be moved by their photographs, Ehrenreich pays somewhat closer attention to the features of the other men's faces. "There is Jeremy Sheets, 26, with the straight brows and almond eyes of a medieval saint." "There is Kevin Nigel Stanford, who has lived 37 years, 18 of them on death row, his soft, tan face glowing with religious resignation."[10] (See figs. 10–12.) Ehrenreich's descriptions of the faces of Sheets and Stanford draw from a kind of Catholic physiognomy in contrast to the criminalized ones studied by the likes of the nineteenth-century Italian physician and physiognomist Cesare Lombroso. Sheets's almond-shaped eyes show no "outward signs of criminality": the "bushy eyebrows that meet across the nose, drooping upper eyelids, squinty eyes," and other facial "anomalies" that supposedly mark out criminals as less than human (see Atwan 1984). That is, as Ehrenreich herself seems to suggest, these men do not *look like* murderers. They look like anyone else. She does not describe the faces of those men whose expressions appear more forceful and direct, their faces marked by scars and deep pockmarks as well as by crooked, broken teeth. Amrine, Sheets, Stanford represent for Ehrenreich "less criminalized" and more beautiful visages. One might say theirs are examples of more Europeanized faces that have come to represent, via thinkers like Lombroso, the hegemonic standards of white Western beauty: the "straight facial angle, a prominent nose and a sharply defined chin" (Atwan 1984, 358–9).

For Emmanuel Levinas, communication in the face-to-face context is a space of ethical exchange that exceeds speech, where one encounters the unspoken dimensions of intersubjective recognition at the boundaries of life and death. The face, according to Levinas, "is not in front of me, but above me; it is the other before death, looking through and exposing death. . . . The face is the other who asks me not to let him die alone, as if to do so were to become an accomplice in his death" (Levinas and Kearney, "Dialogue with Emmanuel Levinas," 23–24, cited in Jay 1993, 557). As

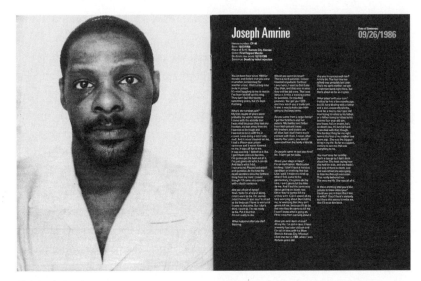

10. Joseph Amrine.

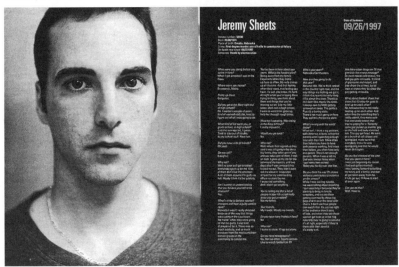

11. Jeremy Sheets.

12. Kevin Nigel Stanford.

Jill Robbins argues, "The face is the privileged figure for the opening of the question of the ethical" (1991, 135). "Encountered neither as a phenomenon nor as a being (something to be mastered or possessed), the other is encountered as a face. It is in the encounter with the face of the other that the other's infinite alterity is revealed" (Robbins 1991, 136).

Benetton's portraits are, nonetheless, gendered and raced products of a corporate-supported campaign that combines branding with anti–death penalty advocacy. Twelve of the inmates in the campaign are racially coded white; eleven, including one woman, are racially coded black; two are coded as Latino; and one as Palestinian. With their insistent focus on the individuality of the inmates as both prisoner and man (or woman), each photograph offers itself to viewers as a truth-telling device, a print witness to the human reality of death row, but one very different from the kind of photographic realism of convict portraits. It purports to offer the truth about life on death row. Convicts speak in their own words next to photos of their faces. The photos also signify the reality of death row. Here are the white cement-block cells, the prison-issued clothing, the wheelchair one inmate uses, the institutional clock on the wall, and the fluorescent lighting. Each of the objects included in the photos stands in for the monotony and bare institutionalism of death row.

If the encounter with the face is an encounter with speech, the death row magazine produced by Benetton both images the face and speaks it through the interview texts. But unless one understands the interview text that runs alongside the prints of the photographs in the campaign's long-form document as speech that corresponds directly to the face, the signifying face may collapse into the signifying act of the witnesses' speech. In the case of "We, On Death Row," the witness and death row inmate are one and the same, for the prisoners pay witness to the conditions of their lives while waiting to be put to death. Levinas theorizes the encounter with another's face as a moment of transformation between the act of seeing and the act of saying. "We, On Death Row" draws attention to the epistemic fissures and gaps that exist between what is seen and what is said (see Peters 2001). One of only two full-body shots included in "We, On Death Row" is that of Carlette Parker. Her interview is the shortest and tersest of all. While we see her whole body—her whole self—we hear very little about her experiences of death row or her memories of life outside of its walls. In moving from the men's facial portraits to the woman's full-body portrait, "We, On Death Row" metaphorizes the male face as speech. For while Parker barely speaks, it is her whole body the reader sees, not the face that could speak. As Jacques Derrida suggested, quoting from Ludwig Feuerbach, "If I see a man's head, it is the man himself who I see; but if I only see his torso, I see no more than his torso" (1978, 101). In a sense, while more of Parker is shown, she is more profoundly de-faced than the men. She barely speaks, while the facial portraits of the others grant men on death row the gift of witnessing and its speech rites (see Robbins 1991, 139) (see fig. 13).

The POMC Campaign

We always know the name of the offender, but we seldom ever see or know the name of the victim. The Murder Wall is a strong and loving reminder, not only of my husband Monte, but of all those who die by violence in our country.
SHARON TEWKSBURY, West Chester, Ohio, from Parents of Murdered Children website (www.pomc.org)

As its slogan, "Behind Every Murderer Lies an Innocent Victim," suggests, POMC's planned anti-Benetton campaign was imagined as a face-based

13. Carlette Parker, the only woman on death row included in "We, On Death Row."

memorial campaign for murder victims. The main proposition of their counterpublicity over whose lives should be memorialized was not only to give face to murder victims, as they do in their online memorials, but also to argue against the representation of death row inmates as people deserving any kind of media depiction. Their planned campaign sought to derail the practice of giving face to convicted murderers. In their view, the representation of death row inmates in life would be an affront to the memories of murder victims.

From the perspective of POMC, the lives of death row inmates matter through their identity as killers. The rest of inmates' lives on death row and their life stories should remain invisible and inaudible. POMC seeks to exclude them from having the means to represent themselves through their proxy, Benetton. To victims' rights advocates who support the death penalty, inmates forfeit the right to be heard and, by extension, the right to be, once they are convicted of capital murder. In the eyes of some families of their victims, stripping them of their rights to representation — their ability to appear to and communicate with the world outside of the prison's walls — takes away a right of communication they no longer deserve. While POMC does not take an explicit stand on the death penalty, they do as-

14. Murder victim billboard, Justice for Murdered Children.
Courtesy of Anna Del Rio and LaWanda Hawkins.

sist the parents of murder victims who seek retribution through the death penalty against the killers of their sons and daughters.[11]

POMC's plan for a billboard campaign included the display of a photo collage of murder victims to counter Benetton's, much like the one created by the organization Justice for Murdered Children to draw attention to the problem of gun violence and gang-related murders in Los Angeles (see fig. 14). It includes the kinds of family snapshots and school photographs that are typical of family-produced commemorations of murder victims, such as the profile of life. These photographic portraits anchor the billboard space and its message.[12] POMC also produced a highly effective letter-writing campaign addressed to Benetton, to magazines that had run or had bought the Benetton advertisements (including *Rolling Stone*), and to stores that had contracted with Benetton to sell their clothing line, such as Sears. Sears canceled an eight-hundred-store contract with Benetton, a decision that cost the label dearly, as prior to the Sears deal Benetton had fewer than two hundred retail outlets in the United States. A further repercussion was that after working on Benetton's United Colors campaigns for eighteen years, Toscani resigned. In addition to POMC, the pro–death penalty victims' rights group Justice For All launched a campaign accusing Benetton of "using the blood of murder victims to promote its commodity. . . . The only reason they are on a poster is because they are capital murderers" (Dianne Clements, president of Justice for All, quoted in Clark 2000).[13]

POMC responded to the Benetton campaign in part as a challenge to the right of death row inmates to be represented in the public sphere, while murder victims, they argue, rarely appear in media depictions except as corpses. As the president of the POMC chapter in Portland, Oregon, states, their goal is "to put a face on murder," and that face constitutes the person-hood of the victim—personhood denied to murder victims through their killing and in their portrayal by the media (phone interview with Mary Elledge, 22 October 2006). The murder wall Sharon Tewksbury describes is an online database of commemorations of murder victims produced by victims' families. They often contain a description of the victim's life before he or she was killed, a description of the status of the police investigation and, where applicable, the prosecution of the person held responsible, and a family snapshot or formal school photograph. They are in many ways like the profile of life format developed by newspapers to commemorate the lives of the dead, but they also give voice to the anger, loss, and, in some cases, desire for punishment many families feel after the murder of their loved one. They also make space for explicit talk of the circumstances of the murder in which their loved one was killed. There is no taboo here, in other words, against talk of their killing. In fact, what makes POMC's victim com-memoration distinctly unlike the profiles of life is their explicit talk of the murder and prosecution of their sons' and daughters' killers. Rather than being a portrait of life, their memorials to murder victims bear more of a contextual burden around the circumstances of the victim's death.

There were two main propositions to POMC's countercampaign against Benetton. The first challenged Benetton's legitimacy as the representatives of inmates. The second was an argument against portraying the lives of death row inmates at all. In their view, the representation of death row in-mates in life was an affront to the memories of the lives of dead murder victims. As one parent of a murdered child, John Peebles, responded in an APBnews.com story on the Benetton campaign to one of the inmate's interviews, "He hasn't played in the rain for 13 years? He didn't even give my son 13 seconds. He just mowed him down" (Chen, 16 February 2000).

Patricia Gioia, the leader of the POMC chapter in the Albany area, expressed in a letter written to *New Yorker* magazine after they ran one of Benetton's death row ads,

> I have just learned of the obviously anti–death penalty campaign by Benetton in seeking to put a human face on the individuals on death row, to the total exclusion of the victims murdered by these inmates. . . . It is our understanding that Benetton did not contact any of the family members of the murdered victims of the inmates featured in its campaign. Benetton has chosen to prominently display some of these inmates on billboards across the country. Can you imagine what it would be like to see your loved one's murderer staring out at you from a large billboard? What kind of feelings would that stir up? I also wonder what the loved ones of the person/s murdered by Jeremy Sheets would think if they opened up your magazine of Feb. 7th [2000] and saw Sheets staring out at them? (letter dated 13 February 2000, to "The Mail" at *New Yorker*, faxed 17 March 2000)

Cindy Finley, the mother of thirteen-year-old Patrick, who was kidnapped and murdered on Christmas day in 1995 by one of the inmates included in Benetton's campaign described how the photograph of the smiling murderer's face brought back the grief she had begun to be able to live with five years after her son was killed. These parents express the shock and dismay they felt coming face to face with the men who killed their children. The shock they express is further linked to the unexpectedness of seeing the photographs in magazines they subscribe to and on billboards along the roads they travel.

Other letters from POMC challenged Benetton's use of the faces of murderers to market sweaters without any understanding of the consequences such representation brought to the families of murder victims. As they suggest, representation itself has the power to re-wound families of murder victims, a re-wounding that occurs through "no mention of the victims that they murdered," as another letter explains (letter from Albany "Capitol District" of New York chapter to chief executive officer of Sears, 12 February 2000). The political project of POMC is to reclaim a right of representation for their dead loved ones against the depiction of death row inmates. According to Mary Elledge, the notable absence in the Benetton campaign was any talk of the crimes the inmates committed. "Why didn't they talk about what they did, their crimes?," Elledge asked me in our phone interview (22 October 2006).[14]

POMC occupies the powerful rhetorical position of parenthood. Like other organizations that can mobilize the moral authority of motherhood, such as Mothers Against Drunk Driving, POMC represents victims from the position of the victimized family. The daughters of some of the parent activists were victims of a boyfriend or a husband. The daughter of the founders of POMC, Charlotte and Bob Hullinger, was killed by her estranged boyfriend. Nancy, the daughter of the founder of the Philadelphia chapter of POMC, Deborah Spungen, was killed by her boyfriend Sid Vicious, the bass player for the punk band the Sex Pistols. In this organization, parenthood, but especially motherhood, is the position from which these advocates speak of themselves as victims. Across the organization itself, however, the violent gender relations through which many of their daughters were killed are rarely questioned or examined, suggesting a distinction between their maternal politics and a more explicitly feminist politics (see Brush 1996).

POMC's powerful maternal politics comes through particularly clearly and movingly in the online memorial page for Shannon Nicole Brown, shot to death by her teenage ex-boyfriend Chasen Schied, who killed her in a jealous rage (see fig. 15). In the memorial her parents, Bill and Debbie, wrote, Shannon appears in her senior year high school portrait. Her long, blond hair falls below her shoulders. She wears an off-the-shoulder, black v-neck sweater and a gold necklace with an *S* charm. Her eyes are clear blue, and she has fine facial features. She is stunningly beautiful. As the text alongside her photograph states, Chasen shot Shannon with a 9mm gun after having beaten her inside of a car wash where he had followed her. The shot pierced the *S* medallion around her neck "about 12 inches from the top of her head, severed the main artery from the heart and exited her back 16 inches below the top of her head" (www.pomc.org/shannonnicolebrown .cfm). Visitors to the page learn that "Chasen shot himself in the head, taking 'the easy way out,'" in that he does not have to live with the consequences of Shannon's murder.

Shannon's memorial text, like so many others on the POMC memorial website, expresses the deep and grievous loss her murder caused for her parents, in terms that speak to both her life and the specifics of her death. In it they indicate that Chasen was a disturbed young man who murdered

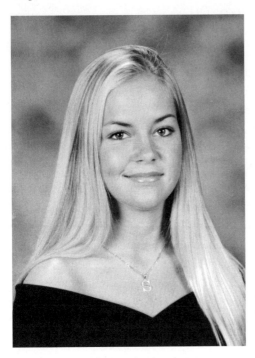

15. Shannon Nicole Brown from her memorial on the website of Parents of Murdered Children. By permission of Bill and Debbie Brown.

Shannon with premeditation after she had broken up with him (at one point he left the scene of the car wash after beating her to retrieve a gun from his car, suggesting that he had planned the murder and armed himself for that purpose). It also tells us that Shannon and Chasen had been dating on and off for four years. The violence in this case is explained as the problem of a troubled teenage boy whose aberrant performance of masculinity led him to commit a brutally violent act. Cases like this one, in which young women are murdered by their boyfriends, are all too common, as POMC's murder wall aptly illustrates. In its memorial webpages, POMC makes visible the dating violence that victims like Shannon Brown and so many other daughters suffer. POMC's own discourse, however, could go further in explaining the social conditions that produce violent boyfriends and male lovers. Without drawing attention to the systemic conditions in which men commit murder against women, the sources of such violence appear as the problem of a few bad men rather than as a condition of the ways in which many boys learn to embody their gender and sexuality within intimate relations.

In the conversations I had with some of the female chapter leaders of POMC, it became clear that the organization works through a form of maternal politics rather than an explicitly feminist framework. Maternalists, as Lisa Brush argues, "claim entitlements to citizenship rights and benefits on the basis of mother-work as a source of women's political personhood." Mother work "involves meeting children's needs for protection, nurturance and moral training" (1996, 430). In the case of POMC, the care and protection toward which the mothers' maternalism is directed focuses on the killing of their children, the circumstances of their assaults, and the memorialization of their lives. Part of that care gets translated into practices of representation that are about telling the stories of their daughters' and sons' murders—asserting a gendered ethic of nurturing motherhood that fuels the political power of its testimony and so often goes unnoticed, is made invisible, or is reprivatized within the contexts of criminal justice. Patricia Gioia wrote and published a book about her daughter's murder to tell the story from the victim's perspective—her own, cultivated as the keeper of her daughter's memory.

POMC's politics of motherhood gives face to the loss and grief work of mothering and the relations of mourning unique to parents whose children have been murdered. Some, as in the case of the countercampaign against Benetton, do so within the context of support for the death penalty, of making the argument for the state killing of another mother's son or daughter. The care work of mothering, in other words, can also be directed toward political positions that call for punishment, retribution, and revenge. "A politics of motherhood," as Marianne Hirsh warns, "can be invoked in the service of any political agenda" (1997, 368; see also Blee 1997; Koonz 1997). "There are war mothers as well as peace mothers, racist as well as anti-racist mothers" (Ruddick 1997, 369).

My point is that there is a potential opportunity for feminists, such as antirape and anti–domestic violence activists, and maternalists to respond together to the problem of male violence against girls and women in ways that could seek out preventive and less deadly responses to even the most murderous of male violence against women. POMC's maternalist voice has incredible symbolic power, enabled by the durable social relations of gender, sexuality, class, and race that define motherhood, often in very circumscribed ways within the family form. At the same time, maternalism offers forms of political agency toward which feminism has, in many contexts, been ambivalent, if not hostile. POMC not only recognizes the political work mothers do, but also creates a platform in which murder can be politicized as an issue of familial and social dependencies.

The voice of this maternal agency is deeply familiar to me. It is located in the spaces of the domestic sphere, constituting a form of kitchen table politics that Linda Kintz (1997) has described. My phone interviews with chapter leaders took place in their homes, not in the offices of the organization. Their homes are the spaces of operation for advocacy on behalf of murder victims' families; chapter leaders are also the political archivists of the organization, and their homes are its storage containers. Some activists, like Gioia, generously went through file boxes of material from her POMC chapter to find copies of letters written during the campaign in response to Benetton's "We, On Death Row." Debbie and Bill Brown scoured through their collection of photographs of their daughter Shannon Nicole to find the one reproduced here. And they did so in the hope that the visibility of their daughter as a murder victim might put a face to the incredible loss that they and so many other parents of murdered children must live with. For these parents, representation is the affective and political grounds for the prevention of others' murder.

I recognize the political maternity—the mother work—of the chapter leaders and members of POMC. I approach their activist mothering as an extension of the mother-child relationship into the context of public talk and action about murder. Their activism occurs in the context-specific conditions of their own grieving, where they see and hear their sons and daughters being misrepresented and misspoken for in courts of law and major media campaigns, if they are given any representation at all. The mothers of POMC see the work of representing murder victims as the means to recognize the former lives of the dead within the family unit. In doing so, they bring them back into representation, away from the dehumanizing forms of depiction in which they are so often represented and into visibility vis-à-vis such high-profile campaigns as Benetton's.

As the feminist epistemologist Sara Ruddick suggests, one should "consider realistically but generously the complex motives and worldly limits of mothers who act politically" (1997, 371). The political agency of mothers who are members of POMC symbolizes the ruptures of attachment they live with as a result of their children's murder (374). From the perspective of POMC, the tragedy of murder is contextualized by "placing the victim within the context of bereaved *families*" (Jermyn 2004, 85). As the profile of life format demonstrated in the aftermath of the Oklahoma City bombing and the 9/11 attacks, murder victims "are never merely or primarily individuals, but parents, children, siblings, spouses" (Jermyn 2004, 85). In various online and artifactual formats, POMC portrays the murder victim through family members' letter writing and practices of remembrance. Because the dead cannot speak for themselves, through POMC the family, but especially mothers, speaks on their behalf.[15]

The parents of murder victims have intimately experienced violence through the killing of their offspring.[16] As they note on their websites and in their meetings, the members of POMC relate to media portrayals of murderers and entertainment centered on murder (e.g., role-play murder games, the exchange of serial killer trading cards) as unique victims of it. Parents of murdered children occupy a unique spectator position from which to view media representations of violent criminality. They not only pay visual witness to media violence, but also have a direct investment in the emotional weight and political imagination of media portrayals that depict murder without showing its consequences, particularly the ways its harms radiate outward to include the families and friends of the person murdered. As one victims' rights activist put it to me, "Popular media shows murders and seldom shows consequences. Parents of Murdered Children hits the nail on the head, especially for young audiences. Who better than someone, a homicide survivor, to address this issue? They are the living, breathing proof of the pain that has to be endured after someone is killed" (Anne Seymour, phone interview, 1 November 2000).

The families of murder victims interpret media programming from the perspective of people who have suffered the killing of a loved one. One audience study of women who had suffered domestic or sexual violence or both and watched the British crime appeal program *Crimewatch UK* found that these viewers wanted "accurate and realistic depictions of their lives, the horror of violence and its negative consequences" (Schlesinger et al. 1992, 68). These viewers, who were experienced in the realities of violence, wanted *Crimewatch UK* to perform a more useful pedagogic role by depicting the aftermath of violence for victims. Many of the women described the importance of television "not in terms of pleasure, escape or fantasy," as so much of scholarship in audience studies has analyzed, "but in terms of relevance and social importance" (1992, 169). In another study, women who had experienced male violence objected to the entertaining character of media depictions of violence against women and found such portrayals to be painful to watch (L. Kelly 1988, cited in Schlesinger et al. 1992, 15).

Like the women in these studies, POMC challenges media portrayals of murder through the interpretative, advocacy-based frameworks that families of murder victims have generated as a secondary class of victim. Through the Murder Is Not Entertainment project, some families of murder victims, as bearers of the emotionally weighted experience of murder, seek to arrest the portrayal of murder as entertaining and the media celebrity of murderers and serial killers. Their position as both the families of murder victims and uniquely situated spectators of media violence gets channeled into their organized counterpublicity in the name of their dead sons and daughters and in their own position as victims. In the process, they give face to the murdered—but not often to themselves.[17]

"We, On Death Row" and POMC represent the politics and political stakes of giving face to murder victims and death row inmates when the lives of the condemned are seen as not worth having. If, as Derrida suggests, "the other is not signaled by his face, he is this face" (1978, 100), then the humanized portraits in which death row inmates are portrayed in "We, On Death Row" signal the very possibility of ethical encounter between murder victims' families and the condemned over capital punishment, murder, and the social and individual sources of violence—and the difficulties and differences that shape these encounters. Both campaigns rest on the idea that portraiture is the act of making those who are dehumanized by murder human again. Their acts of portraiture constitute the actual face of being human—not a transparent lens but a flesh-and-blood point of access to the violence people do to others and to the suffering and grief left in its wake.

Portraiture offers a point of intervention in the politics of victims' rights and the death penalty through the faces of the murdered and their perpetrators. As Margaret Gibson explains, "It is in the face of the other that we are faced not only with the limits of knowledge and representation but also the question of justice. The face commands but it cannot compel respect for the life of the other" (2001, 312). There are no political guarantees when questions of life and death are given a face. Benetton attempted to restore some human dignity to death row inmates in its blatantly branded way.

They gave inmates representation in a political climate that tends to amplify the forces of law and order. POMC restored humanity to those intentionally killed by another, in contexts largely structured by male misogyny. They did so both within a highly capitalized media environment that shut them out of many opportunities for representation and within another, lesser-capitalized (and less visible) environment built around their networks of maternalist activism.

"In a sense," Derrida has argued, "murder is always directed against the face" (1978, 104), for it intentionally takes away the life of an individual. The face mediates the point of contact between who can and cannot claim humanity in the politics of murder and capital punishment. For victims' rights advocates who support the death penalty, it is the victim who occupies the category of human and thereby the category of representable life. Death row inmates, meanwhile, are cast out of the category of human altogether, a status Benetton's anti–death penalty campaign challenged in the process of bringing inmates into portraiture. "We, On Death Row," while a onetime overtly branded publicity campaign, nonetheless called for the fundamental recognition that lives on death row are worthy of life.

POMC gives face to the murdered not only to remember their lives, but also to right the wrongs of their deaths. To the members of this organization, portraits of murder victims restore life narratives to people whose lives were cut short by murder and give face to parental grief and anger, but without making the parents themselves visible. In the case of POMC, victim memorials can function like grief masks for the parents of murder victims. They do not hide their politics behind portraits of the dead, but cover themselves with the portraits. The portraits are their proxies as much as they are the proxies of their sons and daughters.

There are other ways in which families mobilize the faces of murder by putting their own faces on display. In the process, they speak openly of themselves as victims and eschew the ways in which victims' rights activism that is oriented toward law and order purports to speak in the name of victims. Rather than mask the familial face of their politicization of the death penalty—in this case, their abolitionism—behind portraits of murder victims, they instead put their own faces on view. In their refusal to speak for the dead they invest in the recognition of a shared social condition that connects the families of murder victims to the families of death row inmates. The abolitionism advocated by some organizations of murder victims' families demonstrates how encounters with the face of the other might "escape the indifferent, annihilating and/or objectifying look or gaze" (Gibson 2001, 312) and instead embrace a victims' rights orientation grounded not in law-and-order politics but in a human rights framework.

Most political relationships have to be created in the midst of passionate particularity, not outside of it. Maternal politics, because it issues out of particular and familiar allegiances, can inspire a move from one's "own" to "other," from local to more general without ever denying, indeed by continually remembering, irreplaceable and specific loyalties and love.

SARA RUDDICK, "Rethinking 'Maternal' Politics"

conclusion

Giving Face to the Family as Victim

My book ends with the passionate and the particular, that is, with the families of murder victims and the families of death row inmates who find common ground in their agitation against the death penalty. I close this story of victims' rights and the travels it has taken from the 1960s to the present with a consideration of the ethical and political possibilities that lie in the encounter between families who grieve from murder, its commission, and its punishment. While there was no collective identification or political vision shared by the families of victims and inmates in the activism of Parents of Murdered Children and Benetton's anti–death penalty position, in this final chapter I look to some examples in which victims' rights activists find common purpose with death penalty abolitionists around their identification as families of murder.

Parents of murdered children face many of the same issues of grief, loss, and anger as the parents of inmates on death row (Marshall and Oleson 1996; Radelet 2001). In most politics oriented toward victims' rights activists deny this reality, claiming instead that murder creates absolute difference between the families of victims and those of convicted killers—in other words, a state of political alterity rather than commonality. But there are groups of families of murder victims who recognize that they share in the experience of grieving with the families of death row inmates. Organizations like Murder Victims' Families for Reconciliation (MVFR) and Murder Victims' Families for Human Rights (MVFHR) hold this view. The death penalty, these organizations argue, creates a new group of victims: the families of inmates and the executed. While victims' rights activism defined the families of crime victims as victims, these groups define the families of death row inmates as victims too. The victimization of these families is produced by the crime their loved one committed as well as by the criminal justice system. They too constitute a group of secondary victims of murder. They experience loss and incredible grief when their loved ones are incarcerated and executed. In their eyes, they too become murder victims when the state kills their condemned family member. Without denying the violence and losses that murder causes to victims' families, some families of inmates seek to make connections with the families of murder victims around a shared ethical, religious, and moral investment in human life and an unwillingness to dehumanize those who do violence to others.

Following the assertions in Articles 3 and 5 of the UN Declaration of Human Rights that all people share a right to life and that no person shall be subjected to cruel, inhuman, degrading treatment or punishment, Murder Victims' Families for Human Rights argues against the death penalty on the grounds that it is a violation of victims' rights as human rights (see www.mvfr.org). It recognizes that the families of death row inmates not only see themselves as but indeed are victims, although the perpetrator in this case is the state, and their loved one is often guilty of the violent crime they committed (except when there is a question of guilt). These families also often suffer undeniable harm as a result of the execution of their loved one, harm from the grief they suffer after the killing, from social excommunication and marginalization, and from the culture of silence that engulfs communities and families around the death penalty. But "the narrative of victimization does not begin with the execution and its aftermath but rather with original murder and *its* aftermath. As a victims' organization, this is something we never forget or dismiss" (Sheffer and Cushing 2006, 3). Echoing Sara Ruddick's point that maternalist politics can enable ways of thinking about the lives of others, Murder Victims' Families for Human Rights extends victims' rights as a platform for recognizing the human right to a nonviolent life.

Two things about the activism of Murder Victims' Families for Human Rights stand out. The first is the explicit connection it (and organizations like it) draws between the families of murder victims and the families of people living on death row around the struggle to eradicate the death penalty in the United States. The second is the group's open declaration that as victims they possess rights that entitle them to speak against the death penalty *as* and *for* victims. In claiming to speak for others — the murdered and the condemned — they also speak for themselves. They do not seek cover in the depiction of murder victims; they make themselves visible as the faces of murder and death penalty abolition. They do so from the position of murder's victims, as having suffered harm from nonstate murder and the death penalty alike.

Several publications and websites now document the abolitionist activism and storytelling prerogative of murder victims' families and the families of death row inmates.[1] As evidence of their unique victims' rights orientation to the death penalty, their documents picture not the victims of murder or death row inmates, but themselves, the families of murder's victims and perpetrators. Theirs is not the often-hidden familial face of victims' rights which claims to embody the voice of the dead; they openly declare that the family is victimized by murder and other forms of violent crime, but so too is it victimized by the state, which seeks to execute the condemned in the name of victims. Rather than hide the familial face of victims' rights, then, documents such as MVFR's *Dignity Denied* (Cushing and Sheffer 2002) portray the families of murder victims and death row inmates (see also Sheffer and Cushing 2006). Through their abolitionism, these groups represent the familial face of the secondary victims of victims' rights activism more clearly than any other organizations identified with victims' rights advocacy.

When families do assert their rights to represent the imprisoned, states and courts often block their claims on ideological grounds (see Cushing and Sheffer 2002; Sheffer and Cushing 2006). The acknowledgement of their right by states and courts to represent the imprisoned rests on the stipulation that those rights not be used to forward abolitionist and humanitarian claims about the lives of people residing in prison. To speak as the family of a murder victim, let alone the family member of someone on death row, and to be against the death penalty means that one is often "silenced, marginalized, and abandoned, even by the people who are theoretically charged with helping them," including some victim advocates (Cushing and Sheffer 2002, 6). According to MVFR's executive director, opposing the death penalty as a family survivor of murder can lead to a denial by the prosecution of the family's victim status, which they would otherwise be granted in order to speak for their dead loved ones (7). Despite victims' rights protections for families, in states like Maine and Oregon prosecutors deny the families of murder victims who are against the death penalty proxy rights as crime victims. In most states, it is up to the district attorney's discretion to enforce victims' rights to participation and speech in the criminal justice process (Cushing and Sheffer 2002, 8, 13). Who gets to speak as a victim is a matter of prosecutorial discretion; victims' families who oppose the death penalty and other severe sentencing guidelines such as mandatory minimums often find themselves shut out of the process to which victims' rights reforms supposedly give them access, such as the ability to give victim impact statements at sentencings.[2]

The anti–death penalty orientation of these organizations shifts attention away from murder and death toward investments in life and human rights, built on the grief work and political kinship of survivors and secondary victims. They speak against the death penalty not as individuals, as some critics of victims' rights suggest, but as a victim class (see Cole 2006, 173). While so much rights-based legislation in the name of victims does in fact seek to individualize victim claims and avoid talk of social oppression and discrimination, as these activists demonstrate, victims' rights also makes it possible to speak as a class that is linked and identified through a shared ethical commitment and political will to eradicate capital punishment. These activists do not simply use victims' rights as a convenient political language in the debates about capital punishment. They are part of the victims' rights movement, even if the majority of the movement does not recognize or make space for them. Nonetheless, the discourse of victims' rights propels them forward, and it does so on the grounds of its definition of victimization as the harms that arise from encounters with criminal justice.

These organizations and the others I have discussed in this book speak to the power and potential of the political category of secondary victims and the media grammar of victims' rights. Rather than treat the position of victim as a degraded, passive, and vengeful one, in this activism victim becomes a position in which dominant law-and-order victims' rights activism comes into conflict with oppositional, human rights visions of crime, violence, and criminal justice. On this contested political terrain, the language of victimization is still a very useful and necessary one for talking about the harms of social oppression and the violence of many interpersonal relationships. Victim is a category not only worth holding onto out of a grudging recognition of its utility; it is also an incredibly productive concept that expresses, simultaneously, a kind of subjectivity (to become a victim), a quality of institutional encounter, and the character of affective experience (to feel victimized).

There is certainly no shortage of cultural commentary on the pitfalls of public victim talk and the political identity of victim. As Alyson Cole warns, "Most attempts to theorize victimization so far have been rather disappointing — trapped in a liberal calculus of petitions and resources, in the procedures of legalistic discourse, in a therapeutics that reduces grievance to grief, or seeking to eliminate victimhood from politics altogether" (2006, 176). Cole maps out the myriad forms of antivictimism's political demonology — its production of enemies that challenge the status quo that it then casts as subversive threats in order to demonize the political claims making of, among others, civil rights activists, feminists, and child and social welfare agents (4; see also Rogin 1987). Antivictimism "associates victimization with weakness, passivity, dependency and effeminacy. Conversely, it also depicts victims as manipulative, aggressive, and even criminal, at times, as actual or potential victimizers, a danger to themselves and society" (Cole 2006, 3). Antivictimists include Charles Sykes, Francis Fukuyama, Shelby Steele, and even more seemingly progressive authors such as Frank Furedi, Wendy Kaminer, and Wendy Brown. In their work the label victim serves as an insult, a sign of degraded political and personal subjectivity that is chosen voluntarily, a risk-averse, fearing subject (e.g., Furedi 1997) or a marker of "wounded attachments" to political identities mired in historical self-conceptions of injured subjectivity, as Brown (1995) warns.

Neoconservative cultural critics like Sykes and Fukuyama and Nietzschean-identified political theorists like Brown argue that citizenship itself has become a victimized identification. These writers argue that a victim-identified public culture has inhibited the possibilities for social movements to embody political identities that are not defined through injury. The public they discuss is named primarily in stereotypic terms but never in terms of its status as a public or in its relationship to the mass mediation of the victim talk and stories. The "wounded public" Sykes and Furedi discuss constitutes members of political interest groups and major social movements, who in turn wound the "other" public—those defined primarily as working- and middle-class white Americans, who are said to unwittingly suffer from the actions of vengeful, resentment-ridden civil rights movements.

The antivictimists thus attempt to veil their racist, sexist, and classist ideologies about civil rights activism in theses on the wounded identities of those who are oppressed and discriminated against. They suggest that the public prevalence of victim discourses results from the emergence and subsequent cultural dominance of their victimized subject positions. While the antivictimists make this claim in common, Brown's critique differs in some notable ways from those of Sykes, Furedi, and Fukuyama. She argues that new social movements speak through discourses of injury and victimization that fail to enable their constituents to embrace their own possibilities for self-creation and freedom. For Brown, then, this may not be a failure of individuals to make better political decisions—though there is a slippage in her argument between discourses of injury and the political subjects who speak them. Instead, her critique could be aimed more directly against the existing political discursive infrastructures that fail to nurture less victim-identified politics. If there were more of a means to imagine political and social identity outside of one's own sense of victimization or discrimination, she suggests, there could be more ways for individuals to identify and mobilize the freedoms and privileges they already have.

Brown suggests that new social movements embody wounded political identities, not out of conscious choice so much as out of an unthinking clinging to the origins of their political identity in injury. They could occupy different political identifications through their histories of injury, ones that could make a commitment to the future despite the uncertainties and injuries of the past. Brown here is shifting to a theory of consciousness, or "bad thought." Those who identify with victimization are those who are stuck in a mode of bad consciousness, of an unnecessary clinging to past injury for the meaning and constitution of their political subjectivity in the present. Such victimized identities she conflates with a politics of vengeance. "Being victim" politically, in relation to past injuries, can be nothing other than being bound by a politics of *ressentiment*. In this perspective, there is little in the way of a framework to conceive of a victim-identified political subjectivity that could be invested in nonpunitive, nonvengeful, socially just collective action. What would, or could, such a politics of victim identification look like? And how does one politicize victimization and discrimination in ways that directly address them as victim producing?

Absent attention to where public talk of crime and trauma come from and how they are distributed through movement networks, assertions about the meaning of citizenship and the status of public culture as overly victimized require a broad leap of faith: from media coverage of violence and criminal and civil court cases to a public that identifies with victimization and feels victimized (wrongly so, according to antivictimists). Antivictimists claim that citizenship has come to mean woundedness because of the mass distribution of victim stories and victim claims, where mass distribution becomes the evidence for claims that the public identifies with victimization. Furedi's *Culture of Fear* and Sykes's *Nation of Victims*, for instance, pull the majority of their examples of egregious victim claims from news stories, but they do not consider what significance the news media and news values have in publicity about victims, crime, and criminal justice. If the evidence for a form of victim-identified citizenship comes from the news media, then understanding their practices for covering crime and violence might explain why victim stories are so prevalent, and in what form they are most likely to be produced. For instance, as more and more trauma training is incorporated into journalism schools, more emphasis in the news will likely be placed on the experience of victimization rather than the event of crime — not because there are more victims, but because the victims' rights movement has helped to mobilize a victim perspective on news making into journalism education and the news media.

The faces and voices of victims look and sound amplified in the press and other media through the movement grammar of victims' rights, its empowerment of secondary victims, and what this way of representing victims says about their politicization by social movements. One can understand the prevalence and value of victim talk only by shifting attention away from the appearance, or presence, of victims in media representations to consider changes in the movement capacities and representational frameworks for moving victims, especially secondary victims, into the public sphere. It also requires attentiveness to the different political arguments secondary victims and their organizations make. The back-channel and behind-the scenes work of activists, criminal justice agents, families, and politicians crafts the look and talk of victims' rights and distributes them through a networked, national infrastructure of crime victim activism to condition the discourse of victimhood in the United States. In the process, the movement has enlarged the category of victim to not only include families, but also to place them at the center of victims' rights and at the center of public debates about crime, terrorism, punishment, and the death penalty, in ways that are politically disjunctive and diverse.

As Foucault has argued, influence is a rather magical concept because it does not really explain how discourse works or why (1967/1998, 282). My book explains the very notion of discursive influence by locating it among the producers and distributors of the movement's media grammar of victims' rights. For it is their work that has transformed the possibilities for representing victims, whether in the profile of life, the portrait-based campaigns of anti–death penalty and victims' rights activists, or in the abolitionism and antiwar stances of some murder victim family organizations. The influence of victims' rights discourse is as much an issue of building the communication infrastructure through which it would circulate as it is of building a set of conventions for telling stories about victims through the proxies of their families. While so much mass communication research tends to examine the work of media influence according to the effects that can be measured within groups of people that consume media texts, this book offers a different way of thinking about the strategies that advocates and other cultural producers use to influence public debate through the infrastructural, strategic, and pedagogical dimensions of victim-based publicity.

This has been an important story to tell, for it asks and answers the question of what it is possible to do, politically, with the discourse of victims' rights, and it does so in ways that do not presume that the politics of victimization necessarily lead to punishment or to the fueling of a desire for it. Nor can the claims of victims' rights activists be reduced to those of their antivictimist brethren. Claims to victimization are not simply forms of bad politics, bad consciousness, or corruptions of the terms of public debate, as the antivictimists suggest. Instead the victims' rights movement built a public culture of victim-centered activism that transformed the public story of crime and its victims by bringing secondary victims into visibility, and in new ways, some of which have been undeniably and devastatingly punishing.

I share Cole's concern over the political effects of antivictimism (2006, 6) and her acknowledgment that "victimization has been and can be the stepping-stone toward emancipation rather than a corridor to despair, fatalism, enduring powerlessness, and eternal dependence" (176). I have sought to shed light on the ways the victims' rights movement produced victim-based discourse with an eye toward the political variations of its claims makers. Where Cole suspects any grammar of victimization of being implicated in the language of antivictimism, the history of victims' rights and its interesting political genealogy suggest that the politics of victimization in the United States takes many forms, only some of which can be categorized as antivictim within the victims' rights movement. Additionally, in its own internal debates, the movement itself proves that the politics of victimization have been structured by competing claims about who and what a victim is, how victimization is produced, and what should be done about it. Some of these voices have called for forms of vengeful punishment against offenders and support dehumanizing practices of incapacitation and state murder. But other, admittedly more marginalized voices call for the abolition of the death penalty on human rights grounds and invest in prevention-based efforts to end violence. The latter may appear as minoritarian positions in the politics of victims' rights, but that is because they challenge the idea that state punishment is conducted on the grounds that it is what victims and their families want.

While victims' rights is still primarily a law-and-order movement, it creates a political position from which to speak against capital punishment and the state's ventriloquism of victims to legitimate its violent action. From a politically progressive position, dismissing victims' rights as an arm of law-and-order activism, which it is, nonetheless misrecognizes all of the other possible claims to victims' rights, claims that are not grounded in a resentful, vengeful, and punishing politics. The activism of groups such as Murder Victims' Families for Human Rights points to how difficult grief work is, particularly in the high-profile media environments of the death penalty and the 11 September terrorist attacks. Grief is potent affective ground for political affiliation, but it is also a highly contingent one that links the families of those who have been killed to the families of those who have killed. These are the difficult, "messy actualities" of the political work of grieving and grievance in struggles over victims' rights and the families that identify with it (see Ahmed 2008; Larner 2000).

This point is perhaps most forcefully made in regard to the aftermath that wracked the community of Littleton, Colorado, in the wake of Dylan Klebold's and Eric Harris's murderous shooting spree there on 20 April 1999. News images produced by the Denver paper *Rocky Mountain News* captured the deeply religious and faith-based responses to the shock, anger, and grief of students who survived the shooting, their families, and members of the Littleton community. In addition to several Pulitzer Prize–winning spot news photographs, the paper ran individual obituaries for each of the students killed during the shooting at Columbine High School.[3] Obituary after obituary speaks to the exceptional qualities of the dead and their family's love in ways that embody the different ways victims' rights can signify. In one, Rev. George Kirsten refers to Cassie Bernall, who died just after confessing to her killers that she believed in God, that she "went to a martyr's death." The obituary writer, Carla Crowder, tells readers that Cassie had no idea she would be known as "the Colorado girl who died for Christ."[4] Her obituary functions as a kind of evidence for the ways in which victims can still signify sacrifice alongside its more recent connotations in the discourse of victims' rights. In another obituary, Archbishop Charles Chaput Jr. remarks, "Ours is a culture permeated by violence. We *need* to be cut to the heart so that we might work for changes in our society. . . . We are not powerless. We can convert the structures of our society."[5] Chaput speaks to the affective dimensions of social change, the possibility that transformation occurs when people convert their strong feeling into action, where pain becomes the ground of politics.

In these obituaries, one sees how *victim* is one of the keywords of Americans' political lexicon. The significance of such a status lies "not in the clarity [it] bring[s] to public discussions, but just the opposite: [its] very susceptibility to diverse, indeed, opposing, interpretations and appli-

16. Confrontation at the cross for Dylan Klebold on the memorial site for the Columbine dead. By permission of Patrick Davison.

cations" (Cole 2006, 1, 17). Cole attends in particular to how the concept of victim "transforms the meanings of harm, injury and responsibility" in which the term is also "ultimately a sign for an entire discourse whose effects transcend the word itself and no longer depend on its presence." In the language of the two Columbine obituaries cited above, talk of the dead victims brings together religious martyrdom, sacrificial offering, and the concept of murder as an affectively charged, primarily traumatic loss. The language of victimhood, in other words, "rests on a grammar that controls what can be said about personal and political experience" (17), but it also produces a number of ways of talking about victimization that spans crime and criminal justice, interpersonal violence and major acts of terrorism.

The coverage of Columbine also represents the tensions that exist between imagining the victims as those whose lives were ended or injured by the actions of Klebold and Harris, and those who experienced it at a proximate distance, beyond the bodies of the physically injured and murdered to include the parents, friends, and community members of Littleton and the nation itself. Neither representation of victim, however, grants Harris and Klebold any recognition of their humanity, no matter how spoiled it is. While there are no featured obituaries for Klebold or Harris in the *Rocky Mountain News*, they were included in the memorials erected on the hill of Clement Park next to the high school.[6] Fifteen wooden Christian crosses were erected for each of the Columbine dead, including Klebold and Harris. In one photograph by Patrick Davison, a woman is pictured with a black marker in her hand poised in the act of desecrating Klebold's memorial cross (see fig. 16). According to the caption, the message she writes is a derogatory one. Written in large black letters on the cross are the words "HATE BREEDS HATE." The identity of the person who wrote them is unclear.

In the photograph, two female students from Columbine confront the woman as she defaces the cross. In the caption, the reader is told that "debate raged over whether Klebold and fellow gunman Eric Harris should be included in community wide mourning" (see website in n. 6, p. 231). In these commemorative practices, at least some community members felt that Harris and Klebold, despite their murderous violence, had lives that also should be memorialized. Two memorial websites, both run by webmaster Morticia Raven, have since been created specifically in Klebold's memory.[7] While such sites can never erase the murderous violence this young man enacted with his friend, they nonetheless refuse to dehumanize the person who kills. They also recognize the grief of his parents, Sue and Tom Klebold, and refuse to blame them for not knowing how to stop their very troubled son from committing the murders.

It is time to shift the discussion of victims in the media away from claims about the status of victims and victimized speaking subjects toward an examination of the strategic and contested relationships that have developed between the criminal justice system, the national crime victim movement, major news and entertainment media, and educational institutions—and, more directly, between the families of murder victims and the families of perpetrators. Through the political discourse of victims' rights, the crime victim movement in the U.S. has turned the representation of victims into a problem in its own right. These representations of victims' rights not only bring a different conception of the victim into being, but also provide some of the critical tools through which representation itself can be examined as the turbulent, contingent, and often violent ground of human encounter that it is.

introduction

1 On page 50 of the article, information on twelve
missing children and teenagers is printed in a
large sidebar next to a color photograph of Elizabeth in the embrace of her grandparents. Portraits
of the twelve children are included. Four appear to
be Latino, four are African American, three are of
mixed race, and one girl, Erica Baker, appears to be
Caucasian. See "The Miracle Girl" *People*, 31 March
2003, 44–51.

2 As Gumbrecht suggests, "This could also be the case
for some aspects of sex and gender (although they
are not really addressed in this volume—perhaps
because of the situation of gender studies in Ger-
many)" (1994, 400).

3 Scholars who study victims' rights legal reforms, for
instance, have found that most new laws and statutes on victims' rights serve the interests of criminal prosecution while purporting to aid victims,
largely in name only (see Elias 1983; Henderson
1989; Wood 1999, 2005); but others have found that
some reforms, such as the passage of victim compensation laws, create the space in law to articulate that violent crimes happen to people, not to an

abstract state (see Dubber 2002). As a set of laws, victims' rights represents both law-and-order interests in harsher criminal punishments in the name of victims and claims that the law ought to recognize the personhood of victims, not necessarily in terms of punishing offenders.

one Law and Order

1   Law-and-order advocates see the law as a source of crime control, not an effect thereof, a position that differs from the ways in which the inability of law to achieve social order is generally conceived in most bodies of classic social theory, whether Durkheimian, Marxist, or Weberian (see Reiner fn. 7, 200–201).

2   "Concerns about 'black' riots, the growing social scientific interest in victim surveys, and the politicization of the Omnibus Crime Control and Safe Streets Act (1968) passing through US Congress provided the context for a 'fear of crime feedback loop' the likes of which still operate today" (Lee 2007, 56) and helped produce a victims' rights perspective on crime. According to Murray Lee, while "conventional wisdom has assumed that anxiety over civil rights and 'Negro riots,' as well as over the growing 'crime problem,' were symbiotically connected in the public mind and that these anxieties combined to make crime the number one problem for the American public," the crime problem was in fact a manufactured product of the media and politicians (2007, 59). As Lee points out, the discourse of "crime on the streets" was borrowed from a *U.S. News and World Report* editorial dated 29 June 1964, which then was picked up by a speechwriter for Barry Goldwater and used in a speech he gave on the problem of public disorder during his acceptance as the Republican Party candidate for president that year. The *U.S. News and World Report* editorial explicitly defined civil rights demonstrations as crimes (59).

3   Carrington was part of the inner circle of right-wing activism. One of his friends was Richard Viguerie, the well-known and highly successful direct mail fundraiser for the New Right of the 1970s.

4   This policy text has been so significant in the history of victims' rights that twenty years after its publication, the federal Office for Victims of Crime in the Department of Justice funded an oral history project on the movement's leaders that paid special attention to the task force of 1982. The oral history interviews include an extended roundtable discussion with the surviving members of the original task force, including Rev. Pat Robertson, Frank Carrington, and one of its allies in the administration, former U.S. attorney general Edwin Meese (see Task Force "Roundtable Interview Transcript," online at the University of Akron website on the Oral History of the Crime Victim Assistance Field at vroh.uakron.edu).

5   As Galton further mused, "These ideal faces [speaking of portraits] have a surprising air of reality. Nobody who glanced at one of them for the first time would doubt its being the likeness of a living person, yet, as I have said, it is no such thing; it is the portrait of a type and not an individual" (1879, 132–33).

6   The account's language, for instance, moves from the second-person perspective (e.g., "The preliminary hearing was an event for which you were completely unprepared," 7) to the third-person (e.g., "For this victim the ordeal of the trial is over, but the ordeal of being a victim is far from over; it continues with unrelenting pressure," 11).

two   Genealogy of Victims' Rights

1   There are other such attempts to historicize victims' rights from within the movement, including the bullet-pointed chronologies circulated to and among victim advocacy organizations as part of National Crime Victims' Rights Week publicity drives. See, for example, "National Crime Victims' Rights Week Resource Guide: Crime Victims' Rights in America" published in 1997 and available online on the Office for Victims of Crime website at www.ojp.usdoj.gov/ovc. This document highlights the formation of key organizations in the movement, the key funding agencies and their contributions at particular times, and the development of federal resource infrastructures such as the national Victims of Crime Fund in 1984.

2   The first victim compensation programs were started in states whose cities had experienced rebellious disruptions in the mid-1960s. By the mid-1970s, the compensation programs of those same states were plagued by insufficient budgets after the cessation of broad urban unrest, despite the fact that violent crime rates had not decreased (see Elias 1983, 216).

3   National crime commissions of the 1960s established the measurement of victimization as one of their goals. The Commission on Law Enforcement and Administration of Justice during President Lyndon Johnson's administration catalyzed the first victim surveys in 1967. The National Opinion Research Center and the Bureau of Survey Research in Michigan conducted the first surveys; by 1972, they were being conducted by the Bureau of the Census and the Bureau of Justice Statistics. According to the criminologists Dan Lewis and Greta Salem (1986), the early studies funded by the National Commission on Crime in 1967 attempted to determine the level of crime and the level of fear Americans experience, "the assumption being that *levels of fear* would be congruent with the true amount of crime in an area" (4). The importance of measuring the fear of crime was that more people could be counted as victims, albeit potential victims in their own perception. As defined by the surveys, fear of crime meant one's anticipation of a criminal event. A person would score high on fear of crime if she reported an increase in violent criminal events (Lewis and Salem 1986, 4). The surveys emphasized the demographic characteristics associated with victimization and fear of crime rather than criminogenic aspects of the environment. In other words, the Crime Commission and, later, the Department of Justice were more interested in figuring out who the victims of crime are and which people perceive themselves to be potential victims than in investigating the social conditions that enable crime.

4   There is some disagreement over who can be called the founder of victimology.

Mendelsohn asserted that he was the true founder of victimology while von Hentig is generally regarded as its true founder because of the publication and title of his book *The Criminal and His Victim* (1948) and an earlier essay, "Remarks on the Interaction of Perpetrator and Victim" in 1941.

5 Bulow's husband, Claus, was tried and acquitted of attempted murder charges when she became comatose after an apparent overdose of insulin possibly administered by her husband. The founders of the National Center for Victims of Crime, including the children of Sunny von Bulow, built the center to assist high-profile victims in their interactions with the press. (See Weed 1995.)

6 All of these funds come from offenders convicted of federal crimes. The act had placed a cap on fund deposits for the first eight years. In 1993, the cap was lifted, and afterward there was a steady increase in funds being deposited. Under the Anti-terrorism Act of 1996, states must also provide compensation to residents who are victims of terrorist acts within or outside of the United States. See OVC Fact Sheet, "Victims of Crime Act Crime Victims Fund."

7 Bulow's second trial, the civil trial, was underway at this point. Seeking to use the available trust money responsibly, Gurley and Auersperg were looking for an organization that could assist them in responding to the treatment Sunny von Bulow received at the trial and in the news media.

8 As the report says, "Today, as MVFR publishes this account of silencing and discrimination against anti–death penalty victims, *we are not aware of a single protocol in the office of any prosecutor in the United States* that alerts victim assistants to the possibility that some family members of victims may oppose the death penalty and that they are entitled to the same assistance as those who support it" (2002, 7).

three Representing Victims' Rights

1 After the bombing of the Alfred P. Murrah Federal Building in Oklahoma City by Timothy McVeigh and Terry Nichols, family members of the blast victims were gathered together in a church nearby, in part to make service delivery easier and ensure that family members were able to wait in a safe environment away from the press and the public. The media were forced to work through a pool system, and victims who indicated an interest in speaking with the media could do so only with the aid of a victim advocate. Not all family members appreciated the level of control that advocates and the district attorney's office exerted over their participation. Marcia Kight, the mother of Frankie Merrell, a twenty-three-year-old woman killed in the blast, and the director of Families and Survivors United and now a victim activist working for the National Organization for Victim Assistance in Washington, D.C., told me she resented not being able to speak with the media without the assistance of an advocate. She described feeling that her ability to speak with the media and represent herself was curtailed by the procedural system put into

place out of a sense that family members needed to be protected from media intrusion (author interview, 6 June 2000, NOVA office, Washington, D.C.).

2 After being the subject of advocates' stories about the deceptive nature of talk shows for victims, however, in 2007 Montel Williams was given the Leadership Award for "his extraordinary leadership on behalf of victims of crime." As NCVC's online award announcement states, "Mr. Williams has set himself apart from others in the media by treating victims with dignity and compassion while having a significant impact on raising public awareness about the realities of victimization. His respectful treatment of and commitment to crime victims extend to his innovative 'After-Care' program through which victims receive personalized support that continues long after they have been featured on his show" ("The National Center for Victims of Crime 2007 Leadership Awards Reception honors Montel Williams," 2007, accessed online on the National Center for Victims of Crime website at www.ncvc.org).

3 In the United States, with the help of the federal Office for Victims of Crime and national private nonprofit organizations, some of these materials have been made widely available, often for free or at very low cost. Others can be difficult to acquire.

4 These include but are not limited to the following: being treated with dignity and respect by staff, being informed of the format and subject of the show; being informed of who the other guests will be and why they are going to be on the show, being able to object to the format or production decisions, to request measures that will ensure anonymity (if they desire it) and safety, to request that shows not air in markets where they were victimized or where the perpetrator resides; and to end their participation at any time. The guidelines and Bill of Rights seek to make the talk show format as transparent and nondeceptive as possible to victims and their advocates, constituting victims' rights activism around the media as a grand project of media demystification.

four Undisclosed Sources

1 Before the *Rocky Mountain News* ceased publication, 27 February 2009, Denver's competitive newspaper market intensified the pressure on local print journalists to cover multiple details of the shootings, the police investigations, and commemorative community events. Denver reporters covering the shootings felt the stresses of the assignment were amplified by this competition.

2 Trauma curricula are generally integrated into existing courses or are taught as stand-alone outreach seminars for working journalists. The Dart Center for Journalism and Trauma at the University of Washington School of Journalism offers four- to six-hour workshops at which working journalists and journalism students learn how to sensitively conduct interviews with victims by learning the best ways to approach victims posttrauma, if at all (they are encouraged not to interview child victims). In the course "Advanced Reporting," journalism students in the De-

partment of Communication at the University of Washington receive training in a special three-part orientation session devoted to trauma science called "Covering Traumatic Incidents: A Curriculum for Training Student Reporters" (Cane, n.d.). Students are required to enroll in an ethics course, and they can take an additional course on crisis communication. Sherry Ricchiardi, a professor at Indiana University, Roger Simpson at the University of Washington and the news editorial faculty at University of Colorado have all incorporated trauma studies into media ethics and news editorial courses. Indiana University also recently organized a statewide conference on the social and personal effects of crime coverage for journalists, journalism educators, deans of journalism schools, and journalism students. The Center for People and the Media at the University of Central Oklahoma offers training to the newspaper industry in the state to prepare journalists in how to deal with disasters and violence. Three of their faculty, Terry Clark (head of the journalism program), William Hickman, and Kole Kleeman, conduct statewide seminars to assist newspaper staff. Kleeman also teaches a course, "Victims and the Media," on the issue of trauma, news representation of violence, and journalistic practice (author communication with Kleeman, 28 August 2001).

five   Profiles of Life

1   See www.9-11heroes.us/v/Steven_D_Jacoby.php.
2   See http://www.9-11heroes.us/v/Ann_Judge.php.

six   Faces of Murder

1   Local POMC chapters in Wichita, Kan., Portland, Ore., and Albany, N.Y., gathered photographs of murder victims from their families and contacted local billboard owners to buy space on which to display them. According to Executive Director Nancy Ruhe, however, these local affiliates were unable to participate in the billboard campaign because they could not afford the going rate for billboard space and could not acquire a discount from the billboard owners (phone interview with Nancy Ruhe, executive director of Parents of Murdered Children, 11 July 2005). By contrast, the murder victim family organization Justice for Murdered Children, headquartered in Los Angeles, has succeeded in raising the funds to erect 250 billboards depicting victims of murder in that city. The first one they erected was in 2006, and it included photographs of two activists' children who were killed by gun violence: Anna Del Rio's daughter Teresa Del Rio and LaWanda Hawkins's son Reginald Reese. (See fig. 14, where Teresa's and Reginald's portraits appear; they are the two children on the right side of the billboard.)

Additionally, while Benetton's campaign can still be viewed in the magazines in which it was run and in archives of news stories on its controversy, POMC's materials are available only from the organization itself. Based on the relative availability of these counterrepresentation campaigns, Benetton's is far more visible and accessible, while POMC's has nearly disappeared from the physical record. In interviews I conducted with local chapter leaders of POMC, who keep the archives of their organization's materials, often in their own homes, they said the collection of their own records depends upon their space availabilities and record-keeping needs as chapter leaders. Many of the materials from the Benetton countercampaign have been discarded, in part because they hold little current value from an organizational perspective.

2 Author interviews with Patricia Gioia, Nancy Ruhe, and Mary Elledge.

3 The press release quotes from death row inmate Barbara Graham as she made her way to the gas chamber in which she was executed on 3 June 1955.

4 The campaign's ninety-six-page magazine ran as an insert in February 2000 in *Talk* magazine, a short-lived mass-market publication modeled in style and content on the popular style and current affairs magazine *Vanity Fair*. In addition to the *Talk* magazine insert, Benetton bought advertising space for the campaign in *The New Yorker*, *Vanity Fair*, and *Rolling Stone* magazines.

5 They gained access to prisons in other states as well, but no other states have filed suit against them.

6 According to another report, it took three years and the assistance of a number of lawyers to negotiate access for Toscani (Clark 2001).

7 Benetton also admitted to paying two of the death row inmates one thousand dollars each for the right to use their photographs, a clear violation of Missouri's Son of Sam law, which prevents convicted killers from profiting from their crimes (Chen, 16 February 2000). Son of Sam laws, named after the serial killer David Berkowitz, who called himself the "Son of Sam" in reference to the leader of a Satanic cult Berkowitz claims to have followed, were first passed in New York state in 1977 in order to prevent convicted criminals from selling stories about their crimes.

8 This fact alone distinguishes it from the victim composite published in 1982 in the *Final Report of the President's Task Force on Victims of Crime* discussed in chapter 1. While the victim composite was compiled from victim testimony taken at six task force hearings, rather than present an averaged statistical portrait, it sought to dramatize the worst case scenario of a fictive victim repeatedly victimized by her assailant and, most important, by social institutions purportedly there to help her. Carter's and Smith's death row composite fictionalizes a life out of combined statistical data, to put a human face on the conditions of institutional neglect and poverty that explain the circumstances in which so many inmates were sentenced to capital punishment.

9 Fashion designer Kenneth Cole reportedly came out with a death penalty ad campaign right after Benetton; only by then it was old news (O'Leary 2000).

10 Joseph Amrine and Jeremy Sheets have been freed from prison as potentially innocent of the crimes for which they were convicted. Email from Speedy Rice, 11 November 2009.

11 Anti–death penalty advocates consider POMC to be a pro–death penalty group,

despite their apparently neutral stance. The flak campaign against Benetton demonstrates their implicit support of the death penalty.

12 Pictured from left to right are Lori Gonzalez, the granddaughter of a former Los
Angeles police chief; eighteen-year-old Mario Vidal; eighteen-year-old Reginald
Reese, the only son of one of the activist mothers of JFMC; LaWanda Hawkins;
and Teresa Del Rio, the only child of JFMC activist Anna Del Rio. Phone conversation with Anna Del Rio, 11 November 2009.

13 Justice for All was started by Ellen Levin, the mother of murder victim Jennifer
Levin, who was raped and killed while on a date with a college acquaintance,
Robert Chambers.

14 In fact, their lawyers and the prison prohibited the inmates from speaking about
their crimes or their cases for appeal. Toscani and Benetton were also prohibited
from asking them questions about those issues.

15 In addition to offering support groups to the families of murder victims, POMC
has organized several successful campaigns against the parole of convicted murderers. Many of the organization's members also hold memberships in Justice for
All, a pro–death penalty victims' rights lobbying organization (author interview
with Nancy Ruhe, 10 July 2005). According to Executive Director Nancy Ruhe,
POMC has prevented one thousand murderers from getting early release from
parole boards. They also kept one man in prison beyond his minimum sentence
of fifteen years (at the time of my interview with her on 11 July 2005, the man had
been in prison for twenty-one years, according to Ruhe). Ruhe also stated that
the organization had lost fewer than ten cases of early release of prisoners based
upon its letter-writing campaigns to parole boards. As Ruhe suggested, POMC's
letter-writing campaigns are particularly successful in part because the letters are
kept in inmates' files; each time a prisoner comes up for review before the parole
board, the letters collected by POMC are read as part of the parole review process.
Given their focus on the actions of potential parolees and on the portraits of death
row inmates in the Benetton "We, On Death Row" campaign, POMC's approach
to criminality, like the portrayal of crime on crime-appeal programming, "is 'explained' as the irrational violence of dangerous individuals" who should be kept
behind bars, if not executed (A. Williams 1993, 102).

16 Many of the murdered children of these parents were adults when they were killed,
so the label *children* signifies a relationship between parent and victim that does
not necessarily connote age. POMC's website contains a memory wall listing the
names and life spans of the murder victims whom members of the organization
memorialize. As is evidenced from the information included on the twenty-five
panels of the wall, many of the victims were killed as adults, yet their victim status
derives in part from their position as the child of grieving parents.

17 Eric Schlosser's (1997) exposé in *Atlantic Monthly* on the parents of murdered
children reveals how private grief mixes with public anger among homicide's covictims. The grief homicide survivors experience comes not only from the loss of

their murdered love one, but even more significantly from the lack of scripted roles and rights to participation they say they experience in the prosecution and punishment of their sons' or daughters' killer. To rectify this lack of representation, POMC, like many of the other victims' rights organizations I discuss in this book, turn to other practices of representation in which they can claim the right to speak and depict the dead and their own grief.

conclusion

1   These books include Susan Sharp, *Hidden Victims: The Effects of the Death Penalty on Families of the Accused* (Rutgers University Press, 2005); Rachel King, *Don't Kill in Our Names: Families of Murder Victims Speak Out Against the Death Penalty* (Rutgers University Press, 2003); Rachel King, *Capital Consequences: Families of the Condemned Tell their Stories* (Rutgers University Press, 2005); and James Acker and David Karp, eds., *Wounds that Do Not Bind: Victim-based Perspectives on the Death Penalty* (Carolina Academic Press, 2006).

2   Impact statements are typically limited to content on the impact of the crime on the victim physically, emotionally, and financially. Most courts prevent victims from making statements about what sentencing they desire.

3   See http://denver.rockymountainnews.com/shooting/flash/columbinenav.html.

4   Crowder, 27 April 1999, *Rocky Mountain News* website (www.rockymountainnews.com) on the shooting.

5   Meadow, 26 April 1999, *Rocky Mountain News* website (www.rockymountainnews.com) on the shooting.

6   See http://denver.rockymountainnews.com/shooting/flash/columbinenav.html.

7   See www.dylanbennetklebold.com and www.dylanklebold.net.

9/11 Heroes. www.9-11heroes.us.

Acker, J. R., and D. R. Karp, eds. 2006. *Wounds that do not bind: Victim-based perspectives on the death penalty.* Durham: Carolina Academic Press.

Ahmed, S. 2004a. Affective economies. *Social Text* 22: 117–39.

———. 2004b. *The cultural politics of emotion.* Edinburgh: Edinburgh University Press.

———. 2006. *Queer phenomenology: Orientations, objects, others.* Durham: Duke University Press.

———. 2007. 'You end up doing the document rather than doing the doing': Diversity, race equality and the politics of documentation. *Ethnic and Racial Studies* 30: 590–609.

———. 2008. The politics of good feeling. E-journal of *Australian Critical Race and Whiteness Studies Association* 4(1): 1–18.

Aiken, C. 1996. Reporters are victims too. *Nieman Reports* 50: 30–2.

Alcoff, L., and L. Gray. 1993. Survivor discourse: Transgression or recuperation? *Signs* 18: 260–90.

Alderman, E. 1998. Sammy meets Son of Sam. *Columbia Journalism Review* (March/April): 11–13.

Alequin, S., et al. 2001. *In between the lines: How the* New York Times *frames youth.* New York: Youth Force.

Allen, R. C. 1985. *Speaking of soap operas.* Chapel Hill: University of North Carolina Press.

Altheide, D. 1992. Gonzo justice. *Symbolic Interaction* 15: 69–86.

American Press Institute. 2001. *Crisis journalism: A handbook for media response.* Reston, Virginia.

American Psychiatric Association. 1980. *The Diagnostic and Statistical Manual III.* Washington: American Psychiatric Association.

APBnews.com. Fashion ads feature condemned inmates. 2000. 8 January.

Attorney General's Task Force on Violent Crime. 1981. *Final report.* Washington: U.S. Department of Justice.

Atwan, R. 1984. Physiognomy, photography, and prostitution: Cesare Lombroso and the female offender. *Research Communications in Psychology, Psychiatry, and Behavior* 9: 353–64.

Austern, D. 1987. *The crime victims' handbook: Your rights and role in the criminal justice system.* New York: Viking Press.

Aynes, R. L. 1983/84. Constitutional considerations: Government responsibility and the right not to be a victim. *Pepperdine Law Review* 11: 63–116.

Ball, K. 2000. Introduction: Trauma and its institutional destinies. *Cultural Critique* 46: 1–44.

Bandes, S. 1996. Empathy, narrative, and victim impact statements. *University of Chicago Law Review* 63(2): 361–412.

———. 2009. Victims, 'claims,' and the sociology of emotions. *Law and Contemporary Problems* 72(1).

Barker, V. 2007. The politics of pain: A political institutionalist analysis of crime victims' moral protests. *Law and Society* 41(3): 619–63.

Barker-Plummer, B. 1995. News as a political resource: Media strategies and political identity in the U.S. women's movement: 1966–1975. *Critical Studies in Mass Communication* 12: 306–24.

Barnouw, E. 1978. *The sponsor: Notes on a modern potentate.* Oxford: Oxford University Press.

Barsamian, D. 2002. An interview with Charlotte Ryan. *Z Magazine.* Website: www.zcommunications.org/zmag.

Barthes, R. 1981. *Camera lucida: Reflections on photography.* New York: Hill and Wang.

Bayley, J. 1991. The concept of victimhood. *To be a victim: Encounters with the criminal justice system,* ed. D. Sank and D. I. Caplan, 53–62. New York: Plenum Press.

Beckett, K. 1997. *Making crime pay.* New York: Oxford University Press.

Beckman, K. 2004. Dead woman glowing: Karla Faye Tucker and the aesthetics of death row photography. *Camera Obscura* 19: 1–41.

Benetton. 2000. *We, on death row.* Advertising campaign. February.

Benjamin, W. 1955/1986. Paris, capital of the 19th century. *Reflections: Essays, aphorisms, autobiographical writings.* Trans. E. Jephcott, 146–62. New York: Schocken Books.

Bennett, T. 1992. Useful culture. *Cultural Studies* 6: 395–408.

Bennett, W. L., and M. Edelman. 1985. Homo narrans: Toward a new political narrative. *Journal of Communication* 35: 156–71.

Berger, J. 1972. *Ways of seeing.* TV miniseries. London: BBC.

Berlant, L. 1997. *The queen of America goes to Washington City: Essays on sex and citizenship.* Durham: Duke University Press.

———. 2000. The subject of true feeling: Pain, privacy and politics. *Cultural Studies and Political Theory,* ed. J. Dean, 42–62. Ithaca: Cornell University Press.

———. 2008. *The female complaint: The unfinished business of sentimentality in American culture.* Durham: Duke University Press.

Blee, K. 1997. Mothers in race-hate movements. *The politics of motherhood: Activist voice from left to right,* ed. A. Jetter, A. Orleck, and D. Taylor, 247–56. Hanover: University Press of New England.

Blumenfield, et al., producers. 2002. Music Behind Bars. Television program.

Boles, A., and J. Patterson. 1997. Improving community response to crime victims: An eight-step model for developing protocol. Thousand Oaks, Calif.: Sage.

Boltanski, L. 1999. *Distant suffering: Morality, media and politics.* Cambridge: Cambridge University Press.

Booth v. Maryland, 482 U.S. 496 (1987).

Bourdieu, P. 1977. *Outline of a theory of practice.* Trans. R. Nice. Cambridge: Cambridge University Press.

———. 1979. Public opinion does not exist. *Communication and class struggle: 1. Capitalism, imperialism,* ed. A. Mattelart and S. Siegelaub, 124–30. New York: International General.

———. 1990. *The logic of practice.* Trans. R. Nice. Cambridge: Polity.

———. 1999. Understanding. *The weight of the world: Social suffering in contemporary society,* P. Bourdieu et al., 607–26. Stanford: Stanford University Press.

Braidotti, R. 2007. Bio-power and necro-politics: Reflections on an ethics of sustainability. Electronic publication. Originally published in German as 'Biomacht und nekro-Politik. Uberlegungen zu einer Ethik der Nachhaltigkeit,' in *Springerin, Hefte fur Gegenwartskunst,* Band XIII Heft 2, Fruhjahr 2007, 18–23.

Broken lives, broken dreams. 2001/2. *Rolling Stone.* 27 December–3 January, 885–86.

Brown, R. M. 1991. *No duty to retreat: Violence and values in American history and society.* New York: Oxford University Press.

Brown, W. 1995. *States of injury: Power and freedom in late modernity.* Princeton: Princeton University Press.

Brush, L. D. 1996. Love, toil, and trouble: Motherhood and feminist politics. *Signs* 21: 429–54.

Buckland, M. K. 1997. What is a document? *Journal of the American Society for Information Science* 48: 804–9.

Bumiller, K. 1988. *The civil rights society: The social construction of victims.* Baltimore: Johns Hopkins University Press.

———. *In an abusive state: How neoliberalism appropriated the feminist movement against sexual violence.* Durham: Duke University Press.

Butler, J. 2003. Violence, mourning, politics. *Studies in Gender and Sexuality* 4: 9–37.

———. 2004. *Precarious life: The powers of mourning and violence.* London: Verso.

Campbell, N. 2000. *Using women: Gender, drug policy and social justice.* New York: Routledge.

Cane, M. n.d. Covering trauma: UW curriculum offers important training for students. Seattle: University of Washington, Dart Center for Journalism and Trauma. Website: www.dartcenter.org.

Carey, J. 1988. *Communication as culture: Essays on media and society.* Boston: Unwin Hyman.

Carrington, F. 1970. Speaking for the police. *Journal of Criminal Law, Criminology, and Police Science* 61: 244–79.

———. 1975. *The victims.* New Rochelle, N.Y.: Arlington House.

———. 1978. *Neither cruel nor unusual: The case for capital punishment.* New Rochelle, N.Y.: Arlington House.

———. 1983. *Crime and justice: A conservative strategy.* Washington: Heritage Foundation.

Carrington, F., and G. Nicholson. 1984. The victims' movement. *Pepperdine Law Review* 11: 1–13.

Carter, R., and A. L. Smith. 1969. The death penalty in California: A statistical and composite portrait. *Crime Delinquency* 15: 62–76.

Carter, S., and B. Bucqueroux. n.d. *Interviewing victims, tips and techniques.* Lansing: Michigan State University Victims in the Media Program. website: victims.jrn.msu.edu.

Caruth, C. 1996. *Unclaimed experience: Trauma, narrative, history.* Baltimore: Johns Hopkins University Press.

———, ed. 1995. *Trauma: Explorations in memory.* Baltimore: John Hopkins University Press.

Catherine Genovese memorial conference: Law, social science, public policy. 1984. 10–12 March, Fordham University, New York.

Center for Community Change. 1998. How to tell and sell your story: A guide to developing effective messages and good stories about your work. *Community Change,* vol. 20 (spring). Special issue. Washington.

———. 1999. How to tell and sell your story: A guide to media for community groups and other nonprofits. *Community Change,* vol. 18. Special issue, 2nd ed. Washington.

Chancer, L. 1998. Playing gender against race through high-profile crime cases: The Tyson/Thomas/Simpson pattern of the 1990s. *Violence Against Women* 4: 100–113.

Chen, H. 10 January 2000. Death row fashion ads spark outrage. *APBnews.com.*

―――. 16 February 2000. Victims' parents blast Benetton death row ads. *APBnews .com*.

Chermak, S. 1995. *Victims in the news: Crime and the American news media*. Boulder: Westview Press.

Chibnall, S. 1977. *Law and order news: Crime reporting in the British press*. London: Tavistock.

Chimel v. California, 395 U.S. 752 (1969).

Christie, N. 1981. Conflict as property. *Perspectives on crime victims*, ed. B. Galway and J. Hudson, 234–44. London: C. V. Mosby.

Chun, W. 1999. Unbearable witness: Toward a politics of listening. *differences* 11: 112–49.

Clark, M. 2000. Benetton on death row. *New Statesman*. 24 January, 129: 43–45.

Clayman, S., and J. Hermitage. 2002. *The news interview: Journalists and public figures on the air*. Cambridge: Cambridge University Press.

Clifford, J. 9 March 1996. Stark ads urge action against abuse. *San Diego Union-Tribune*, E1.

Cloud, D. 1998. *Control and consolation in American culture and politics: Rhetoric of therapy*. Thousand Oaks, Calif.: Sage.

Coe, T. n.d. Memo to the field. Mothers Against Drunk Driving National Office.

Cohen, S. 2002. *Folk devils and moral panics: The creation of the mods and rockers*. 3rd ed. London: Routledge.

Cole, A. 2003. Trading places: From black power activist to 'anti-Negro Negro.' *American Studies* 44(3): 37–76.

―――. 2006. *The cult of true victimhood: From the war on welfare to the war on terror*. Stanford: Stanford University Press.

Comaroff, J., and J. Comaroff. 2006. Figuring crime: Quantifacts and the production of the un/real. *Public Culture* 18: 209–46.

Connolly, W. 1995. *The ethos of pluralization*. Minneapolis: University of Minnesota Press.

Corner, J. 2000. 'Influence': The contested core of media research. *Mass media and society*, ed. J. Curran and M. Gurevitch, 376–97. London: Arnold.

Coté, W., and B. Bucqueroux. 1996. *Covering crime without re-victimizing the victim*. Paper presented at Newspapers and Community Building Symposium, National Newspaper Association's Annual Convention, Opryland Hotel, Nashville, 25 September. Available on Michigan State University's Victims in the Media website: victims.jrn.msu.edu.

Coté, W., B. Bucqueroux, and R. Simpson. 2000. *Covering violence: A guide to ethical reporting about victims and trauma*. New York: Columbia University Press.

Couldry, N. 2000. *The place of media power: Pilgrims and witnesses of the media age*. London: Routledge.

Crime victims' rights. 1994. *CQ Researcher* (4 July) 22: 625–48.

Crowder, C. 27 April 1999. Your courage and commitment to Christ have gained you a special place in heaven. *Rocky Mountain News*.

Cushing, R. R., and S. Sheffer. 2002. *Dignity denied: The experience of murder victims' family members who oppose the death penalty.* Cambridge, Mass.: Murder Victims' Families for Reconciliation.

Cvetkovich, A. 2003. *An archive of feelings: Trauma, sexuality, and lesbian public cultures.* Durham: Duke University Press.

Dart Center for Journalism and Trauma. 2001. Journalism and trauma. Self-study training module. Website: www.dartcenter.org/content/self-study-unit-1-journalism-trauma.

————. 2002. The Languages of Emotional Injury. Conference, 23–26 April. Seattle.

————. 2003. *The languages of emotional injury.* DVD.

Das, V. 2002. Violence and translation. *Anthropological Quarterly* 75: 105–12.

Davis, C. 2001. A killer campaign. *Columbia Journalism Review* (January/February) 39: 9.

Davis, J. 2005. *Accounts of innocence: Sexual abuse, trauma and the self.* Chicago: University of Chicago Press.

Davis, M. 1990. *City of quartz: Excavating the future in Los Angeles.* New York: Verso.

DeCastillo, R., and C. McNeil, 1999. Constituents speak: Preparing to tell your story to the media. *New England Non-Profit Quarterly* 6(1): 36–37.

De La Roche, L. 2000. Columbine: Images of tragedy. Slideshow. *Rocky Mountain News.*

Deleuze, G., and F. Guattari. 1994. *What is philosophy?* New York: Columbia University Press.

Derrida, J. 1978. *Writing and difference.* Trans. A. Bass. Chicago: University of Chicago Press.

Donovan, Brian. 13 September 2001. The lost. *Newsday,* W14.

Dorfman, L., and V. Schiraldi. 2001. *Off balance: Youth, race and crime in the news.* Washington: Building Blocks for Youth.

Dorfman, L., E. Thorman, and J. E. Stevens. 2001. Reporting on violence: Bringing a public health perspective into the newsroom. *Health Education and Behavior* 28: 402–19.

Douglass, A., and T. Vogler, eds. 2003. Introduction to *Witness and memory: The discourse of trauma,* 1–53. New York: Routledge.

Dubber, M. D. 2002. *Victims in the war on crime: The use and abuse of victims' rights.* New York: New York University Press.

Edmunds, C., K. McLaughlin, M. Young, and J. Stein. 1985. *Campaign for victims' rights practical guide: 1985.* Washington: National Organization for Victim Assistance.

Edwards, P. 1996. *The closed world: Computers and the politics of discourse in cold war America.* Cambridge: MIT Press.

Ehrenreich, B. 2000. Dirty laundry. *Aperture* 160: 20–25.

Ehrenreich, B., and D. English. 1973. *Complaints and disorders: The sexual politics of sickness.* New York: CUNY Feminist Press.

Elias, R. 1983. The symbolic politics of victim compensation. *Victimology: An International Journal* 8: 213–24.

———. 1990. Which victim movement? *Victims of crime: Problems, policies and programs*, ed. A. J. Lurigio, W. G. Skogan, and R. C. Davis, 226–50. Newbury Park, Calif.: Sage.

Eliasoph, N. 1998. *Avoiding politics: How Americans produce apathy in everyday life.* Cambridge: Cambridge University Press.

Ellis, C. A., K. Ho, and A. Seymour. 2006. The impact of the death penalty on crime victims and those who serve them. *Wounds that do not bind: Victim-based perspectives on the death penalty*, ed. J. R. Acker and D. R. Karp, 431–44. Durham: Carolina Academic Press.

Enloe, C. 2000. *Maneuvers: The international politics of militarizing women's lives.* Berkeley: University of California Press.

Escobedo v. Illinois, 378 U.S. 478 (1964).

Faludi, S. 2007. *The terror dream: Fear and fantasy in post-9/11 America.* New York: Metropolitan Books.

Family Violence Prevention Fund. 1998. It's your business. Publicity campaign, dist. American Urban Radio Network.

———. n.d. *The backlash book: A media and political guide for battered women's advocates.* San Francisco.

Fattah, E. 1986. On some visible and hidden dangers of victim movements. *From crime policy to victim policy*, ed. E. Fattah, 1–16. New York: St. Martin's Press.

Feinstein, A. 2004. The psychological hazards of war journalism. *Nieman Reports* 58: 75–76.

Felman, S., and D. Laub. 1992. *Testimony: Crises of witnessing in literature, psychoanalysis and history.* New York: Routledge.

Fine, M., and L. Weis 1998. *The unknown city: Lives of poor and working class adults.* Boston: Beacon Press.

Finkelhor, D. 1988. The trauma of child sexual abuse: Two models. *Lasting effects of child sexual abuse*, ed. G. E. Wyatt and G. J. Powell, 61–82. Newbury Park, Calif.: Sage.

Fishman, M. 1978. Crime waves as ideology. *Social Problems* 25: 531–43.

Fitzpatrick, T. 1991. The figure of captivity: The cultural work of the Puritan captivity narrative. *American Literary History* 3: 1–26.

Foucault, M. 1967/1998. On the ways of writing history. *Michel Foucault: Aesthetics, method, and epistemology*, ed. J. Faubion, 279–96. New York: New Press.

———. 1972. *The archaeology of knowledge.* New York: Pantheon.

———. 1977. What is an author? *Language, counter-memory, practice*, ed. D. Bouchard. Trans. D. Bouchard and S. Simon, 113–38. Ithaca: Cornell University Press.

———. 1978/1990. *The history of sexuality volume one: An introduction.* Trans. R. Hurley. New York: Vintage.

————. 1988. The dangerous individual. *Politics, philosophy, culture: Interviews and other writing, 1977–1984*, ed. L. Kritzman, 125–51. New York: Routledge.

————. 1990. Questions of method. *The Foucault effect: Studies in governmentality*, ed. G. Burchell, C. Gordon, and P. Miller, 87–104. Chicago: University of Chicago Press.

Fraser, N. 1992. Rethinking the public sphere: A contribution to the critique of actually existing democracy. *Habermas and the public sphere*, ed. C. Calhoun, 109–42. Cambridge: MIT Press.

Freedom Forum. 2001. *Risking more than their lives: The effects of post-traumatic stress disorder on journalists*. Washington.

Fried, J. 14 November 1995. Killer of Kitty Genovese is denied a new trial. *New York Times*, B4.

Frosh, P. 2006. Telling presences: Witnessing, mass media, and the imagined lives of strangers. *Critical Studies in Media Communication* 23: 265–84.

Frosh, P., and A. Pinchevski, eds. 2008. Introduction: Why media witnessing? Why now? *Media witnessing: Testimony in the age of mass communication*, 1–22. New York: Palgrave Macmillan.

Fukuyama, F. 1992. *The end of history and the last man*. New York: Free Press.

Furedi, F. 1997. *Culture of fear: Risk-taking and the morality of low expectation*. London: Cassell.

Furman v. Georgia, 408 U.S. 238 (1972).

Gal, S. 2003. Movements of feminism: The circulation of discourses about women. *Recognition struggles and social movements: Contested identities, agency, and power*, ed. B. Hobson, 93–118. Cambridge: Cambridge University Press.

Gallagher, L. 2001. About face. *Forbes*, 19 March, 178–80.

Galton, F. 1879. Composite portraits, made by combining those of many different persons into a single resultant figure. *Journal of the Anthropological Institute of Great Britain and Ireland* 8: 132–44.

Gans, H. 1979. *Deciding what's news: A study of CBS Evening News, NBC Nightly News, Newsweek, and Time*. New York: Vintage.

Gansberg, M. 27 March 1964. 37 who saw murder didn't call the police. *New York Times*, 1, 38.

Gaonkar, D., and E. Povinelli. 2003. Technologies of public forms: Circulation, transfigurations, recognition. *Public Culture* 15: 385–97.

Garland, D. 2001. *The culture of control: Crime and social order in contemporary society*. Chicago: University of Chicago Press.

Gates, K. 2005a. Biometrics and post-9/11 technostalgia. *Social Text* 23: 35–53.

————. 2005b. Technologies of identity and the identity of technology: Race and the social construction of biometrics. *Race, identity, and representation in education*, ed. C. McCarthy et al., 59–71. 2nd ed. New York: Routledge.

Geis, G. 1990. Crime victims: Practices and prospects. *Victims of crime: Problems, policies and programs*, ed. A. Lurigio, W. Skogan, and R. Davis, 251–68. London: Sage.

Gert, H. 1995. Family resemblances and criteria. *Synthese* 105: 177–90.

———. 1999. The death penalty and victims' rights: Legal advance directives. *Journal of Value Inquiry* 33: 457–73.

Gever, M. 2005. The spectacle of crime digitized. *European Journal of Cultural Studies* 8: 445–63.

Gibson, M. 2001. Death scenes: Ethics of the face and cinematic deaths. *Mortality* 6: 306–20.

Gideon v. Wainwright, 372 U.S. 335 (1963).

Gilmore, R. 1998/1999. Globalisation and U.S. prison growth: From military Keynesianism to post-Keynesianism militarism. *Race and Class* 40: 171–88.

Ginzburg, C. 2004. Family resemblances and family trees: Two cognitive metaphors. *Critical Inquiry* 30: 537–56.

Gitlin, T. 2001. *Media unlimited: How the torrent of images and sounds overwhelms our lives*. New York: Metropolitan Books.

Glaser, D. 1970/1974. Victim survey research: Theoretical implications. *Victimology*, ed. I. Drapkin and E. Viano, 31–41. Lexington, Mass.: Lexington Books.

Glassner, B. 1999. *The culture of fear: Why Americans are afraid of the wrong things*. New York: Basic Books.

Goldenberg, E. 1975. *Making the papers: The access of resource-poor groups to the metropolitan press*. Lexington, Mass.: Lexington Books.

Gordon, A. 2008. *Ghostly matters: Haunting and the sociological imagination*. Minneapolis: University of Minnesota Press.

Green, D. 1985. Veins of resemblance: Photography and eugenics. *Oxford Art Journal* 7: 3–16.

Greenlee, S. 2001. Look for the ways people respond to events. *Crisis journalism: A handbook for media response*, ed. C. Hazlett, 40. Reston, Va.: American Press Institute.

Grossberg, L. 1992. *We gotta get out of this place: Popular conservatism and postmodern culture*. New York: Routledge.

Grosz, E. 1995. *Space, time and perversion: Essays on the politics of bodies*. New York: Routledge.

Guillory, J. 2004. The memo and modernity. *Critical Inquiry* 31: 108–32.

Gumbrecht, H. U. 1994. A farewell to interpretation. *Materialities of communication*, ed. H. U. Gumbrecht and K. L. Pfeiffer. Trans. W. Whobrey, 389–402. Stanford: Stanford University Press.

Gumbrecht, H. U., and K. L. Pfeiffer, eds. 1994. *Materialities of communication*. Trans. W. Whobrey. Stanford: Stanford University Press.

Gunning, T. 1997. In your face: Physiognomy, photography, and the Gnostic mission of early film. *Modernism/modernity* 4: 1–29.

Gutierrez, G. 8 October 2000. Ventura County perspective: For too many women, home is a place of assault and pain. . . . *Los Angeles Times*, B19.

Gwin, P. 2000. United Colors of the condemned. *Europe* (November): 12.

Habermas, J. 1964/1974. The public sphere: An encyclopedia article. *New German Critique* 1: 49–55.

———. 1989. *The structural transformation of the public sphere: An inquiry into a category of bourgeois society.* Trans. T. Burger. Cambridge: Polity.

Hacking, I. 1986/1999. Making up people. *The Science Studies Reader*, ed. M. Biagioli, 161–71. London: Routledge.

———. 1996. Memory sciences, memory politics. *Tense past: Cultural essays in trauma and memory*, ed. P. Antze and M. Lambek, 67–88. London: Routledge.

———. 2002. *Historical ontology.* Cambridge: Harvard University Press.

Halberstam, J. 1993. Imagined violence/queer violence: Representation, rage and resistance. *Social Text* 37: 187–201.

Hall, S. 1984. The narrative construction of reality: An interview with Stuart Hall. *Southern Review* 17: 3–17.

———, et al. 1978. *Policing the crisis: The state, mugging, and law and order.* London: Macmillan.

Hartley, J. 1992. *Tele-ology: Studies in television.* London: Routledge.

Hazlett, C. 2001. *Crisis journalism: A handbook for media response.* Reston, Va.: American Press Institute.

Henderson, L. 1985. The wrongs of victims' rights. *Stanford Law Review* 37: 937–1021.

Herbst, S. 1993. *Numbered voices: How opinion polling has shaped American politics.* Chicago: University of Chicago Press.

———. 1994. *Politics at the margin: Historical studies of public expression outside the mainstream.* New York: Cambridge University Press.

———. 1996. Public expression outside the mainstream. *Annals of the American Academy of Political Science and Sociology* 546: 120–31.

———. 2001. Public opinion infrastructures: Meanings, measures, media. *Political Communication* 18: 451–64.

Herman, E., and N. Chomsky. 1988. *Manufacturing consent: The political economy of the mass media.* New York: Pantheon.

Herman, J. 1992. *Trauma and recovery.* New York: Basic Books.

———. 1994. Presuming to know the truth. *Nieman Reports* 48: 43–44.

Hesford, W. 1999. Reading rape stories: Material rhetoric and the trauma of representation. *College English* 62: 192–221.

———. 2004. Documenting violations: Rhetorical witnessing and the spectacle of distant suffering. *Biography* 27: 104–44.

Hight, J., and F. Smyth. 2004. *Tragedies and journalists: A guide for more effective coverage.* Seattle: University of Washington, Dart Center for Journalism and Trauma.

Hirsch, M. 1997. Feminism at the maternal divide. *The politics of motherhood: Activist voice from left to right*, ed. A. Jetter, A. Orleck, and D. Taylor, 352–68. Hanover: University Press of New England.

———, ed. 1999. Introduction: Familial looking. *The familial gaze*, xi–xxv. Hanover: University of New England Press.

Hirsch, S. 2000. Victims for the prosecution: A survivor of the Embassy bombings on the limits of impact testimony. *Boston Review* (October/November), 21–25.

Hochschild, J. L. 1989. Review: The politics of victimization makes strange bedfellows. *Michigan Law Review* 87: 1584–98.

Holstein, J., and G. Miller. 1990. Rethinking victimization: An interactional approach to victimology. *Symbolic Interaction* 13: 103–22.

Honig, B. 1998. Immigrant America? How foreignness 'solves' democracy's problems. *Social Text* 56: 1–27.

Iyengar, S. 1991. *Is anyone responsible? How television frames political issues.* Chicago: University of Chicago Press.

Iyengar, S., and D. Kinder. 1987. *News that matters: Television and American opinion.* Chicago: University of Chicago Press.

Jay, M. 1993. *Downcast eyes: The denigration of vision in twentieth-century thought.* Berkeley: University of California Press.

Jeffords, S. 1989. *The remasculinization of America: Gender and the Vietnam War.* Bloomington: Indiana University Press.

———. 1991. Rape and the new world order. *Cultural Critique* 19: 203–15.

Jenkins, P. 1998. *Moral panic: Changing concepts of the child molester in modern America.* New Haven: Yale University Press.

Jermyn, D. 2003. Photo stories and family albums: Imagining criminals and victims on *Crimewatch UK*. *Criminal visions: Media representations of crime and violence,* ed. P. Mason, 175–91. Cullompton: Willan.

———. 2004. 'This *is* about real people': Video technologies, actuality and affect in the television crime appeal. *Understanding Reality Television,* ed. S. Holmes, and D. Jermyn, 71–90. London: Routledge.

Johnson, M. 2007. *The dead beat: Lost souls, lucky stiffs, and the perverse pleasures of obituaries.* New York: Harper Perennial.

Justice for All. Website: www.jfa.net/index.html.

Justice Solutions. 2002. An oral history of the Crime Victim Assistance Fund: Task Force roundtable interview transcript. University of Akron. Website: vroh.uakron.edu.

Kaminer, W. 1995. *It's all the rage: Crime and culture.* Reading, Mass.: Addison-Wesley.

Kaplan, E. A. 2005. *Trauma culture: The politics of terror and loss in media and literature.* New Brunswick: Rutgers University Press.

Karmen, A. 1984. *Crime victims: An introduction to victimology.* Pacific Grove, Calif.: Brooks/Cole.

Katz, J. 1987. What makes crime 'news'? *Media, Culture and Society* 9: 47–75.

Kelley, C. M. 1975. What about the victims of crime? *U.S. News and World Report,* 24 February, 43.

Kelly, D. 1983/1984. Victims' perceptions of criminal justice. *Pepperdine Law Review* 11: 15–22.

Kelly, L. 1988. *Surviving sexual violence.* Minneapolis: University of Minnesota Press.

Kennedy, L., and V. Sacco. 1998. *Crime victims in context*. Los Angeles: Roxbury.

Kennedy, R. 1994. The state, criminal law, and racial discrimination: A comment. *Harvard Law Review* 107: 1255–78.

King, R. 2003. *Don't kill in our name: Families of murder victims speak out against the death penalty*. New Brunswick: Rutgers University Press.

———. 2005. *Capital consequences: Families of the condemned tell their stories*. New Brunswick: Rutgers University Press.

King, R., and B. Hood. 2003. *Not in our names: Murder victims' families speak out against the death penalty*. Cambridge, Mass.: Murder Victims' Families for Reconciliation.

King, S. 2006. *Pink ribbons, inc.: Breast cancer and the politics of philanthropy*. Minneapolis: University of Minnesota Press.

Kintz, L. 1997. *Between Jesus and the market: The emotions that matter in right-wing America*. Durham: Duke University Press.

Klaver, E., ed. 2004. *Images of the corpse: From the Renaissance to cyberspace*. Madison: University of Wisconsin Press.

Klein, E., et al., 1997. *Ending domestic violence: Changing public perceptions/halting the epidemic*. Thousand Oaks, Calif.: Sage.

Kolodny, A. 1981. Turning the lens on 'The Panther Captivity': A feminist exercise in practical criticism. *Critical Inquiry* 8: 329–45.

Koonz, C. 1997. Motherhood and politics on the far right. *The politics of motherhood: Activist voice from left to right*, ed. A. Jetter, A. Orleck, and D. Taylor, 229–46. Hanover: University Press of New England.

Kozol, W. 1995. Fracturing domesticity: Media, nationalism, and the question of feminist influence. *Signs* 20: 646–67.

LaCapra, Dominick. 2001. *Writing history, writing trauma*. Baltimore: Johns Hopkins University Press.

Lamb, S. 1999. Constructing the victim: Popular images and lasting labels. *New versions of victims: Feminists struggle with the concept*, ed. S. Lamb, 108–38. New York: New York University Press.

Langer, J. 1998. *Tabloid television: Popular journalism and the 'other news.'* London: Routledge.

Larner, W. 2000. Post-welfare state governance: Towards a code of social and family responsibility. *Social Politics* (Summer): 244–65.

Lee, M. 2007. *Inventing fear of crime: Criminology and the politics of anxiety*. Cullompton: Willan.

Lee, R. E. April 24 1995. 'That was Dad's dream, to retire and raise cattle.' *Oklahoman*, A12.

Levin, E. 1995. The victim: Twice wounded. *The culture of crime*, ed. C. L. LaMay, and E. E. Dennis, 49–54. New Brunswisk: Transaction.

Levinas, E., and R. Kearney. 1986. Dialogue with Emmanuel Levinas. *Face to face with Levinas*, ed. R. A. Cohen, 56–62. Albany: State University of New York Press.

Lewis, D., and G. Salem. 1986. *Fear of crime*. New Brunswick, N.J.: Transaction.

Leys, R. 2000. *Trauma: A genealogy*. Chicago: University of Chicago Press.

Lippman, W. 1927. *Public opinion*. New York: Macmillan.

Livingstone, S., and P. Lunt. 1994. *Talk on television: Audience participation and public debate*. London: Routledge.

Lloyd, J. 2001. Come on: Look at me! *New Statesman* 130: 13–15.

Lull, J., and S. Hinerman, ed. 1997. *Media scandals*. New York: Columbia University Press.

Lyon, J. 1992. Militant discourse, strange bedfellows: Suffragettes and vorticists before the war. *differences* 4: 100–133.

———. 1999. *Manifestoes: Provocations of the modern*. Ithaca: Cornell University Press.

Macek, S. 2006. *Urban nightmares: The media, the right, and the moral panic over the city*. Minneapolis: University of Minnesota Press.

Madigan, L., and N. C. Gamble. 1989. *The second rape: Society's continued betrayal of the victim*. New York: Lexington Books.

Madriz, E. 1997. *Nothing bad happens to good girls: Fear of crime in women's lives*. Berkeley: University of California Press.

Mandel, E. 1986. *Delightful murder: A social history of the crime story*. Minneapolis: University of Minnesota Press.

Manning, P. 1998. Media loops. *Popular culture, crime and justice*, ed. F. Y. Bailey and D. Hale, 25–39. Belmont, Calif.: Wadsworth Publishing.

Mapp v. Ohio, 367 U.S. 643 (1961).

Marshall, M., and A. Oleson. 1996. MADDer than hell. *Qualitative Health Research* (February): 6–23.

Marx, K. 1963. *The 18th Brumaire of Louis Bonaparte*. New York: International.

Massachusetts Office for Victim Assistance. 2001. High-profile cases and their impact on victims and survivors. Panel discussion from Massachusetts Victim Rights Conference. Boston, April 17.

Matthews, N. 1994. *Confronting rape: The feminist anti-rape movement and the state*. London: Routledge.

McCarthy, A. 2006. From the ordinary to the concrete: Cultural studies and the politics of scale. *Questions of method in cultural studies*, ed. M. White and J. Schwoch, 21–53. Malden, Mass.: Blackwell.

McManus, J., and L. Dorfman. 2000. Youth and violence in California newspapers. *Berkeley Media Studies Group*, Issue 9 (April).

Meadow, J. 26 April 1999. Teens 'radiant, forever young.' *Rocky Mountain News*.

Mendolsohn, B. 1974. The origin and doctrine of victimology. In *Victimology*, ed. I. Drapkin and E. Viano, 3–12. Lexington, Mass.: Lexington Books.

Miller, N. 2003. 'Portraits of Grief': Telling details and the testimony of trauma. *differences* 14: 112–35.

Mills, C. W. 1959. *The sociological imagination*. Chicago: University of Chicago Press.

Miranda v. Arizona, 384 U.S. 436 (1966).

Moeller, S. 1999. *Compassion fatigue: How the media sell disease, famine, war and death.* New York: Routledge.

Moore, E. 16 October 2001. Devoted to the value of life. *Newsday*, A49.

Moorti, S. 1998. Cathartic confessions: Framing a popular discourse of race on Oprah Winfrey. *Social Text* 57 (winter): 89–126.

Moritz, M. 2001. *Covering Columbine.* Documentary film.

MurderVictims.com. Website: www.murdervictims.com.

National Center for Victims of Crime. 1991. America speaks out: Citizens' attitudes about victims' rights and violence—executive summary. Fort Worth.

———. 1992. Rape in America: A Report to the Nation. Arlington, Va.

———. 1993. Crime and victimization in America: Statistical overview. Arlington, Va.

———. 1998a. The national center for victims of crime does not support SJR3. Arlington, Va.

———. 1998b. Strategies for action: National crime victims' rights week. Arlington, Va.

———. 2000. *Privacy and dignity: Crime victims and the media.* Arlington, Va.

———. 2002. Bringing honor to victims. Arlington, Va.

———. 2007. Invitation to Leadership awards reception. Honoree Montel Williams.

———. n.d. Talk show guidelines. Arlington, Va.

National Clearinghouse for the Defense of Battered Women. 1997. Position paper on proposed victims' rights amendment. Philadelphia.

National Network to End Domestic Violence. 1997. Position statement on proposed victims' rights constitutional amendment. Washington.

National Organization for Victim Assistance. 1983. *Campaign for victim rights.* Washington.

Newman, E., and C. Bull. 2002. *Covering terrorism.* Seattle: University of Washington, Dart Center for Journalism and Trauma. Website: http://www.dartcenter.org.

Newman, E., and B. Monseu. n.d. *Understanding journalists' experience of September 11, 2001: The need for a research agenda.* Seattle: University of Washington, Dart Center for Journalism and Trauma (unpublished manuscript).

Newsday. 8 October 2001. Richard Y. C. Lee: Renaissance man never forgot about people, A22.

———. 21 October 2001. Places of grief, A13.

———. 4 November 2001. Jennifer Smith: Loving woman, a savior of cats, A38.

———. 2 December 2001. Pamela J. Boyce: She lived life to its fullest, with no regrets, W16.

———. 31 December 2001. 9/11/01: The lost, B8–9, B26–30.

———. 2002. *American lives: The stories of the men and women lost on September 11.* Philadelphia: Camino Books.

New York Times. *Portraits 9/11/01: The collected 'Portraits of Grief' from the* New York Times. 2002. New York: Times Books.

Nietzsche, F. 1990. *On the genealogy of morals*, ed. W. Kaufmann. New York: Vintage.

Noys, B. 2007. *The culture of death.* Oxford: Berg.

Ochberg, F. 1996. A primer on covering victims. *Nieman Reports* 50: 21–26.

O'Driscoll, P. 2000. Trauma 'never ends' for Columbine: On April 20, high school and community will mark the 1-year anniversary of the worst school shooting in USA. *USA Today*, 20 March, 3A.

Offen, E., J. Stein, and M. Young. 1996. *The victim advocate's guide to the media.* National Organization for Victim Assistance: Washington.

Oklahoman. 25 April 1995. Those who died: Zackary Chavez, A11.

———. 25 April 1995. Those who died: Ashley Megan Eckles, A11.

———. 25 April 1995. Those who died: Colton Wade Smith and Chase Dalton Smith, A11.

———. 26 April 1995. Those who died: Kayla Titsworth, A11.

———. 27 April 1995. Those who died: Aaron Coverdale and Elijha Coverdale, A15.

———. 28 April 1995. Bobby Ross, Jr. Child's ready smile, affection remembered, A21.

———. 29 April 1995. Those who died: Jaci Rae Coyne, A19.

———. 29 April 1995. Those who died: Dominque London, A19.

———. 2 May 1995. Those who died: Danielle Bell, A8.

———. 4 May 1995. Those who died: Blake Ryan Kennedy, A12.

———. 4 May 1995. Those who died: Lakesha R. Levy, A12.

———. 6 May 1995. Those who died: Tevin Garrett, A17.

———. 7 May 1995. A split second of destruction, A19.

———. 7 May 1995. Those who died: Tyler Eaves, A18.

———. 8 May 1995. Those who died: Peachlyn Bradley, A9.

———. 9 May 1995. Those who died: Gabreon DeShawn Lee Bruce, A5.

———. 9 May 1995. Those who died: Antonio Ansara Cooper Jr., A5.

———. 9 May 1995. Those who died: Kevin 'Lee' Gottshall II, A5.

O'Leary, N. 2000. Ad infinitum. *Print* (May/June): 42–44.

Orbach, S. 1999. *Toward emotional literacy.* London: Virago Press.

Parents of Murdered Children. Website: www.pomc.org.

Payne v. Tennessee, 501 U.S. 808 (1991).

Pearce, R. H. 1947. The significances of the captivity narrative. *American Literature* 19:1–20.

Peters, J. D. 1994. The gaps of which communication is made. *Critical Studies in Mass Communication* 11:117–40.

———. 2001. Witnessing. *Media, Culture and Society* 23: 707–23.

Potorti, D., ed. 2003. *September 11 Families for Peaceful Tomorrows: Turning our grief into action for peace.* New York: RDV Books.

President's Task Force on Victims of Crime. 1982. *Final Report.* Washington.

Priest, P. J. 1995. *Public intimacies: Talk show participants and tell-all TV*. Cresskill, N.J.: Hampton Press.

Pryse, M. 2000. Trans/feminist methodology: Bridge to interdisciplinary thinking. *NWSA Journal* 12: 105–18.

Quinney, R. 1972. Who is the victim? *Criminology* 10: 314–23.

Radelet, M. 2001. Humanizing the death penalty. *Social Problems* 48: 83–88.

Rapping, E. 1996. *The culture of recovery: Making sense of the self-help movement in women's lives*. Boston: Beacon Press.

———. 1999. Aliens, nomads, mad dogs and road warriors: Tabloid TV and the new face of criminal violence. *Mythologies of violence in postmodern media*, ed. C. Sharrett, 249–74. Detroit: Wayne State University Press.

———. 2003. *Law and justice as seen on TV*. New York: New York University Press.

Rasenberger, J. 8 February 2004. Kitty, 40 years later. *New York Times*, Section 14.

———. 2006. Nightmare on Austin Street: It was a story so disturbing that we all still remember it. But what if it wasn't true? *American Heritage* 57: 65–67.

Reiner, R. 2002. Media-made criminality. *The Oxford Handbook of Criminology*, ed. R. Reiner, M. Maguire, and R. Morgan, 376–416. Oxford: Oxford University Press.

———. 2007. *Law and order: An honest citizen's guide to crime and control*. Cambridge: Polity.

Rentschler, C. 2003. Expanding the definition of media activism. *Blackwell companion to media studies*, ed. A. Valdivia, 529–47. Malden, Mass.: Blackwell.

———. 2007. Risky assignments: Sexing "security" in hostile environment reporting. *Feminist Media Studies* 7: 257–79.

———. 2010. Trauma training and the reparative work of journalism. *Cultural Studies* 24(4): 447–77.

Reporting on Victims of Violence and Catastrophe. 1999. East Lansing: Michigan State University Victims in the Media Program.

Reporting on Victims of Violence and Catastrophe: Instructor's guide. 1999. East Lansing: Michigan State University Victims in the Media Program.

Rhode Island Coalition Against Domestic Violence. 1998. Stopping the perpetrators, serving the victims: Working together to stop domestic violence. Press release. Warwick, R.I., 24 March.

———. 1999. Domestic violence: It *is* your business. Public awareness campaign. Warwick, R.I.

———. 2000a. Annual communication plan—worksheet. Warwick, R.I., 7 January.

———. 2000b. Communication plan. Warwick, R.I., 7 January.

———. 2000c. Domestic violence: A handbook for journalists. Media guide. Warwick, R.I.

———. 2000d. Public relations/publications calendar for 2000. Warwick, R.I., 13 March.

Ricchiardi, S., and T. Gerczynski. 1999. Confronting the horror. *American Journalism Review* 21: 34–39.

Riggs, C., and D. Kilpatrick. 1990. Families and friends: Indirect victimization by crime. *Victims of crime*, ed. A. Lurigio, W. Skogan, and R. Davis, 120–38. Thousand Oaks, Calif.: Sage.

Riles, A. 1998. Infinity within the brackets. *American Ethnologist* 25: 378–98.

———. 2006. Introduction to *Documents: Artifacts of modern knowledge*, ed. A. Riles, 1–38. Ann Arbor: University of Michigan Press.

Roach, K. 1999. *Due process and victims' rights: The new law and politics of criminal justice.* Toronto: University of Toronto Press.

Robbins, B. 1993. Introduction: The public as phantom. *The phantom public sphere*, ed. B. Robbins, vii–xxvi. Minneapolis: University of Minnesota Press.

Robbins, J. 1991. Visage, figure: Reading Levinas's totality and infinity. *Yale French Studies* 79: 135–49.

Rock, P. 1988. On the birth of organizations. LSE *Quarterly* 2: 123–53.

———. 1990. *Helping victims of crime: The Home Office and the rise of victim support in England and Wales.* Oxford: Clarendon Press.

———. 1998. *After homicide: Practical and political responses to bereavement.* Oxford: Clarendon Press.

———. 2004. *Constructing victims' rights: The home office, new labour, and victims.* Oxford: Oxford University Press.

Rogers, P., and M. Eftimiades. 1995. Bearing witness. *People* 44: 42–43.

Rogin, M. 1987. *Ronald Reagan the movie and other episodes in political demonology.* Berkeley: University of California Press.

Roper, R. 1996. The justice system should consider the rights of victims. *America's victims: Opposing viewpoints*, ed. P. Winters, 154–57. San Diego: Greenhaven Press.

Rose, F. 1989. Celebrity victims: Crime casualties are turning into stars on tabloid TV. *New York* (July) 22: 38–44.

Rose, G. 1995. *Love's work: A reckoning with life.* New York: Schocken Books.

Rose, N. 2001. The politics of life itself. *Theory, Culture and Society* 18: 1–30.

Rosenthal, A. M. 1964. *Thirty-eight witnesses.* New York: McGraw-Hill.

Rubin, L. 1986. *Quiet rage: Bernie Goetz in a time of madness.* Berkeley: University of California Press.

Ruddick, S. 1997. Rethinking 'maternal' politics. *The politics of motherhood: Activist voice from left to right*, ed. A. Jetter, A. Orleck, and D. Taylor, 369–81. Hanover: University Press of New England.

Ryan, C. 1991. *Prime-time activism: Media strategies for grassroots organizing.* Boston: South End Press.

———. 1999. Why take media seriously? *New England Nonprofit Quarterly* (spring): 8–13.

Sapolsky, R. 1994. *Why zebras don't get ulcers.* New York: Holt.

Sarat, A. 1996. Narrative strategy and death penalty advocacy. *Harvard Civil Liberties–Civil Rights Review* 31: 353–81.

————. 1997. Vengeance, victims and the identities of law. *Social and Legal Studies* 6: 163–89.

————. 2001. *When the state kills: Capital punishment and the American condition.* Princeton: Princeton University Press.

Scannell, P. 2000. For-anyone-as-someone structures. *Media, Culture and Society* 22: 5–24.

Scarry, E. 2002. Citizenship in emergency. *Boston Review* (October/November).

Schafer, S. 1968/1974. The beginnings of 'victimology.' *Victimology*, ed. I. Drapkin and E. Viano, 17–30. Lexington, Mass.: Lexington Books.

Scheingold, S. 1984. *The politics of law and order: Street crime and public policy.* New York: Longman.

————. 1991. *The politics of street crime: Criminal process and cultural obsession.* Philadelphia: Temple University Press.

————. 1995. Politics, public policy, and street crime. *The Annals of the American Academy of Political and Social Sciences* 539: 155–68.

Scherer, M. 1996. For victims who go public. *Nieman Reports* 50: 36.

Schivelbusch, W. 1986. *The railway journey: The industrialization of time and space in the 19th century.* Berkeley: University of California Press.

Schlesinger, P., et al. 1992. *Women viewing violence.* London: BFI.

Schlosser, E. 1997. A grief like no other. *Atlantic Monthly* 280: 37–76.

Schudson, M. 1995. *The power of news.* Cambridge: Harvard University Press.

Schwanbeck, K. 2004. Dealing with trauma: Some journalists fell victim to stress after the Station nightclub fire. *News Photographer* 59: 34–37.

Scott, J. 2002. Introduction to *Portraits 9/11/01: The collected 'Portraits of Grief' from* The New York Times. New York: Times Books.

Scott, W. 1990. PTSD in DSM-III: A case in the politics of diagnosis and disease. *Social Problems* 37: 294–310.

Sedgwick, E. 2003. *Touching feeling: Affect, pedagogy, performativity.* Durham: Duke University Press.

Sekula, A. 1986. The body and the archive. *October* 39: 3–64.

Seltzer, M. 1998. *Serial killers: Death and life in America's wound culture.* New York: Routledge.

September 11 Families for Peaceful Tomorrows. 2002. *Afghan portraits of grief: The civilian/innocent victims of U.S. bombing in Afghanistan.* New York.

————. 2005. *Beyond retribution.* Film short.

————. 2007. Shaping the legacy of 9/11.

Seymour, A. 1990. *Crime victims and the media.* Arlington, Va.: National Center for Victims of Crime.

————. 1999a. Innovative technologies and the information age. In *National Victim Assistance Academy Manual.* Washington: National Victim Assistance Academy. Website: www.ojp.usdoj.gov/ovc. Accessed 24 April 2000.

————. 1999b. The news media's coverage of crime and victimization. In

National Victim Assistance Academy Manual. Washington: National Victim
      Assistance Academy. Website: www.ojp.usdoj.gov/ovc. Accessed 24 April 2000.

Shapiro, B. 1995a. One violent crime. *Nation,* 3 April.

———. 1995b. Unkindest cut. *New Statesmen and Society,* 14 April, 23–26.

———. 1997. Victims and vengeance: Why the victims' rights amendment is a bad
      idea. *Nation,* 10 February, 11–19.

Sharp, S. 2005. *Hidden victims: The effects of the death penalty on families of the accused.*
      New Brunswick: Rutgers University Press.

Shay, J. 1994. *Achilles in Vietnam.* New York: Atheneum.

Sheffer, S., and R. Cushing. 2006. *Creating more victims: How executions hurt the
      families left behind.* Cambridge, Mass.: Murder Victims' Families for Human
      Rights.

Shell. 17 February 1999. Predator: How to avoid being the prey. Print advertisement.
      New York Times, A13.

Sherer, M. n.d. *Training steps: A guide to teaching students about trauma.* Seattle:
      University of Washington, Dart Center for Journalism and Trauma.

Sherman, D. 2006. Naming and the violence of place. *Terror, culture, politics:
      Rethinking 9/11,* ed. D. Sherman, and T. Nardin, 121–45. Bloomington: Indiana
      University Press.

Showalter, E. 1985. *The female malady: Women, madness and English culture.* New
      York: Pantheon.

Simmel, G. 1959/2004. The aesthetic significance of the face. *The body: Critical
      concepts in sociology,* ed. A. Blaikie and the Aberdeen University Body Group, 5–9.
      London: Routledge.

Simpson, R. A., and J. G. Boggs. 1999. An exploratory study of traumatic stress
      among newspaper journalists. *Journalism and Communication Monographs* 1: 1–26.

Singhal, A., and E. Rogers. 1999. *Entertainment-education: A communication strategy
      for social change.* Mahwah, N.J.: Lawrence Erlbaum Associates.

Slotkin, R. 1973. *Regeneration through violence: The myth of the American frontier,
      1600–1860.* Middletown, Conn.: Wesleyan University Press.

Smith, B., and C. R. Huff. 1992. From victim to political activist: An empirical
      examination of a statewide victims' rights movement. *Journal of Criminal Justice*
      20: 201–15.

Smith, D. 1990. *Texts, facts and femininity: Exploring the relations of ruling.* London:
      Routledge.

Sobieski, R. 1993. MADD study finds: Most victims satisfied with law enforcement.
      MADDvocate 6: 30–31.

Sontag, S. 2003. *Regarding the pain of others.* New York: Farrar, Straus and Giroux.

Sound Portraits. 2004. Remembering Kitty Genovese. Broadcast on *Weekend Edition
      Saturday.* Prod. M. Ozug. Exec Prod. D. Isay. Original airdate 13 March.

South Carolina v. Gathers, 490 U.S. 805 (1989).

Spencer, C. 1987. Sexual assault: The second victimization. *Women, the courts, and
      equality,* ed. L. Crites and W. Hepperle, 54–73. Newbury Park, Calif.: Sage.

Spivak, G. C. 1988. Can the subaltern speak? *Marxism and the interpretation of culture*, ed. C. Nelson and L. Grossberg, 217–316. Champaign: University of Illinois Press.

Sproule, J. M. 1989. Progressive propaganda critics and the magic bullet myth. *Critical Studies in Mass Communication* 6: 225–46.

Spungen, D. 1983. *And I don't want to live this life*. New York: Villard Books.

———. 1998. *Homicide: The hidden victims*. Thousand Oaks, Calif.: Sage.

Stabile, C. 2006. *White victims, black villains: Gender, race, and crime news in U.S. culture*. New York: Routledge.

———. 2007. No shelter from the storm. *South Atlantic Quarterly* 106: 683–708.

Star-Ledger. 1 January 2002. New Jersey's terror victims, 30.

Steele, S. 1990. *The content of our character: A new vision of race in America*. New York: St. Martin's Press.

Stein, J. 2007. An oral history of the crime victim assistance field. Interview. University of Akron.

Stevens, J. 1997. *Reporting on violence: A handbook for journalists*. Berkeley: Berkeley Media Studies Group.

———. 1998. Integrating the public health perspective into reporting on violence. *Nieman Reports* 52: 38–40.

Stormer, N. 1997. Embodying normal miracles. *Quarterly Journal of Speech* 83: 172–91.

Strathern, M. 2006. Bullet-proofing: A tale from the United Kingdom. *Documents: Artifacts of modern knowledge*, ed. A. Riles, 181–205. Ann Arbor: University of Michigan Press.

Sturken, M. 1997. *Tangled memories: The Vietnam War, the AIDS epidemic, and the politics of remembering*. Berkeley: University of California Press.

———. 2007. *Tourists of History: Memory, kitsch, and consumerism from Oklahoma City to Ground Zero*. Durham: Duke University Press.

Sturma, M. 2002. Aliens and Indians: A comparison of abduction and captivity narratives. *Journal of Popular Culture* 36: 318–34.

Surette, R. 1994. Predator criminals as media icons. *Media, process, and the social construction of crime: Studies in newsmaking criminology*, ed. G. Barak, 131–58. New York: Garland.

Sykes, C. 1992. *A nation of victims: The decay of American character*. New York: St. Martin's Press.

Symonds, M. 1975. Victims of violence: Psychological effects and aftereffects. *American Journal of Psychoanalysis* 35: 19–26.

Tagg, J. 1988. *The burden of representation: Essays on photographies and histories*. Amherst: University of Massachusetts Press.

Tait, S. 2006. Autoptic vision and the necrophilic imaginary in CSI. *International Journal of Cultural Studies* 9(1): 45–62.

Taussig, M. 1998. Crossing the face. *Border fetishisms: Material objects in unstable spaces*, ed. P. Spyer, 224–44. New York: Routledge.

Terry v. Ohio, 392 U.S. 1 (1968).

Thomason, T. 1986. Compassion, concern mark symposium. *Crime Victims and the*

News Media, ed. T. Thomason and A. Babbili, 3. Fort Worth: Texas Christian University.

Thomason, T., and A. Babbili. 1986. *Crime victims and the news media*. Texas Christian University: Department of Journalism.

Toobin, J. 1994. Buying headlines. *Quill* 82: 20–24.

Treichler, P. 1999. *How to have theory in an epidemic: Cultural chronicles of AIDS*. Durham: Duke University Press.

Trenholm, S., and A. Jensen. 2000. *Interpersonal communication*. Belmont, Calif.: Wadsworth Publishing.

Tresniowski, A., et al. 2002. The miracle girl. *People* 59: 44–51.

Trimble, M. 1981. *Post-traumatic neurosis: From railway spine to whiplash*. Chichester: John Wiley.

Tumber, H., and M. Prentoulis. 2004. Journalists under fire: Subcultures, objectivity and emotional literacy. *War and the media*, ed. D. Thussu and D. Freedman, 215–30. Thousand Oaks, Calif.: Sage.

Tunnell, K. 1992. Film at eleven: Recent developments in the commodification of crime. *Sociological Spectrum* 12: 293–313.

Turner, F. 2001. *Echoes of combat: Trauma, memory and the Vietnam War*. Minneapolis: University of Minnesota Press.

Twitchell, J. 1989. *Preposterous violence: Fables of aggression in modern culture*. New York: Oxford University Press.

U.S. Department of Justice, Office for Victims of Crime. 1995. National Victim Assistance Academy training manual. Washington.

———. 1996/2000. Victim empowerment: Bridging the systems—mental health and victim service providers. Pennsylavania Coalition Against Rape, Harrisburg, and Office for Victims of Crime. Washington.

———. 1997. *Crime victims' rights in America: An historical overview*. National Crime Victims' Rights Week Resource Guide. Washington.

———. 1998a. From pain to power: Crime victims take action. Monograph. Washington.

———. 1998b. *New Directions from the Field: Victims' Rights and Services in the 21st Century*. Washington.

———. 1998c. Victims of Crime Act crime victims fund: Fact sheet. Washington.

———. 1999a. Criminal fine collection efforts benefit victims. Press release. 22 September. Washington.

———. 1999b. The news media coverage of crime and victimization. Videotape. Washington.

———. 2008a. *Justice for victims, justice for all*. National Crime Victims' Rights Week Resource Guide. Washington.

———. 2008b. National Crime Victims' Rights Week theme video. Transcript on website: ovc.ncjrs.gov/ncvrw2008/transcript_themevideo.html. Accessed 20 February.

Van Alphen, E. 1999. Nazism in the family album: Christian Boltanski's *Sans Souci*.

The familial gaze, ed. M. Hirsh, 32–50. Hanover, N.H.: University Press of New England.

Viano, E. 1987. Victims' rights and the Constitution: Reflections on a bicentennial. *Crime and Delinquency* 33: 438–51.

———. 1990. The recognition and implementation of victims' rights in the United States: Developments and achievements. *The victimology handbook: Research findings, treatment and public policy*, ed. E. Viano, 319–36. New York: Garland.

———. 1992. The news media and crime victims: The right to know versus the right to privacy. *Critical issues in victimology: International perspectives*, ed. E. Viano, 24–34. New York: Springer Publishing.

von Hentig, H. 1941. Remarks on the interaction of perpetrator and victim. *Journal of Criminal Law and Criminology* 31: 303–9.

———. 1948. *The criminal and his victim*. New Haven: Yale University Press.

Wacquant, L. 2005. Pointers on Pierre Bourdieu and democratic politics. *Pierre Bourdieu and democratic politics*, ed. L. Wacquant, 10–28. Cambridge: Polity.

Walklate, S. 2005. *Criminology: The basics*. New York: Routledge.

Walsh, J. 1997. *Tears of rage*. New York: Pocket Books.

———. 1998. *No mercy*. New York: Pocket Books.

———. 2002. *Public enemies*. New York: Pocket Books.

Warner, M. 2002. Publics and counterpublics. *Public Culture* 14: 49–90.

Warshaw, R. 1988. *I never called it rape: The Ms. report on recognizing, fighting and surviving date and acquaintance rape*. New York: Harper and Row.

Websdale, N., and A. Alvarez. 1998. Forensic journalism as patriarchal ideology: The newspaper construction of homicide-suicide. *Popular culture, crime and justice*, ed. F. Y. Bailey and D. C. Hale, 123–42. Belmont, Calif.: West/Wadsworth Publishing.

Weed, F. 1995. *Certainty of justice: Reform in the crime victim movement*. New York: Aldine de Gruyter.

Weis, L., and M. Fine. 1998. Crime stories: A critical look through race, ethnicity, and gender. *International Journal of Qualitative Studies in Education* 11: 435–59.

Weis, M. 1999. The production of a media campaign. A case study: Rhode Island Coalition Against Domestic Violence. *New England Nonprofit Quarterly* (spring): 30–35.

Werner, J. 2001. The detective gaze: Edgar A. Poe, the flâneur, and the physiognomy of crime. *American Transcendental Quarterly* 15: 1–31.

Whittier, N. 2009. *The politics of child sexual abuse: Emotion, social movements, and the state*. New York: Oxford University Press.

Williams, A. 1993. Domestic violence and the etiology of crime in *America's Most Wanted*. *Camera Obscura* 3: 96–109.

Williams, J. E., and K. A. Holmes. 1981. *The second assault: Rape and public attitudes*. Westport, Conn.: Greenwood Press.

Williams, L. 2001. Melodrama in black and white: Uncle Tom and The Green Mile. *Film Quarterly* 55: 14–21.

Williams, P. 1991. *The alchemy of race and rights*. Cambridge: Harvard University Press.

Wolf, N. 1993. *Fire with fire: The new female power and how it will change the 21st century*. New York: Random House.

Wood, J. 1999. Refined raw: On the symbolic violence of victims' rights. *College Literature* 26: 150–69.

———. 2003. Justice as therapy: The victim rights clarification act. *Communication Quarterly* 51: 296–311.

———. 2005. In whose name? Crime victim policy and the punishing power of protection. *NWSA Journal* 17: 1–17.

Woodall, J., ed. 1997. *Introduction to Portraiture: Facing the subject*. Manchester: Manchester University Press.

Wray, R. J. 2000. Alternative explanations: Examining exposure recall, selective perception, and response bias in the evaluation of a domestic violence prevention radio campaign. Ph.D. diss., University of Pennsylvania.

Young, A. 1995. *The harmony of illusions: Inventing post-traumatic stress disorder*. Princeton: Princeton University Press.

———. 1996. *Imagining crime: Textual outlaws and criminal conversations*. Thousand Oaks, Calif.: Sage.

Young, I. M. 2003. The logic of masculinist protection: Reflections on the current security state. *Signs* 29: 1–25.

Young, M. A. 1988. The crime victims' movement. *Post-traumatic therapy and victims of violence*, ed. F. Ochberg, 319–29. New York: Brunner/Mazel.

———. 1991. Survivors of crime. *To be a victim: Encounters with crime and justice*, ed. D. Sank and D. I. Caplan, 24–71. New York: Plenum Press.

———. 1997. Victims rights and services: A modern saga. *Victims of crime: Problems, policies and programs*, ed. R. Davis, A. Lurigio, and W. Skogan, 194–210. Thousand Oaks, Calif.: Sage.

Zalin, L. 2001. Stress on the press. *University of Washington Alumni Magazine*. March.

Zedner, L. 2002. Victims. *Oxford handbook of criminology*, ed. M. Maguire, R. Gordon, and R. Reiner, 419–56. 2nd ed. New York: Oxford University Press.

Zelizer, B. 1998. *Remembering to forget: Holocaust memory through the camera's eye*. Chicago: University of Chicago Press.

———. 2002. Photography, journalism, and trauma. *Journalism after September 11*, ed. B. Zelizer and S. Adam, 48–68. London: Routledge.

———. 2004. When facts, truth and reality are God-terms: On journalism's uneasy place in cultural studies. *Communication and Critical/Cultural Studies* 1: 100–119.

Zielinski, S. 1999. *Audiovisions: Cinema and television as entr'actes in history*. Amsterdam: Amsterdam University Press.

CARRIE A. RENTSCHLER is an associate professor and William Dawson Scholar of Feminist Media Studies in the Department of Art History and Communication Studies at McGill University.

Library of Congress Cataloging-in-Publication Data

Rentschler, Carrie A., 1971–
Second wounds : victims' rights and the media in the U.S. /
Carrie A. Rentschler.
p. cm.
Includes bibliographical references and index.
ISBN 978-0-8223-4930-3 (cloth : alk. paper)
ISBN 978-0-8223-4949-5 (pbk. : alk. paper)
1. Victims of crimes — Legal status, laws, etc. — United States.
2. Victims of crimes — Civil rights — United States.
3. Victims of crimes in mass media.
4. Victims of crimes — Press coverage — United States.
I. Title.
HV6250.3.U5R47 2011
362.880973 — dc22   2010039973